Anti-Movements in America

This is a volume in the Arno Press series

Anti-Movements in America

Advisory Editor
Gerald N. Grob

Editorial Board
Ray Allen Billington
Nathan Glazer
Irving Louis Horowitz

*See last pages of this volume
for a complete list of titles.*

THE TROJAN HORSE IN AMERICA

MARTIN DIES

ARNO PRESS
A New York Times Company
New York / 1977

E 743.5 .D54 1977

Editorial Supervision: JOSEPH CELLINI

Reprint Edition 1977 by Arno Press Inc.

Copyright © 1940 by Dodd, Mead & Company, Inc.
Copyright Renewed 1968 by Martin Dies.

Reprinted by permission of Dodd, Mead
 & Company, Inc.

ANTI-MOVEMENTS IN AMERICA
ISBN for complete set: 0-405-09937-1
See last pages of this volume for titles.

Manufactured in the United States of America

Library of Congress Cataloging in Publication Data

Dies, Martin, 1901-1972.
  The Trojan horse in America.

  (Anti-movements in America)
  Reprint of the ed. published by Dodd, Mead, New York.
  1. Subversive activities--United States--1917-
3. Propaganda, Communist--United States. 4. United
States--Politics and government--1933-1945. I. Title.
II. Series.
E743.D54 1977   322.4'2'0973   76-46072
ISBN 0-405-09945-2

THE TROJAN HORSE IN AMERICA

THE TROJAN HORSE IN AMERICA

By
MARTIN DIES

DODD, MEAD & COMPANY
New York   1940

COPYRIGHT, 1940
BY DODD, MEAD AND COMPANY, INC.

ALL RIGHTS RESERVED
NO PART OF THIS BOOK MAY BE REPRODUCED IN ANY FORM
WITHOUT PERMISSION IN WRITING FROM THE PUBLISHER

PRINTED IN THE UNITED STATES OF AMERICA
BY THE CORNWALL PRESS, CORNWALL, N. Y.

CONTENTS

CHAPTER		PAGE
I.	The Whole World Becomes a Modern Troy	1
II.	Looking the Trojan Horse in the Mouth	13
III.	Stalin's League for War and Dictatorship	25
IV.	Successors to a Dead Trojan Horse	36
V.	Stalin Bids for American Youth	47
VI.	A Trojan Horse as an Insurance Agent	68
VII.	A Trojan Horse for the Unemployed	80
VIII.	A Trojan Horse in the Courts	106
IX.	A Trojan Horse for Negroes	118
X.	Communist Theory of Labor Unions	130
XI.	Communism in the Labor Unions	142
XII.	Wheels and the Revolution	162
XIII.	An Australian Communist Controls American Shipping	176
XIV.	The Communist Party is Run From Moscow	196
XV.	Communism Preaches Violence	204
XVI.	Stalin's Agents of Crime	217
XVII.	Treason is a Communist Virtue	229
XVIII.	Communism is the Opiate of the People	237
XIX.	Browder Runs a Big Business	248

CONTENTS

CHAPTER		PAGE
XX.	A Trojan Horse on the Ballot	257
XXI.	A Railroad Mechanic Becomes an International Spy	266
XXII.	A Little Man and a Big Battleship	273
XXIII.	The Trojan Horse in Government	285
XXIV.	Kuhn Rides a Trojan Horse for Hitler	304
XXV.	A Trojan Horse of German War Veterans	316
XXVI.	Pelley Tries to Sell Silver Shirts	324
XXVII.	Mussolini's Trojan Horse in America	332
XXVIII.	America's Answer to the Trojan Horse	347

THE TROJAN HORSE IN AMERICA

CHAPTER I

THE WHOLE WORLD BECOMES
A MODERN TROY

OUTWARDLY Moscow was in gala mood on August 2, 1935. The Seventh World Congress of the Communist International was in session. Streamers of red bunting were everywhere in evidence. They bore the slogans of communism in many languages. "Workers of the World Unite!" "Down with Capitalism!" "Fight against Imperialist War!" "Long Live Stalin!" The citizenry of Moscow had been ordered to stage "spontaneous" demonstrations. Huge pictures of Stalin, some of them thirty feet in length, were draped from all of the principal buildings. The emblem of the Hammer and Sickle was ubiquitous.

The ancient city of the czars was thronged with visitors from the five continents and sixty countries. Many of them were delegates from the communist parties of the world. This was the first congress of the Communist International which "Czar" Stalin had called in seven years, although the Constitution of the organization explicitly commands that "the World Congress shall be convened once every two years."

The delegates—thousands of them—were moving upon the Hall of Columns, an unimpressive but commodious building in the heart of Moscow. Almost without exception they were professional revolutionists and, therefore, well fed and well clothed. They appeared even prosperous by contrast with the dire poverty of Moscow's proletariat

—a mass of humanity whose physical existence has altered little from Ivan to Stalin the Terrible.

Among the delegates, there was a veritable babel of tongues which bespoke the world-embracing character of the communist plan for revolution. Oddly enough, some fifty or more governments of the world had issued passports upon which these agents of sedition and revolt were enabled to make the journey to Moscow in order to receive fresh instructions on ways and means to destroy the very governments which issued them the passports. Stalin does not issue passports to his subjects for any such purposes, even where the possibility of revolt against him is remotely suspected; but Stalin, of course, does not entertain the fantastic conception of civil liberties which holds it a "progressive" act to facilitate treason.

When the Hall of Columns was filled and the proceedings were about to begin, William Z. Foster of Massachusetts, the chairman of the American Communist Party, took his seat on the platform, only three seats removed from Stalin himself. In the vast audience were Earl Browder of Kansas, the general secretary of the Communist Party in the United States; James W. Ford of Alabama, Negro Communist candidate for the vice-presidency this year; Gil Green of New York, head of the Young Communist League in the United States; Sam Darcy of California; and many others, all of whom had traveled to Russia on American passports which they had obtained only after swearing falsely to defend the Constitution of the United States. In former years, American communist leaders—hundreds of them, including Foster and Browder—had gone to Moscow to conspire against the United States government, on passports which they had obtained under false names.

On August 2, 1935, the Hall of Columns was filled with

an atmosphere of expectancy. Many of the delegates were to have their first opportunity to hear the fiery, stocky Bulgarian, Georgi Dimitroff, who had recently been freed from his imprisonment in Germany where he had been the chief defendant in Hitler's Reichstag fire trial. The Congress was already a week old, and Dimitroff's scheduled speech was a carefully planned climax. Less dramatic figures from the communist world had spoken their pieces, each ending with much verbal groveling at the feet of Stalin. Two days earlier, Browder had recited American communist successes in launching the American Youth Congress and the American League Against War and Fascism. From the rostrum in Moscow, Darcy had served long-distance notice on California that the Communists were preparing for a revolutionary uprising of seamen. Communist speeches are notoriously long-winded. A four-hour exposition of the currently true Marxist-Leninist-Stalinist doctrine is nothing extraordinary for the faithful to endure. But it also begets a disposition on the part of the listeners to engage in proportionately long demonstrations of cheering, shouting, singing, and marching—before, during, and after the delivery of the speech.

When Dimitroff appeared on the platform, there was prolonged cheering. The "Internationale" was sung in three score tongues. When Stalin took his place on the platform, the assembled delegates were careful to measure their cheering so that it came out at least twice as long and twice as loud as that which had been accorded Dimitroff. The "Internationale" was sung twice. When Wilhelm Pieck, German communist leader, finally introduced Dimitroff, there was a ten-minute ovation with more singing of the "Internationale." Then Dimitroff spoke. Three sentences in his speech made it an historic utterance. Out of those three sentences, the world got its clearest characterization of communist strategy. Thereafter the main communist strategy throughout the world was to be known as that of the Trojan Horse.

Stalin had called the Seventh World Congress for the sole purpose of making a tactical renovation of the world communist plot. Dimitroff acted as his mouthpiece for the renovating.

It was near the end of the second hour of his discourse that Dimitroff used the story of the Trojan Horse to illustrate the strategy which communists were instructed to employ in their campaign for world revolution. "Comrades," said Dimitroff, "you remember the ancient tale of the capture of Troy. Troy was inaccessible to the armies attacking her, thanks to her impregnable walls. And the attacking army, after suffering many sacrifices, was unable to achieve victory until with the aid of the famous Trojan Horse it managed to penetrate to the very heart of the enemy's camp."

There is more to the story of the Trojan Horse than Dimitroff told the delegates in his address that day. We must supply the missing points: The attacking Greeks did not limit their tactic of deceit to the concealing of some of their best warriors in the sides of the wooden horse. An equally shrewd piece of trickery was their use of a fake refugee. Having built the horse, the Greeks pretended to withdraw from the siege of Troy, but they left behind them one of their own soldiers, a man named Sinon, who told the Trojans that he was under a sentence of death at the hands of the Greeks. Sinon begged the Trojans to give him a refugee's asylum. After they had listened to his carefully rehearsed and pitiful tale, they allowed him to come into the city of Troy along with the wooden horse. They were tremendously impressed with his "sincerity." It was this fake refugee who, taking advantage of the gullibility and hospitality of the Trojans, waited for the cover of darkness and then arose from his feigned sleep to let the Greek soldiers out of the wooden horse. The liberated warriors then opened the gates of the city *from the inside*, and the Greek army, rushing from its concealment, fell upon Troy and sacked it. Ten years of military siege had failed to break through the defenses of Troy. One day's work with a wooden horse which concealed a mere handful of its enemies brought about the city's downfall.

Not all of the refugees from the tyranny of the modern dictators are fake caretakers of a Trojan Horse by any means, and no such implication should be read into the stressing of the story of Sinon at this point. Nevertheless, it is true that Stalin's Trojan Horse methods have involved the use of ostensible refugee relief to get their agents into the United States or into Mexico where they may operate in conjunction with their American associates. The Spanish Refugee Relief Campaign is a notable example of Stalin's Trojan Horse organizations.

In his speech to the Seventh World Congress, Earl Browder admitted that only forty per cent of the members of the American Communist Party were native Americans. A few years ago, he conceded, only ten per cent of the Party's members had been born in the United States. In other words, a very large proportion of the Communists who now plot through Trojan Horse methods to destroy the American government and institutions came to this country as refugees. Any one of scores from among these thousands of foreign-born Communists would serve to illustrate the manner in which Communists who came here ostensibly to find a haven of opportunity (and have, indeed, found opportunities never before experienced by them in their European countries) have used America's hospitality as a cover under which to plot revolution. To mention only a few of the more prominent cases, Welwel Warzower, alias William Weiner, came here from Poland; Max Bedacht migrated from Germany; and Alexander Trachtenberg fled from Russia. These three are among the foremost leaders of the American Communist Party who are now, like Sinon in Troy, engaged in opening Trojan Horse doors. In the same fashion, it is clear from a vast amount of evidence that a very large proportion of the members of the German-American Bund and other Nazi Trojan Horses came to the United States ostensibly as refugees. Fritz Kuhn and James Wheller-Hill are among the more prominent of the Nazi Trojan Horsemen who belong to this group. Ambassador William C. Bullitt has declared that the undoing of France was in large measure attributable to the work of the refugee-spies, both Nazi and Communist, who swarmed into France in the days of that country's sentimental liberalism.

Sinon succeeded not only in manufacturing the ring of sincerity for his tale of persecution, but also in convincing the Trojans that the wooden horse was an object worthy of their religious veneration—an excellent substitute for the image of their goddess Pallas.

It is appropriate to recall at this point that communism works to make its philosophy of dialectical materialism a substitute for religion.

Dimitroff commissioned the assembled agents of Stalin to return to their countries and build Trojan Horses. Browder, Foster, Ford, Darcy, and Gil Green heard and applauded Dimitroff's speech.

Browder returned to the United States—on his good

American passport—and announced that the American Communist Party had received "a new tactical orientation" from the deliberations of the Seventh World Congress of the Communist International in Moscow. This new tactical orientation was the People's Front in which the Trojan Horse was the most cunning of the tactics.

The picture changes now. We are in Berlin. There is no tumultuous gathering to hear the exposition of the Nazi strategy for world domination. The scene is a private conference between Adolf Hitler and one of his trusted lieutenants. The familiar rasping oratory of the Nazi Fuehrer is absent. He is talking earnestly but in a simple conversational style of how he proposes to open the gates of foreign countries *from the inside*. It is the Nazi version of the Trojan Horse.

Hitler's sole listener on that occasion was Dr. Hermann Rauschning of Danzig.* In great detail, the Nazi dictator outlined his Trojan Horse method to the Danzig Nazi leader. According to Dr. Rauschning, Hitler said:

> When I wage war, troops will suddenly appear . . . they will march through the streets in broad daylight . . . No one will stop them. Everything has been thought out to the last detail. They will march to the headquarters of the general staff. The confusion will be beyond belief. But I shall long have had relations with the men who will form a new government—a government to suit me. I shall find such men; we shall find them in every country. We shall not need to bribe them. They will come of their own accord. Ambition and delusion, party squabbles and self-seeking arrogance will drive them . . . Our strategy is to destroy the enemy from within, to conquer him through himself.

* *The Voice of Destruction*, published by G. P. Putnam's Sons, 1940.

The Fuehrer expounded his plan to use systematic blackmail to advance his program. He continued:

> I am building up a great organization of my own. It costs a lot of money, but it gets things moving for me. I have drawn up a questionnaire covering details of the persons I am interested in. I am having a comprehensive card index compiled of every influential person in the world. The cards contain every detail of importance. Will he take money? Can he be bought in any other way? Is he vain? Is he sexual? In what way? Is he homosexual? That is of the utmost value, because it provides close associations that can never be escaped from. Has he anything in his past to conceal? Can he be subjected to pressure? What is his business? His hobby, his favorite sport, his likes and dislikes? Does he like travel? And so on. It is on the strength of these reports that I choose my men. That really is politics. I get hold of men who will work for me. I create a force of my own in every country.

Next the Nazi dictator outlined his scheme for using persons of German blood who reside, either as aliens or citizens, in other countries. He said:

> It is a good idea to have at least two German societies in every country. One of them can then always call attention to its loyalty to the country in question, and will have the function of fostering social and economic connections. The other one may be radical and revolutionary. It will have to be prepared to be frequently repudiated by myself and other German authorities. I want to make it quite clear, too, that I make no distinction between German nationals and Germans by birth who are citizens of a foreign country. Superficially we shall have to make allowances for such citizenship. But it will be your special task to train all Germans, without distinction, unconditionally to place their loyalty to Germandom before their loyalty to the foreign state.

The dictators, Stalin and Hitler, are alike in many ways. Long before Hitler cynically abandoned his anti-communist pretense and entered into an alliance with Stalin, the Nazi dictator had appropriated almost all of the tactics of the communists. In no other respect is this similarity between the red and brown dictators more striking than in their common use of Trojan Horse methods of conquest.

The words of Dimitroff, puppet for Stalin, and the words of Hitler spoken to Dr. Rauschning were not idle threats. Already their words have been translated into deeds. Their imperialistic ambitions of conquest and their methods of achieving those ambitions have made the whole world into a modern Troy. When they say that their respective empires must be extended throughout the world, their words may not be discounted as mere pipe-dreams. The record to date precludes that. In recent months, Stalin has annexed the whole of three countries and large parts of three others. Hitler has added the whole of six countries and large parts of two others to the new German empire.

The imperialistic appetites of the dictators have only been whetted. There is no people or territory so remote that Stalin and Hitler do not include it within their scheme to conquer. Hitler's marching legions sing:

> Today we own Germany,
> Tomorrow the whole world.

Stalin is not less ambitious. "The ultimate aim of the Communist International is to replace world capitalist economy by a world system of communism," says the Official Program of the Communist International. Eventually, of course, the ambitions of Stalin and Hitler must clash; but for the present they are leagued together in an alliance for conquest.

Both Stalin and Hitler have expressly included the United States in their plans for a world-embracing revolution along the lines of their respective ideologies. In an address to delegates of the American Communist Party in Moscow years ago, Stalin called special attention to the strategic position of the United States in his scheme of world revolution. "When a revolutionary crisis develops in America," said Stalin, "that will be the beginning of the end of world capitalism as a whole." In the same speech, Stalin commanded the representatives of the American Communist Party to remember that "their" party was "one of the few Communist Parties in the world upon which history has laid tasks of a decisive character from the viewpoint of the world revolutionary movement." Stalin left no shred of doubt about who controls the Communist Party of the United States—the party which, in his view, occupies such strategic importance in the world revolutionary movement. "The American comrades," he declared, "will unhesitatingly submit to the decisions of the Executive Committee of the Communist International and actively carry them into effect."

Hitler's intentions with respect to the United States are equally clear. "National Socialism alone," he said, "is destined to liberate the American people from their ruling clique and give them back the means of becoming a great nation." Hitler is the self-appointed liberator of the American people. "I shall undertake this task simultaneously with the restoration of Germany to her leading position in America," the Nazi Fuehrer declared.

Americans are to be "liberated" by Stalin if his announced plans succeed. On the other hand, we are to be "liberated" by Hitler if his avowed schemes materialize.

Ironically, we are still on friendly terms with the governments of both of our would-be "liberators."

Stalin's group of Trojan Horse organizations is far more developed than Hitler's. Communism is a much older system than national socialism, and its strategy is proportionately more elaborate and subtle. The agents of Russian communism have been at work in the United States three times as long as the agents of German nazism.

It is important that we make distinctions between the various types of Trojan Horse or—as some prefer to call them—fifth column organizations. Espionage and propaganda are different activities. A fifth column for propaganda must operate largely in the open even though its purposes and controls remain secret. A fifth column for espionage or sabotage must be entirely secret or at least attempt to be so. Millions of gullible Americans have been hoodwinked into joining or working for the fifth columns of propaganda, whereas relatively few have been drawn into the activities of the fifth columns of espionage and sabotage. In the last analysis, however, the fifth column of propaganda may be more menacing to our national security than the fifth column of espionage. Also, it must be borne in mind that there is an area where the propaganda organization of the totalitarian dictator overlaps the espionage organization. Both types of penetration into our national life have the ultimate objective of destroying American institutions. Both constitute un-American and subversive activities. Our discussion in this volume must of necessity, however, deal chiefly with the Trojan Horses or fifth columns of propaganda.

It is of vital importance that we neither exaggerate nor underestimate the menace of the dictators' declared intentions. The Trojan Horse may be viewed with hysterical alarm. Such an attitude is both dangerous and ineffective. On the other hand, the Trojan Horse may be viewed with indifference or complaisance. That is equally or more dangerous. Between undue excitement on the one hand and calm acquiescence on the other, we must follow a course of prompt and courageous action to guard against the extension of totalitarian rule to our shores.

First, let us look at the facts.

CHAPTER II

LOOKING THE TROJAN HORSE IN THE MOUTH

OUT of the hundreds of Trojan Horse organizations which the Communists and the Nazis have set up in this country, not one of them will admit its subservience to its builders. In fact, each one denies emphatically that it is in any way dependent upon or controlled by Communists or Nazis. We must be prepared for sweeping denials when we confront a Trojan Horse outfit with the evidence of its hidden connections.

Despite the denials of stooges, whether they be persons of high rank or low, the Trojan Horse organizations are here. Communists and Nazis have both said pointedly that they advance their respective causes by the use of such organizations. Both have declared on occasion that they have succeeded in setting them up. Otto Kuusinen, member of the secretariat of the Communist International, declared:

> We must create a whole solar system of organizations and smaller committees around the Communist Party, so to speak, smaller organizations working actually under the influence of our Party.

Such a "solar system" exists. The Communists have not been negligent in carrying out Moscow's instructions; nor Nazis those of Berlin. It is our business to find these "solar systems" and all of their satellites.

Deception is the chief characteristic of the Trojan Horse.

Stalin does not intend for even the average member of one of his Trojan Horse organizations to know what secret purposes and control are hidden within the creature. Neither does he intend that the people of a country into which he has sent one of his Trojan Horses shall know what it carries within it.

The Trojan Horse is an instrument of revolution, and revolution must of necessity use methods of deception, concealment, and intrigue. The Trojan Horse must, therefore, look like one thing on the outside; and it must be quite a different thing on the inside. It must appear to be innocent, while it actually works for its revolutionary objectives. It must appear to be concerned solely with things that appeal to all men of good intentions, while it actually is concerned with the one purpose of preparing for the revolution. It must appear to be loyally American, while it is actually and entirely un-American.

Notwithstanding all the deception and concealment which are used in the best Trojan Horse which Stalin ever constructed and sent into the United States, there is no good reason why any American should be deceived by one of Stalin's devices. There are guiding principles by which any alert citizen may readily recognize a Trojan Horse when he sees one. Americans are not altogether helpless in the face of the Trojan Horse tactics of Moscow. They have only to throw off their carelessness, and then to use their minds in order to be able to identify any and all of the organizations which serve the cause of the Communist revolution. The carelessness of the average citizen is among the best aids which the Communist cause utilizes. Without such indirect assistance from the careless citizen, the Communists would be and remain far less dangerous to our institutions.

LOOKING THE TROJAN HORSE IN THE MOUTH 15

Ignorance, too, is one of the assets upon which the Communists rely heavily in their Trojan Horse operations. Americans must now dispel any remaining ignorance about the methods which foreign dictators use in penetrating the countries which they hope to conquer. Carelessness and ignorance combined have cost a dozen European countries their very existence as separate and independent nations. The time has come when those who choose to remain careless or ignorant of the Trojan Horse tactics of Stalin and Hitler must share in the guilt for these dictators' designs against our well-being and independence. To become a sponsor for a Trojan Horse organization, to lend it prestige by speaking at one of its meetings, to increase its influence by joining it—all these things have become inexcusable for any citizen, high or low, official or private, who wishes to serve his country with unquestioned patriotism.

What are some of the guiding principles by which any one may be able to recognize a Communist Trojan Horse organization when he sees one?

1. Does the organization have a substantial number of Communist Party members and fellow travelers on its highest governing board? Take, for example, the International Labor Defense. On its National Committee, are the following persons who are avowed members of the Communist Party: William L. Patterson, Ben Davis, Jr., Leo Gallagher, Angelo Herndon, Yetta Land, and Henry Shepard. All of the foregoing individuals have been candidates for public office on the ticket of the Communist Party. In addition to these publicly known members of the Communist Party, there are other Party members on the National Committee of the International Labor Defense, such as Anna Damon, Dirk De Jonge, Lawrence Simpson, and Louise Thompson. Besides the Communist Party members, there

are numerous fellow travelers on the National Committee of the International Labor Defense. A fellow traveler is one who goes along with the program and activities of the Communist Party and whose name appears frequently as a supporter of organizations controlled by the Communist Party.

2. Does the organization appear to make a point of having one or more of the nationally prominent Communists address its important congresses, conferences, or meetings? For example, Earl Browder has been a prominent speaker on the annual programs of the American Student Union, the International Workers Order, and the American League for Peace and Democracy. Clarence Hathaway, editor of the *Daily Worker*, has been a featured speaker at the American Youth Congress.

3. Are the key positions, especially the secretaryship, of the organization held by members of the Communist Party? By and large, Trojan Horse organizations have secretaries who are members of the Party. The secretaryship is usually a much more important office than the chairmanship, from the standpoint of organizational control. Herbert Benjamin, an outstanding Communist Party member, was for years the general secretary-treasurer of the Workers Alliance. He is now general secretary of the International Workers Order. Anna Damon, an avowed Party member, is secretary of the International Labor Defense. Max Bedacht, one of the most prominent members of the Party, was for years general secretary of the International Workers Order. Donald Henderson, an avowed member of the Communist Party, was secretary of the American League Against War and Fascism. Marcel Scherer, openly known as a Party member, was national secretary of the Friends of the Soviet Union. John Santo, a known member of the

LOOKING THE TROJAN HORSE IN THE MOUTH

Communist Party, is secretary-treasurer of the Transport Workers Union.

4. Is the editor of the organization's publication a member of the Communist Party? It is important in a Trojan Horse organization that its editorial policy be rigidly controlled by the Party. The editor is, therefore, usually a Party member or a dependable fellow traveler. Corby Paxton, a member of the Communist Party, is editor of the *Pilot*, official organ of the National Maritime Union.

5. Is the literature of the organization published by the Prompt Press? This printing establishment is controlled by the Communist Party, and uses printers' union label No. 209. Organizations whose publications, periodicals, leaflets, and flyers bear union label No. 209 have, as a rule, close connections with the Communist Party. This union label, for example, may be found on the printed matter of the following organizations: Transport Workers Union, American Youth Congress, Workers Alliance, Workers Library Publishers, Communist Party, Young Communist League, and the *Daily Worker*.

6. Are the legal documents of the organization notarized by Max Kitzes? Secure in their belief that their efforts at deception are successful, Communists overlook many small matters. The name of Max Kitzes, erstwhile secretary-treasurer of the *Daily Worker* and notary public, appears on the legal documents of many Communist Party organizations and publications. Among these are the following: The *Working Woman*, The *Champion, Health & Hygiene*, and the *New Pioneer*.

7. Are the headquarters of the organization to be found at well-known Communist addresses, such as 799 Broadway or 80 East 11th Street? In the past at least, Communists have tended to concentrate their organizations in a few

buildings. Among the many organizations which have had headquarters at 799 Broadway, New York, are the following: Friends of the Soviet Union, International Labor Defense, National Unemployment Councils, and the Young Communist League.

8. Is the treasurer of the organization a responsible official handling its funds directly, or is his function limited to signing checks? Is the treasurer a member of the Communist Party? Does the organization make complete and accurate accounting of all funds to its national board or membership? Are any of the funds of the organization diverted to the Communist Party, either directly or indirectly? Does the organization advertise extensively in the press of the Communist Party, thereby granting what amounts to a subsidy of the Party's publications? The International Workers Order, for example, spends $50,000 for advertising in the *Daily Worker*. World Tourists, ostensibly a regular travel organization, spent large sums of money for advertising in the needy journals which were under Party control.

9. Is the accountant of the organization a member of the Communist Party or a dependable fellow traveler?

10. Is the office staff of the organization drawn largely from the circle of Communist Party members? In numerous instances, the Trojan Horse organizations provide an extremely helpful patronage set-up for the Communist Party, providing employment for Party members. At least three fourths of the staff of Consumers Union, for example, are members of the Party.

11. Does the organization use for entertainment such well-known Communists or communist-controlled groups as Earl Robinson, TAC, and Freiheit Gesangs Verein? Does it popularize camps such as Unity and Beacon?

12. Does the organization get much favorable publicity in the Communist Party press? A former member of the staff of the *Daily Worker* says that all Trojan Horse organizations belong in the "must" category when their press releases and other stories of activities come to the desk of the city editor of the *Daily Worker*.

13. Is the organization frequently found in association with other Trojan Horse organizations, in joint demonstrations, united fronts, and federations? Lists are frequently published in the *Daily Worker* and the *New Masses* which provide a clue to the suspected organization's political orientation. In a recent mass meeting in New York, for example, the following organizations were present as sponsoring groups: International Workers Order, Jewish People's Committee, American Friends of the Chinese People, Coordinating Committee Against Profiteering, and United American Artists. The meeting was under the auspices of the New York Peace Association.

14. Does the organization participate in the May Day parades which are controlled by the Communist Party? Usually, the complete list of the May Day parade participants is published in the *Daily Worker*. In 1940, this list included the following organizations: National Maritime Union; United Electrical, Radio, and Machine Workers of America; Communist Party; International Workers Order; Veterans of the Abraham Lincoln Brigade; International Labor Defense; and the American Student Union.

15. Does the organization follow in general the "line" of the Communist Party, using the same slogans, supporting the same causes, and denouncing the same individuals and organizations? It is the function of the Communist Party "fraction" in a Trojan Horse organization to introduce

resolutions which support the Party's "Line" on all major issues which the Party considers important.

16. Does the organization's policy or "line" shift in strict accordance with the shifts of the Communist Party, working energetically for a boycott of Nazi Germany at the time the Communist Party is doing so and dropping all mention of the boycott of Hitler when the Party drops the subject?

17. Does the organization, through its official publication, lectures, and public speakers, endeavor to popularize the Soviet Union?

18. Has the organization ever gone on record as clearly and emphatically opposed to communism and the Communist Party?

The foregoing guiding principles for the identification of a communist Trojan Horse organization are not all applicable to any single group. Obviously, for example, many organizations which belong in the Trojan Horse category cannot be identified as subversive simply by the address of their headquarters. Likewise, many Trojan Horse organizations do not use the printers' union label No. 209.

No single point in this set of guiding principles is sufficient, as a rule, to justify the conclusion that a given organization is one of Stalin's Trojan Horses. In looking for the marks of identification which point to Moscow's control over any particular group, these guiding principles will assist in compiling cumulative evidence. If, for example, an organization has five or six clear marks of identification as a Trojan Horse, there is cumulative evidence to support a conclusion. Many Trojan Horse groups have a dozen or more marks of Stalin upon them.

It is of the greatest importance that patriotic Americans should not be deceived by the various forms of camouflage which are used by Trojan Horse groups to conceal their real character and control.

In the first place, it is more than likely that the Trojan Horse organization will have among its officers, national committee, or list of sponsors a number of individuals who cannot in any way be branded as Communists. Communist tacticians make a special point of using such individuals as window-dressing to divert suspicion.

In the second place, no one should be deceived by the fact that Trojan Horse organizations frequently, if not as a rule, obtain the services of outstanding citizens as speakers. The fact that a member of the President's cabinet or some other high government official addresses an organization is no proof whatever that the organization is not subversive. It would indeed be difficult to find a single Trojan Horse group which has not been able to command the services of cabinet officers, members of Congress, college presidents, or distinguished clergymen. The Communist theory is that the presence of such distinguished citizens of large reputation on the program of one of their Trojan Horse organizations establishes "innocence by association." For example, when Harold Ickes, Mrs. Roosevelt, or Bishop Francis J. McConnell addresses a meeting or convention, it is argued that this distinguished American citizen establishes the innocence of the whole organization. This tactic of "innocence by association" was the chief method of deception used by the Communists during the late People's Front period, and it is still used on a wide scale. No one should be deceived by it.

In the third place, no patriotic American should be deceived by the name which has been chosen for the Trojan Horse organization. As a rule there is not the slightest suggestion of revolution or un-Americanism in the name of a

Trojan Horse organization. Here again is a use of the tactic of "innocence by association." For example, such a name as the American League for Peace and Democracy, when considered by itself and without reference to any of the guiding principles which have been cited, is so completely disarming that its innocence and good Americanism appear to rate 100 per cent. What is said here with respect to the names of Trojan Horse organizations applies equally to the innocent-sounding objectives which are announced to the public. Communists do not hesitate in their attempt to bring large numbers of people under their influence by setting up an organization whose publicly announced objective is to obtain more and better milk for babies. There is, in fact, scarcely any worthy social objective which Communists refuse to exploit in their drive to extend Stalin's influence among the American people.

We have examined some of the criteria by which the Communist Trojan Horse may be identified. Let us now consider the marks of the Nazi Trojan Horse.

1. Does the organization through its leaders and literature laud the achievements of Adolf Hitler? Take, for example, an illustration from a magazine which bears the name *Southern Progress*. "Adolf Hitler is the George Washington of Germany (and, maybe, of all Europe)," declared this obscure paper. Ironically, the same publication announced Hitler's contribution to peace, only five months before the outbreak of the present European war, in the following language: "The banning of jewish (*sic*) communist activities in Germany and other countries reduces war possibilities to the merest minimum."

2. Does the organization use the swastika as its emblem? The German-American Bund, the Nordic Aryan Federation, the Federation for Nordic Revival, the Russian Na-

tional Revolutionary Party, the American Guard, the American Nationalist Confederation, and the Crusader White Shirts are examples of organizations which have used the official Nazi emblem, the swastika, as one of their own insignia.

3. Is the Nazi salute used at the gatherings of the organization or when its members greet each other?

4. Does the organization use German consular and diplomatic officers as speakers for its gatherings? It must be remembered that all such representatives of Adolf Hitler are convinced Nazis and, as abundant evidence shows, use every occasion to propagandize for nazism.

5. Does the organization circulate or reprint official Nazi propaganda emanating from the propaganda ministry in Germany?

6. Does the organization have fraternal or cooperative relations with Nazi-minded groups? For example, Joseph E. McWilliams, head of the Christian Mobilizers, has been a speaker at gatherings of the German-American Bund.

7. Has the organization gone on record against nazism and fascism as unequivocally as it has against communism? Organizations which are duly concerned to leave no doubt about their Americanism do not hesitate to condemn all totalitarian philosophies with equal clarity and vigor. Whenever an organization is forthright in its denunciation of communism and is pussyfooting or silent on nazism (or vice versa), it leaves itself properly suspect in the minds of all thinking and loyal Americans.

8. Does the organization have uniformed "storm troopers" or advocate the formation and use of private military groups for dealing with its chosen enemies? William Dudley Pelley, for example, advocated the setting up of a

"Christian militia" under the auspices of his Silver Shirt Legion.

9. Does the organization advocate and disseminate racial hatred? Anti-Semitism is the stock-in-trade of the average Nazi group. In this connection, does the organization circulate the forged document in which Benjamin Franklin is made to advocate the exclusion of Jews from the United States? Does it circulate the spurious list of Lenin's cabinet in which it is made to appear that Russian communism was a strictly Jewish affair? Does it reprint or circulate the forged *Protocols of the Elders of Zion?* Does it circulate false or distorted quotations from the Jewish Talmud?

10. Does the organization follow the "line" of the Nazis in promulgating an anti-democratic and pro-totalitarian system of government? Do its leaders scoff at parliamentary institutions? Do they advocate the set-up of the "corporate state" for the administration of a nationally "planned economy"? Do they teach the doctrine of "fuehrership" or the "strong man" in national affairs?

As in the matter of applying the criteria for identifying Communist Trojan Horses, so in the use of the foregoing criteria for discovering Nazi Trojan Horses, we must not depend upon any one criterion in particular as a safe guide. Substantial evidence to justify the conclusion that a given organization is a Nazi Trojan Horse will be cumulative in character.

We shall deal first with some of the more important Communist Trojan Horse organizations and with the nature and aims of the Communist Party which controls them, and then turn our attention to the Trojan Horses of Hitlerism.

CHAPTER III

STALIN'S LEAGUE FOR WAR AND DICTATORSHIP

ANY fruitful examination of Communist Trojan Horse tactics may begin appropriately with the organization which Earl Browder himself described in Moscow, as the Communist Party's "most successful application of the united front."

They called it the American League for Peace and Democracy. Millions of Americans were deceived by the name. Long after the Special Committee on Un-American Activities established its true character as an agency for Stalin's foreign policy—which ultimately spells war and dictatorship—the deception was successfully perpetuated in wide circles. Eventually, however, the exposure of the nature and purposes of this Trojan Horse brought about its abandonment by the Communists themselves. The League was dissolved in February, 1940. It is now only a memory and a lesson—a very important lesson for those who wish to understand the tactics by which Stalin penetrates his enemy's territory, the territory of peaceful men and their democratic institutions.

The League began with Stalin's decision to build a worldwide front against fascism for his own special brand of totalitarianism. This most ambitious of Moscow's fronts was to serve two purposes: first, to combat the rival totalitarianism which Hitler was setting up; and, second, to utilize this anti-Nazi agitation for advancing Stalin's own program among the democratic peoples.

One of Moscow's secret agents, a man named Urevich, came to the United States to confer with leading Communists and prominent sympathizers on the first steps in launching the movement.

Urevich held a meeting at the home of A. A. Heller in the Bronx. Heller had once made a fortune out of an oxygen concession in the Soviet Union. In return for Lenin's favor, Heller has given generous financial support to more than one of Stalin's Trojan Horse enterprises in the United States. He has been a benefactor of International Publishers, the Friends of the Soviet Union, the American Committee for Struggle Against War, the American League Against War and Fascism, and *Soviet Russia Today*. Urevich, Heller, and the other assembled Party members and fellow travelers made plans for the support of the World Congress Against War which was to convene in Amsterdam, Holland, in August, 1932.

According to its own publications, the American League grew out of the Amsterdam World Congress Against War in 1932. That congress was convened on the call of the famous French Communist, Henri Barbusse, acting under instructions of the Communist International. It was attended by 2,196 delegates, of whom 830 were avowed members of the Communist parties of the world. In addition to these avowed Communists, there were 291 delegates who styled themselves "Social Democrats" but whose position, according to their own publication, was in complete agreement with that of the Communists. These self-styled Social Democrats pledged themselves to work for civil war in their respective countries in the event of another international conflict! The Amsterdam congress unanimously adopted a program which declared that it would not allow the Soviet Union "to be touched." This program was adopted as its own by the American Section of the world committee which was set up at Amsterdam. Of the thirty-two American delegates to the Amsterdam congress, a large majority were well-known Communist Party members or came from organizations such as the John Reed clubs, whose affiliations with the Communist Party were clear beyond dispute.

The American Section of the Amsterdam movement first called itself the American Committee for the Struggle Against War. Its secretaries, Oakley Johnson and Donald Henderson, were well-known Communists. It was this committee which called the First United States Congress Against War, at which the founding of the American League Against War and Fascism took place. Donald Henderson, now head of a C.I.O. union, became the first secretary of the organization.

In three successive programs adopted by the annual congresses of the American League, the organization boldly declared its first objective to be the work of interfering with the preparation of our national defense. Point I in these programs stated this purpose in the following language:

To work toward the stopping of the manufacture and transport of munitions and all other materials essential to the conduct of war.

At its second annual congress, Harry F. Ward, national chairman of the American League, declared this program to be "sound." Earl Browder, one of the main speakers at that congress and vice-president of the American League at that time, joined Harry F. Ward in this declaration concerning the League's program. Shortly before that, Browder, who was also secretary of the Communist Party, had gone in person to Moscow to report to the Executive Committee of the Communist International that the program of the American League was "politically satisfactory." Browder also declared in Moscow that the Communist Party had led the First United States Congress Against War "quite openly." In 1937, the American League Against War and Fascism changed its name to the American League for Peace and Democracy. This change of name was in keeping with the Communist Party's new "line" on the People's Front.

According to the minutes of the Washington, D. C., branch of the American League, it was decided "to set up League committees in the units of government agencies with [its] present membership in those agencies as a nucleus." These nuclei of the League were formed in more than a score of government agencies. H. C. Lamberton, a government attorney and chairman of the Washington branch of the League, testified under oath before the Special Committee on Un-American Activities that there were 700 government employees who were members of the American League for Peace and Democracy.

Both the financial secretary of the Communist Party, William Weiner (convicted since his testimony before the Committee as an impostor falsely posing as an American citizen in obtaining a passport), and the national chairman of the American League for Peace and Democracy, Harry F. Ward, testified under oath that the Communist Party was the only national organization which contributed any appreciable sum of money to the work of the American League. According to these two witnesses, this amounted to the sum of two or three thousand dollars annually and represented approximately fifteen per cent of the total annual budget of the American League. This financial contribution from the Communist Party continued down to the time the League dissolved, despite the fact that the Communist Party formally severed, for tactical reasons, its affiliation with the American League more than two years ago.

The Chicago branch of the American League for Peace and Democracy sent out a letter in which its executive secretary, Gilbert Rocke, boosted the Communist Party's newspaper, the *Midwest Daily Record*. Rocke wrote:

> I have sent you about a dozen copies of the May 10 *Record* under separate cover. I am sending copies of this issue to all of our branches calling attention to the invaluable role of the *Midwest Record* in this important phase of our activity and urging their support by subscriptions, etc. It is a shame that the *Midwest Record* does not have one hundred times its present circulation.

When the American League backed an avowed Communist Party publication in that manner, it was clear that the League and the Communist Party had a link with each other which the leaders of the two organizations had attempted to conceal from the general public.

A member of the national committee of the American League, Mrs. Clinton A. Barr, appeared as a witness before the Special Committee on Un-American Activities and told how a radio address which she had been asked to deliver under the auspices of the American League shortly after the signing of the Soviet-Nazi pact was completely revised by the secretary of the Communist Party of the State of Wisconsin. The Committee found that among the changes which the secretary of the Wisconsin Communist Party made in this radio address of the national committeewoman of the American League was the deletion of uncomplimentary references to Adolf Hitler. Mrs. Barr refused to deliver the revised radio address and resigned from the League.

The League's position on the Soviet-Nazi pact clearly stamped it as an organization subservient to the Communist Party. A statement prepared by the executive committee of the Washington branch of the American League read, in part, as follows:

> This pact is a real contribution to world peace and to the peace and security of the United States. . . . The signing of the nonaggression pact between the U.S.S.R. and Germany is not a war alliance between the two powers. It is not an agreement for the partition of Poland. . . . In this sense the pact between the U.S.S.R. and Germany is the only real contribution to the security of Poland that has been made to date. . . . In doing this, the Soviet Union has made a real contribution to an understanding of the present crisis in Europe. It has made a real contribution to the peace and security of Europe, the world, and the United States.

In answer to the question "Is the American League against communism as well as fascism?" the League stated officially:

> So far as the economic and political organization of society is concerned, fascism and communism are opposites. Fascism is for war; the Fascist state is the war-breeding and war-making state. Communism is for the abolition of war. We can't in any sense be against both. Communists—in Germany and other countries—have shown themselves to be hard, courageous, and sincere fighters against war and fascism. The same is true here in the United States.

Despite all the customary denials of Communist Party control which leaders of the American League for Peace and Democracy have made, the evidence of the League's Communist character and program is overwhelming.

James Lerner, Communist Party member and Youth Secretary of the American League, described the treasonable aims of the League in his speech at one of its annual congresses. Lerner was speaking as an officer of the League. Harry F. Ward, national chairman of the organization, was presiding over its sessions when Lerner spoke. "We pledged," said Lerner, "to carry on work within the armed forces of the United States Government, to make the soldiers feel that they must unite with the working class against war."

At two of the League's annual gatherings, the Communist Party produced a man—unidentified—in a soldier's uniform. On both occasions, the anonymous "soldier" delivered a revolutionary speech which greatly aroused the enthusiasm of the League's assembled delegates. On the first occasion, James W. Ford, leading Negro Communist in the United States, was in the chair. On the second occasion, Harry F. Ward, professor of Christian Ethics at Union Theological Seminary, was presiding. Without protest, Professor Ward heard the "soldier" declare: "We will struggle relentlessly until the workers' democracy has removed this dangerous development and if the capitalists call upon us to wage war, we will wage war, but it will be a war against the war makers." This declaration was simply an announcement of the Communist Party's familiar doctrine that it will do its utmost to turn any war in which the United States might become involved into a civil war for the overthrow of the American government.

Professor Ward's own position is clear enough from the

record. Speaking at one of the League's annual gatherings, he said: "You all heard the speech of Earl Browder last night. You heard him make a clear historical judgment that there was only one choice before mankind now and that was between fascism and communism." In a statement published in *Soviet Russia Today*, Professor Ward declared: "There is no way to constructively organize peace except by adopting throughout the world the basic principle of economic organization on which the Soviet Union is founded."

At its third annual congress, the League revealed its allegiance to Stalin by pledging itself "to promote a wider understanding of the peace policies of the Soviet Union and to cooperate with other agencies to prevent an attack on the Soviet Union."

The purposes for which the Communist Party intended to use the American League were set forth with clarity in Party publications. Writing in the *Communist*, Alex Bittelman declared that it was the duty of the Communist Party to build groups of the American League in factories, especially in those factories which produced ammunition, and to organize the American League among marine and transport workers. Bittelman stated bluntly that the Party intended to use these groups of the American League "to attack the vital parts of the war machine of imperialism."

While he was still vice-president of the American League, Earl Browder said that the program of the organization was "so clear and definite in facing the basic issues, that to carry it out in practice entailed clearly revolutionary consequences." At no time did the League repudiate this utterance of its vice president.

The *Daily Worker* called upon all Communist Party members in the American League to use the organization as a feeder for membership in the Party. The American League was, in other words, a true Communist Party "transmission belt."

Shortly before the Communist Party decided to put the American League out of existence, the organization claimed that its supporting affiliates had a combined membership of seven and a half million persons. There can be no doubt that the American League reached far into trade unions, peace organizations, schools, and even into the government itself.

Many government employees belonged to the American League for Peace and Democracy. In the Washington chapter of the League, as has been pointed out, there were about 700 government employees. These 700 persons of dubious loyalty to the United States are still on the government payroll. The Special Committee on Un-American Activities published the names of these League members which were taken from the organization's own files.

When the names of these government employees were made public, the Special Committee on Un-American Activities was bitterly assailed by so-called liberal groups. President Roosevelt characterized the procedure of the Committee in making public these names as "sordid." As a matter of fact, the Committee had announced more than a year prior to the publication of this list of federal servants that the American League for Peace and Democracy was controlled by Communists and was a "front" organization of the Communist Party. Government employees were fully apprised of the true nature of the organization, but the officers of the League, who occupied important government positions, denounced the Committee and ridiculed its finding that the League was Communist. In fact, some of these government officials stated that they were proud to be officers of the League and announced their determination to increase the membership of the League as rapidly as possible. The committee's announcement of the subversive character of the organization had given these government employees every opportunity to withdraw from the League, but with few exceptions they stubbornly refused to do so. The Special Committee on Un-American Activities, after due consideration, decided that it had no right to withhold from the country the names of these government employees—all of whom were receiving their support from taxpayers funds—when it was clear that they insisted upon retaining their affiliation with a Moscow-controlled organization.

The fact that the Communist Party, through one of its subsidiary organizations, had been able to enlist the support of such a large number of persons in the Federal Government was convincing proof that Communism had made considerable headway in this country, at least to the extent of winning sympathizers and fellow travelers.

Government employees in Chicago, New York, and other cities were also affiliated with the League. It has been estimated that the total number of government employees who were members of this Stalinist agency throughout the country ran to several thousand. Some of them had key positions in government, with salaries in excess of $5,000.

Despite the fact that the President of the United States branded the procedure of the Special Committee on Un-American Activities as "sordid," it was only six months later that investigators from the White House itself requested the Committee to let them examine the list and material in the Committee's files in order to obtain information concerning "fifth column" activities being carried on inside government agencies.

Two years ago the World Committee Against War and Fascism, with which the American League was affiliated, held a congress in Mexico City. Among the outstanding delegates to the gathering were Leon Jouhaux and John L. Lewis. Jouhaux was head of the trade union movement in France. He was the power behind the People's Front government of France which did so much to prepare the way for Hitler's conquest of the country. At the Mexico City gathering of the World Committee Against War and Fascism, Jouhaux paid a tribute to the late Henri Barbusse, eminent French Communist who has been described in Communist publications as the founder of both the World Committee Against War and Fascism and its American branch. According to the *Daily Worker's* reports of the Mexico City gathering, Edwin S. Smith, member of the National Labor Relations Board, was elected a member of its presiding committee. Smith also addressed the gathering.

The League is dead. It was killed by exposure, but Stalin and Browder are not easily discouraged. On the death of the League, they went to work immediately to set up new organizations, with new names, to take its place.

Stalin and Browder, with all of their obedient followers in the United States, are carrying on in their unchanging determination to build their Trojan Horses in our country to the end of destroying our government and free institutions.

We shall next consider some of the successors to the late American League for Peace and Democracy.

CHAPTER IV

SUCCESSORS TO A DEAD TROJAN HORSE

The American League for Peace and Democracy is dead. It was killed by the same Communist hands that brought it into existence. It had outlived its usefulness. Its complete exposure as a Trojan Horse for Stalin's foreign policy was brought about by revelations made before the Special Committee on Un-American Activities and by the sudden shift from an extreme anti-Nazi to a pro-Nazi position in the foreign relations of the Russian dictator.

The Communists have gone right ahead more energetically than ever before, in the construction of Trojan Horses of the anti-war variety. In fact, Browder and his agents have been able to utilize popular anti-war sentiment in this country during the past six months to an extent that was not possible before the appearance of the present international crisis.

The sole issue before us in this discussion is the question of Communist control of various so-called peace organizations. We are not concerned with the announced objectives of these organizations. Whether the Communists are pro-peace or pro-war at any given moment is altogether beside the point. The fact that they are Communists means that they are always, at all times and in all places, un-American. This is true regardless of the programs which they pretend to support. Because they are un-American, it is our business to know what organizations they have set up and what organizations they have gained control of for the purpose

SUCCESSORS TO A DEAD TROJAN HORSE

of advancing the cause of Communist revolution. One does not have to be in favor of war in order to oppose a Communist "peace" organization, just as one does not have to be anti-labor in order to fight against Communist leadership in a labor union. In fact, one cannot be genuinely in favor of peace without being opposed to all Communist "peace" groups; just as one cannot be genuinely pro-labor without being unqualifiedly opposed to all Communist leadership of labor.

The American League for Peace and Democracy was a highly centralized organization, although national in scope. The new Communist tactic in Trojan Horse "peace" organizations is "decentralization." Scores of organizations which are apparently purely local or regional affairs have taken the place of the American League. These organizations bear different names. They form a national network, but the Communist control is better concealed because of the apparently decentralized structure.

The decentralization of its anti-war Trojan Horse organizations has been a clever move on the part of the Communist Party. It is more difficult to detect the Party's hand in a movement when that movement is apparently split up into a large number of wholly unrelated units, each having its own name. Nevertheless, we can and must expose these Trojan Horses as fast as they appear. The mere recital of the unadorned facts concerning the organizations may be tedious for the reader, but it should be remembered that a good deal of Communist strategy is successful simply because it is a tedious process for the average citizen to examine it.

When the Washington branch of the American League for Peace and Democracy mailed the notice of its dissolution to its members, it enclosed in the same envelope an announcement of the formation of a new organization to be known as the Washington Committee for Democratic Rights. The leading personnel of the new organization was practically identical with that of the old. Alice Barrows of the Department of Interior, Henry C. Lamberton of the Rural Electrification Administration, Gardner Jackson of Labor's Non-Partisan League, and Eve Budd of the Communist Party were all carried over as officials from the defunct American League to the new Washington Committee for Democratic Rights

In New York, the American League died and the New York Peace Association was promptly born. The new organization held a mass meeting on June 13th of this year. The list of sponsors for the meeting tells all that we need to know about the political complexion of the New York Peace Association. Here they are: Bishop Francis J. McConnell, William Lloyd Imes, Bella V. Dodd, George Seldes, Congressman Vito Marcantonio, Rockwell Kent, Margaret Schlauch, Rabbi Michael Alper, Robert K. Speer, Arthur T. Goold, Edwin Berry Burgum, Arthur Kallet, and Randolph B. Smith. With the lone exception of Arthur Goold who is a newcomer on such lists, all of these persons have appeared so frequently as window dressing for Communist fronts that their names instantly identify the New York Peace Association as one of Moscow's newly constructed Trojan Horses. The organization publishes a monthly magazine called *Peace Reporter*. In its June issue, the magazine announces Morris Engel, former president of the notorious Commonwealth College in Mena, Arkansas, as one of the new organization's lecturers.

Functioning in New York at the present time is the New York Emergency Peace Mobilization Committee. The manner in which the personnel of Communist Trojan

Horses invariably interlocks is seen in the fact that the chairman of this committee is Jean Horie who is also executive secretary of the New York Youth Congress.

Across the East River from Manhattan, there is an organization known as the Brooklyn Community Peace Congress. It has just come into existence. Speakers at its rally in August were Congressman Vito Marcantonio, Michael Quill (about whose Communist connections we shall have more to say later), Rabbi Moses Miller, president of the Jewish People's Committee, John P. Davis, secretary of the National Negro Congress, Bella V. Dodd, chairman of the Trade Union Women's Peace Committee, and Jean Horie, secretary of the New York Youth Congress. These six speakers, appearing on any program, show clearly enough who is behind the affair. The Jewish People's Committee was formerly headed by two nationally prominent Communists, Ben Gold and William Weiner. Daniel S. Gillmor, publisher of the magazine *Friday*, presided at the Brooklyn meeting.

Out in Pittsburgh, there has been set up what is known as the Conference for the Protection of Constitutional Rights. One Richard H. Lawry is chairman of the organization. Lawry appeared before the Special Committee on Un-American Activities this year, and freely admitted that he had spoken at meetings of the Communist Party and the Communist-controlled Unemployment Councils, and further that he was head of the Pittsburgh branch of International Workers Order (about which we shall have more to say in a later chapter). Lawry is also supervisor of the United States Census in the district which centers in Pittsburgh. His record of Communist associations is a long one, and he appears to take much pride in it. Despite this fact, he has been appointed to a highly important position in the Census.

The Emergency Peace Mobilization Committee is a new Communist front which recently staged a "gigantic rally" on Randall's Island, New York. The *Daily Worker* featured Martha Dodd's endorsement of this rally. The daughter of the former United States Ambassador to Germany has supported many Communist-controlled meetings and organizations. Speakers at the Randall's Island affair were Congressman Vito Marcantonio, John P. Davis of the National Negro Congress, and Jean Horie of the American Youth Congress. Earl Robinson's chorus was also one of the attractions. Robinson's "Ballad for Americans" is an American version of the "Internationale," the international anthem of the Communist movement. Again and again, the *Daily Worker* has analyzed "Ballad for Americans" to show how Robinson skillfully set the "class struggle" to new words and music. (The "Ballad" was used to open the recent Republican National Convention in Philadelphia.)

One of the largest efforts of a Trojan Horse character in the anti-war movement is the Committee to Defend America by Keeping Out of War. The entire apparatus of the Communist Party, with all of its front organizations, was set in motion to back this committee's Chicago meeting in August. Among the principal committee members are Jack McMichael of the American Youth Congress, Franz Boas of the American Committee for Democracy and Intellectual Freedom, Joseph Curran of the National Maritime Union, and Max Yergan of the National Negro Congress—all familiar stars in the galaxy of Communist supporters. Paul Robeson, Negro singer and Communist fellow traveler, sang Robinson's "Ballad for Americans" at the Chicago rally.

In California, the American Peace Crusade has been established under the leadership of Herbert Biberman, John Stapp, Dalton Trumbo, Sam Ornitz, and Carey McWilliams. Some of these are members of the Communist Party; others are enthusiastic fellow travelers.

The limitations of space make it impossible to deal, even sketchily, with all of the scores of successors to the American League for Peace and Democracy. Some of the remaining ones are:

> The Northern California Peace Mobilization Committee
> The Seattle Peace Coordinating Committee
> The Minnesota Emergency Peace Crusade
> The American Peace Committee of Detroit
> The Massachusetts Peace Council
> The Baltimore People's Peace Committee
> The Washington (D. C.) Peace Mobilization Committee
> Trade Union Women's Peace Committee

These organizations and scores of others which could be named show the extent to which the Communist Party has decentralized (in names at least) its anti-war movement.

In addition to the foregoing organizations, the Communists are energetically sponsoring an anti-war movement which is organized around the slogan, "The Yanks Are Not Coming." In many communities, Yanks Are Not Coming Committees have taken the place of the American League for Peace and Democracy.

It is noteworthy that the German-American Bund has also taken up the Yanks Are Not Coming slogan. When Wilhelm Kunze's car was stopped by the State Troopers of New Jersey recently, it was found to contain a large supply of Yanks Are Not Coming literature. It is obvious, of course, that the anti-war stand of both the Communists and the German-American Bund is determined by the current foreign policy of Moscow and Berlin. It has nothing to do with the vital interests of the American people.

The author of the slogan, the Yanks Are Not Coming, is the well-known Communist Party member, Mike Quin. In the *Daily Worker* for May 15, 1940, Quin is described as the "popular People's World columnist." The *People's World* is a Communist Party newspaper published in San Francisco. The editor-in-chief of the *People's World* is Harrison George. George is also a member of the National Committee of the Communist Party of the United States.

Quin's writings are praised in the *Daily Worker* by such well-known Communist Party members and fellow travelers as Ruth McKenney, editor of the *New Masses*, Anna Louise Strong, prominent Soviet propagandist in the United States, Theodore Dreiser, novelist who was one of the three men who summoned the congress which founded the American League Against War and Fascism, and Clifford Odets, playwright and leader of a Communist Party delegation to Cuba.

In the first issue of the strongly pro-Communist, weekly magazine *Friday*, Quin was described as "an Irish-American, seaman, radio commentator and newspaperman." *Friday* did *not* inform its readers that Quin is a Communist. Only the highest praise is bestowed by *Friday* on Quin's pamphlet which bears the title *The Yanks Are Not Coming*. In its boost for the pamphlet, *Friday* declared that "some 250,000 people have read it, talked about it, acted because of it."

The Special Committee on Un-American Activities is in possession of an original letter from Corby Paxton to Mike

Quin. This letter indicates that both Quin and Paxton are members of the Communist Party. Corby Paxton is editor of the *Pilot*, official organ of the National Maritime Union headed by Joseph Curran.

District Council No. 2 of the Maritime Federation of the Pacific publishes a bulletin which is devoted exclusively to the promotion of the Yanks Are Not Coming Committee. *Bulletin* No. 1 announced that "Windshield Stickers," "Celluloid Buttons," and "Signature Petitions" for the Yanks Are Not Coming movement are available for distribution. Yanks Are Not Coming windshield stickers have been distributed to government employees in various departments of the Federal Government in Washington, according to evidence in the possession of the Special Committee on Un-American Activities. Mike Quin is one of the writers in the *Bulletin* of the Yanks Are Not Coming Committee of the Maritime Federation of the Pacific. Quin's interpretation of the European war, as well as that of the other writers in the *Bulletin*, follows strictly the Communist Party "line," including a defense of the Russian invasion of Finland.

Quin's pamphlet, *The Yanks Are Not Coming*, has been printed and circulated by the Maritime Federation of the Pacific. According to the Maritime Federation's edition of the Quin pamphlet, the American Youth Congress and the National Maritime Union have made themselves a part of the Yanks Are Not Coming movement.

In its issue of February 9, 1940, the *Daily Worker* reported that the Washington representative of the Maritime Federation of the Pacific, Bjorne Halling, had announced the formation of a Yanks Are Not Coming committee composed of himself, M. Hedley Stone of the National Maritime Union, and Dan Driesen legislative representative of the American Communications Association.

The Communist Party of Massachusetts has issued a circular which features the Yanks Are Not Coming slogan.

The Communist Party of California has issued a mimeographed statement on the Yanks Are Not Coming Movement which reads, without regard to the facts of the Soviet invasion of Finland, as follows:

> Remember that the Soviet Union, with 185,000,000 people, is anti-war. Join the defense of the peace policy of the only socialist country in the world, the Soviet Union.

Two branches of the Young Communist League in New York have put out a circular on the Yanks Are Not Coming movement which summarizes the Communist Party's position on the European war, the Soviet invasion of Finland, the defense program of the Washington Administration, and support of the brand of socialism which has been adopted in the Soviet Union.

The Worcester (Massachusetts) *Worker*, published by the local unit of the Communist Party, shows how the local units generally are backing the Yanks Are Not Coming movement.

On college campuses, under the leadership of the American Student Union, students have organized local committees of the Yanks Are Not Coming. An instance of this is found in the *People's World* which reports the organization of such committees in Los Angeles.

The Communist Party of Rhode Island issued a leaflet which featured the Yanks Are Not Coming slogan along with a sweeping endorsement of the Soviet invasion of Finland.

The front organizations of the Communist Party have

been following the Party "line" in their support of the Yanks Are Not Coming movement. The Workers Alliance of America, for example, has issued a leaflet which features the movement's slogan. Superimposed indistinctly on copies of this leaflet is the stamp of the "Helen Lynch Center of the Workers Alliance." Helen Lynch was an active Communist Party member in New York for a number of years. She died recently, and the Workers Alliance in New York named one of its centers in her honor.

The Communist Party has made its intentions with respect to anti-war work crystal clear. These intentions are not those of the familiar pacifist movement. They go much beyond such attitudes, and clearly involve treasonable plans to turn a national war emergency into a civil war against the United States government.

When he was a witness before the Special Committee on Un-American Activities, Earl Browder stated categorically that he would attempt to plunge this country into civil war in the event of a war between the United States and the Soviet Union.

The Agit-Prop (agitation and propaganda) Department of the Communist Party of the United States has published a pamphlet written by Leon Platt, alias Martin Young, which sets forth in unmistakable language the intentions of the Communist Party on the subject of a war emergency involving the United States and the Soviet Union. Leon Platt wrote in this pamphlet, as follows:

> The American workers when called upon to go into this war against the Soviet Union must refuse to fight the Russian workers, and go over on the side of the Red Army. The American workers, like the Russian workers in 1917 must turn the imperialist war into a civil war against their real enemies—the

capitalist class of the United States which exploits and oppresses the American working class.

When Clarence Hathaway, editor of the *Daily Worker*, addressed the American Youth Congress, he said:

I am sure that the American youth guided and led by the American Youth Congress will be a force for the defense of the Soviet Union, our Socialist Fatherland, and for the defeat of our own robber imperialist government and for the victory of the American toiling masses (Prolonged applause).

William Weinstone, one of the leading American Communists, wrote in the *Communist*, as follows:

Only if our anti-war campaign is developed in the factories, munition plants, docks and ships can our struggle against war be effective. Only by such means can we actually paralyze the war plans of the American bourgeoisie; only in this way can the Soviet Union be defended from American imperialist intervention. . . . The next strategic places for the anti-war activities of the Party and the Y.C.L. must be within the armed forces . . .

The foregoing quotations are only a few among hundreds which might be cited from official Communist Party sources. They set forth without concealment or equivocation the anti-war plans of the Communist Party.

Any anti-war movement, such as the Yanks Are Not Coming movement, in which the Communists play a dominant role, is a movement which aims at the revolutionary overthrow through violent civil war of the American government and American free institutions in favor of a Soviet system.

CHAPTER V

STALIN BIDS FOR AMERICAN YOUTH

THE wife of the President of the United States has made a public issue out of the question of the Communist control of the American Youth Congress.

On May 8th of this year, Edward J. Flynn, chairman of the Democratic National Committee, gave a dinner at his home. The letter of invitation which he sent to his wealthy guests reads as follows:

> At the suggestion of Mrs. Franklin D. Roosevelt, I am asking a small group of people to my home, 2728 Henry Hudson Parkway, for a buffet supper, on Wednesday evening, May 8th, at 7:30 o'clock. I should be delighted if you could join us.
>
> The purpose of the gathering is to introduce a few representatives of the American Youth Congress who are anxious to present their problem to people who are in a position to help them financially. As you know, Mrs. Roosevelt is keenly interested in assisting these young people, and she will be with us on that evening to introduce their members.
>
> Will you be good enough to let me know if it will be possible for you to join us? Would you address your reply to 2728 Henry Hudson Parkway.
>
> Yours very truly,
EDWARD J. FLYNN

A recent book entitled *American Youth Today* * purports to tell the facts concerning the American Youth Con-

---

* *American Youth Today* by Leslie Gould, published by Random House, 1940.

gress. It contains a foreword by Eleanor Roosevelt. Inasmuch as the book was written as a piece of propaganda for the Youth Congress, it goes without saying that the vast array of evidence which establishes the fact of Communist control over the organization is omitted. On the other hand, the book contains many serious distortions—too numerous to mention without writing a companion volume. A sample distortion will give an idea of what the book is like. Frances Williams, secretary of the American Youth Congress, is quoted as saying: "Yes, Communists are represented in the Congress through the Young Communist League." The whole truth of the matter is that the Communists are represented in the American Youth Congress by the American Student Union, the International Fur Workers Union, the International Workers Order, the National Negro Congress, the Southern Negro Youth Congress, the Workers Alliance, and a dozen other organizations which, like the foregoing, are completely under the control of the Communists. It is a standard communist tactic to put its members into such an organization as the American Youth Congress by providing them with credentials from another communist-controlled front. Earl Browder, for example, was a delegate to the American League for Peace and Democracy from the International Workers Order and not from the Communist Party. Browder is still Browder, head of the American Communist Party, no matter what credentials he holds.

American Youth Today contains The Creed of the American Youth Congress. No more admirable document could be used as a guide for youth, but that is wholly beside the point. The question is not what the Youth Congress says it believes in, but what it actually does believe in as

STALIN BIDS FOR AMERICAN YOUTH 49

shown by its deeds, its week-to-week policies, its personnel, and its constituent organizations.

The American Youth Congress purports to speak for 4,700,000 young Americans. As a matter of fact, any group of young Americans as large as that would be shocked to learn that their spokesman is the American Youth Congress. The figure is arrived at by a type of mathematics peculiar to Communists. An individual who happens to hold membership in a bona fide organization, simply because he has been sent into it by the Young Communist League to bore from within, declares that he represents the whole organization. He may have no authorization whatever from the membership of the organization to repersent it in the Youth Congress. He simply puts himself down as representing 100,000 or more young people, and that figure goes to swell the grand total which the Youth Congress claims. There is, of course, no way of knowing how many young Americans are satisfied to have the American Youth Congress speak on their behalf. They must be a very much smaller group than the 4,700,000 claimed, and even the smaller group, for the most part, represents those who have been duped by the high ideals expressed in the Creed of the Youth Congress into supporting the organization.

Let us look at some of the facts about the Youth Congress!

Last February several thousand young men and women stood in a drenching rain on the lawn of the White House. The President of the United States was addressing them. When he ventured to suggest that Russia belonged in the category of modern dictatorships, these American youth booed lustily. It was the American Youth Congress in action. A day or two later, these same American youth swarmed into the gallery of the House of Representatives of the United States Congress, and there again they booed and hissed when procedures were not to their liking.

These incidents of rank discourtesy did more, perhaps, to open the eyes of thousands of gullible liberals with respect to the real nature and aims of the American Youth Congress than had ever been done by the vast amount of evidence concerning the completely Communist control of the organization.

The American Youth Congress has long been one of Stalin's most successful Trojan Horses in the United States, and the disrespect which its members demonstrated for the American government was exactly what any informed person would have expected from those whose only real loyalty—regardless of their citizenship—is to the Soviet Union.

The Youth Congress was launched in August, 1934, at a gathering held in New York University. Miss Viola Ilma was in charge. She was soon to lose control to the Communists, however.

Communists alleged at the outset that Miss Ilma was of nazi or fascist sympathies. This allegation was elaborated several months later in the *New Masses* in an article by John L. Spivak. Mr. Spivak's article was entitled "Who Paid Viola Ilma's Way to Nazi Germany?" According to the official version of the history of the Youth Congress, set forth in a pamphlet entitled "Youngville, U.S.A.," Miss Ilma made a trip to Germany and Italy in 1934, and during her stay in those countries was inspired with the idea of launching a youth congress. The pamphlet declares:

> She invited representatives from national youth organizations, reaching all the way from the Boy Scouts to the Young Communist League. Her arrangements were remarkably efficient and all-inclusive. And that was her mistake.

The plain meaning of this official version of the origin of the American Youth Congress is that Viola Ilma, herself, was responsible for the Communist capture of the organization. It was she who invited the Communists to participate; the Communists did the rest.

In his book entitled *Communism in the United States*, Earl Browder also stated that the first American Youth Congress was "captured away from Ilma."

In describing the capture of the organization, Browder said:

A unique achievement of the youth united front movement was the building of an anti-fascist bloc inside the American Youth Congress, which was called together by a certain young woman named Viola Ilma with the backing of Mrs. Roosevelt, Anne Morgan, a half-dozen State Governors, members of the Roosevelt cabinet, etc., with the purpose of adopting a program for American youth which was distinctly fascist in its tendencies.

It will be noted that Browder's comment ante-dated the period of the People's Front, and that accounts for the glibness with which he pinned the label "Fascist" on Mrs. Roosevelt. There was certainly no hint in Browder's pre-People's Front comment that Mrs. Roosevelt would one day be welcomed as the principal sponsor of the American Youth Congress after it had come completely under the control of Browder's organization.

The importance which we are to attach to any of Browder's claims concerning Communist capture or control of an organization depends entirely on whether or not those claims are borne out by other evidence of a substantial character.

Discussing the work of the American Youth Congress, a

writer in the *Daily Worker* for January 5, 1935, recounted the capture of the organization from Miss Ilma as follows:

The program to be acted upon in the two-day congress of seven sessions here was formulated by the first American Youth Congress, a broad assemblage brought together by Viola Ilma with the direct connivance of administrative officials. At that time, the overwhelming majority of the delegates, including those from the Young Communist League and Young Peoples Socialist League, becoming disgusted with the machine rule, entered into a united front around a working class program of action, and repudiated the reactionary sponsorship of the congress.

In the *Daily Worker* for July 19, 1935, the success of the Communists and Socialists in their joint action in the American Youth Congress was reported as follows:

In the past period of time, we have learned to work together and to act together despite the fundamental differences in program and policy which still separate our two organizations. Working relationships have now existed between the Young Peoples Socialist League and the Young Communist League for over a year. Joint activity for realizing the program of the American Youth Congress resulted in the inspiring student strike of April 12, participated in unitedly by Socialist and Communist students.

In his report to the Sixth World Congress of the Young Communist International, Wolfe Michal described the way in which the young American Communists and Socialists captured the American Youth Congress, as follows:

Thanks to the joint participation and work of the young American comrades with the Socialist and other non-fascist youth at the Youth Congress, originally called by a reactionary group desirous of fascist honors, our Young Communist

League of the United States helped to bring about the unity of several non-fascist organizations with a membership of over a million.

Michal characterized the strategy of the young Communists in the American Youth Congress as "an example of how to *influence* the masses of youth."

At the Seventh World Congress of the Communist International, Otto Kuusinen repeated the story of the capture of the American Youth Congress in the following language:

> Our American comrades achieved a great success at this youth congress. The agents of fascism were completely isolated, and the congress was transformed into a great united front congress of the radical youth. And when, somewhat later, a second general youth congress was held, our young comrades already enjoyed a position of authority at it.

Kuusinen, whom Stalin recently made head of his Finnish puppet state, declared that the young Communists, in their strategy in the American Youth Congress, had followed the principles enunciated by Dimitroff at the Seventh World Congress of the Communist International. Kuusinen described the success of the young American Communists in their penetration of non-communist organizations in the following language:

> The comrades of the Young Communist League of the United States have learned that it is essential to enter the *big* youth *organizations* led by the *bourgeoisie*. And not only that, they have also learned how to work in these organizations.

Kuusinen further declared:

> In the course of not quite a year, the Young Communist League in the United States has succeeded in creating 175 fractions in these mass organizations. (Applause.)

Before he concluded his speech to the Seventh World Congress, Kuusinen spoke of the "Soviet country, the fatherland of the workers of all countries." In the conclusion of his address, he gave clearest expression to the tactic of Stalin's "fifth column" in France and the United States. Kuusinen said:

We want to attack our class enemies in the rear . . .
We often repeat the slogan of transforming the imperialist war into a civil war against the bourgeoisie. In itself, the slogan is a good one, but it becomes an empty and dangerous phrase if we do nothing serious in advance to create a united youth front. (loud applause.)
We need a revolutionary youth movement at least ten times as broad as our parties, and a united youth front hundreds of times broader still. That this is entirely possible in many countries is shown by the achievements of our French and American young comrades.

It is noteworthy that Kuusinen explicitly classified the "achievement" of the American young comrades in the Youth Congress as a demonstration of the possibilities of forming a Communist "fifth column" in the United States.

After Viola Ilma was deposed from the leadership of the American Youth Congress, Waldo McNutt was installed as chairman. McNutt retained the chairmanship of the American Youth Congress for about a year. He then became national organizer of the American League Against War and Fascism, with which we dealt in Chapter III.

Waldo McNutt contributed an article in the July, 1936, issue of *The New Order*, official publication of the International Workers' Order. The Special Committee on Un-American Activities has found that the International Workers' Order is a communist-controlled organization.

When Earl Browder came out of Russia after the Seventh World Congress in 1935, he lost his brief case. The contents of that brief case included correspondence from Waldo McNutt which clearly established his membership in the Communist Party. This is the sort of evidence which is omitted from Leslie Gould's book, *American Youth Today*.

For a few months in the latter part of 1935, William W. Hinckley was executive secretary of the American Youth Congress. In January, 1936, he was elected chairman of the organization, and continued in that position until July, 1939.

On Friday, March 11, 1938, Mr. Hinckley appeared as a witness before a sub-committee of the Committee on Education and Labor of the United States Senate. On page 242 of the Hearings before this sub-committee, the following testimony appears:

Mr. Hinckley: I believe that there is certainly no organization on the National Council of the Youth Congress that believes in subversive doctrines.
Senator Lee: Not on the council, no; but in your organization?
Mr. Hinckley: So far as I know, no organization believes in subversive doctrines.

At the conclusion of Mr. Hinckley's testimony, Senator Lee (Oklahoma) made the following comment:

I wanted to give you a good chance to repudiate communism as far as your organization is concerned, but you have not done it. If you have nothing further, that will be all.

Following this comment by Senator Lee, Mr. Hinckley said nothing.

On April 2, 1939, Hinckley appeared on the program of the People's Platform—a broadcast feature of the Columbia

Broadcasting System. In the transcript of this broadcast, we find the following exchange between Mr. John B. Trevor and Mr. Hinckley:

Trevor: I'd like to ask Mr. Hinckley whether; in view of the positive stand he's taken in regard to the Bund, whether he would take precisely the same stand in regard to a communist meeting in Madison Square Garden.

Hinckley: I think that, in that case, I would say absolutely no. The Communists, it seems to me, are no threat of aggression from without or from within.

The Special Committee on Un-American Activities has been informed by one of the departments of the Federal Government that in 1936 the Communist Party arranged and paid for Mr. Hinckley's transatlantic passage to Europe where he was in attendance at the First World Youth Congress. It should be noted that Mr. Hinckley was at that time chairman of the American Youth Congress.

Hinckley was recently appointed assistant to the administrator in the Office of Education of the Department of the Interior.

Among the leaders of the American Youth Congress, at least three have been on the staff of the publication, *Champion*. These are Edward Strong, Abbott Simon, and Rose Terlin. Strong has been a member of the administrative committee of the American Youth Congress, representing the National Negro Congress, and chairman of the Southern Negro Youth Congress. He was also a member of the national committee of the American League for Peace and Democracy. Simon has been legislative director for the American Youth Congress. Terlin has been a member of the administrative committee of the American Youth Congress.

Proofs that *Champion* was a communist publication are to be found in the following facts: The Young Communist League gave *Champion* subscriptions to all members who paid their initiation fee. *Champion* was published at 799 Broadway, New York, N. Y., which is also the headquarters of the Young Communist League and many Communist Party auxiliary organizations. *Champion* was used as an official publication of the International Workers' Order. The minutes of the National Resident Board meeting of the Young Communist League for March 26, 1938, contain a discussion of the financial problems of *Champion*. Among those on the staff of *Champion* were many known Communists, including Sam Pevzner, Louis Gordon, James Murphy, James Lerner, Angelo Herndon, Morris Schnapper, Francis Franklin, Langston Hughes, Frederick N. Meyers, Richard Pack, John Groth, Gregor Duncan, Frank Beebe, Eli Jaffe, Jo Page, and Colin Allen.

Prompt Press, one of the income-producing enterprises conducted by the Communist Party of the United States, printed *Champion* under union label No. 209. Most of the literature, pamphlets, and flyers of the American Youth Congress also have been printed under this label. Mrs. Roosevelt has offered the explanation that the American Youth Congress has used the Communist Party's printing establishment because purely commercial considerations, namely, lower costs than could be obtained elsewhere.

One of the witnesses who appeared before the Special Committee on Un-American Activities in 1939 was Kenneth Goff, of Delavan, Wisconsin. Mr. Goff was a member of the Communist Party and also of the Young Communist League until the day that he appeared as a witness. Mr. Goff testified that he used the alias, John Keats, in both the Communist Party and the Young Communist League, and he turned over to the Special Committee on Un-American Activities his membership books and cards in both organizations.

Goff was a delegate to the Eighth National Convention of the Young Communist League in New York in May 1936. While he was in attendance at this convention, his delegate's card was autographed by Joseph Curran, head of the National Maritime Union.

Goff was a member of the administrative committee of the American Youth Congress. He was listed on this committee as a representative of the Wisconsin Townsend Club.

Because of the importance of Mr. Goff's testimony, in expressing the manner in which the Communists recruited the youth in their movement, we shall quote him at length. He was asked to state the circumstances of his connection with the Workers' Alliance and the seizure of the State House at Madison, Wisconsin. His answer was as follows:

> Well, prior to joining the Workers' Alliance, I attended the Workers' Educational School which was sponsored by the Federal Government at Madison. It was held in one of the student houses and was for a period of six weeks, in which all of the expenses were paid for while we were there. That is where I first came in contact with any communist leanings. In other words, one of the teachers—I can't remember her name at the present time—was a member of the Muscovite group from New York. This school was just sponsored one summer there. While we were there, we learned to sing the "Internationale." We learned to sing other songs, anti-capitalistic songs of different types; and we studied some history of different movements, labor movements, Leftist movements in America. During the period of time we were there one night—well, from time to time, we were given different pamphlets by different people in the school, different students. This one night a group of us were told to go to a certain place. We rode down the

back street, and landed up in the basement of a man's house. I guess the man's name was John Gary. That is all I know him by. There we had a talker, a Jewish boy from New York. He told us about the new things that were taking place in this country and in the Communist Party. That was in 1935, when there was a change in the Communist Party. He explained first that the Communist Party was the vanguard of the people of the working class.

After I left the school, I got a letter, quite some time after, to come to Milwaukee to hear an address by Earl Browder, a report on the International meeting of the Communist Party that he attended in 1935. After that I joined up with the Workers' Alliance at Delavan. Some men came from Racine to organize an alliance there. I joined it and became secretary of it. In the spring of 1936, word went out through Lyle Olson and Finski that there would be a march of the Alliance workers and the W.P.A. from the surrounding territories. We were not sure whether to bring the Walworth county group or not. I went with two other men, who were either Socialists or Social Labor people. They belonged to the party in England. They were from the W.P.A. At Madison I was put on the committee in charge for having the strikes. We held our committee meetings—the private ones were held in the book store, the Vanguard Book Store.

That is, the leadership of the strike, the striking committee, the strikers' committee, those were all made up of members of the Communist Party. A young fellow, Barney Seigal, who was a U.W. student, a boy from New York, was the one who gave us instructions how to carry on, how to act.

Question: How long did you hold the Capitol?

Goff: Ten days.

Question: Do you know of your own personal knowledge that the leaders of the Workers' Alliance on this occasion at least were members of the Communist Party and the Young Communist League?

Goff: Yes.

Question: Did your experience in the Workers' Alliance confirm that for you?

Goff: Yes.

Question: Now, you have had connection with other so-called front organizations of the Communist Party?

Goff: Yes. The American League for Peace and Democracy. It has changed its name now.

Question: At that time it was the League Against War and Fascism?

Goff: Yes, sir.

Question: Now, as the American League for Peace and Democracy, have you attended meetings of that organization?

Goff: I belonged to that organization. My office in the Manhattan building in Milwaukee was next to it. I did a lot of work for it, spoke for it. I have a paper where I spoke on some of their programs.

Question: Did the leaders of the Young Communist League receive instructions as to what they should do in the American League for Peace and Democracy?

Goff: Yes; there were caucuses in that organization as to the control of the other organization, and to determine its policy.

Question: In those caucuses the party members would receive instructions how to act in the League as a matter of policy?

Goff: Yes.

Question: You were told in the Young Communist League about the policy of the American League for Peace and Democracy, and how to act?

Goff: Yes, sir.

Question: What other organizations were you a member of?

Goff: The American Youth Congress. I was a member of the National Committee of the American Youth Congress; and was responsible for bringing the American Youth Congress to Milwaukee.

Question: In what year?

Goff: In 1937. I had charge of all activities.

Question: You were in charge of arrangements for bringing the American Youth Congress to Milwaukee?
Goff: Yes, sir.
Question: Was that the National Congress?
Goff: That is the National Congress.
Question: What leaders of the American Youth Congress did you meet on that occasion?
Goff: I met most all of the leaders.
Question: Did you meet Joseph Cadden?
Goff: I met Joseph Cadden, Jim Lerner, William Hinckley, Miriam Bogorad, Rose Terlin, Rose Troiano, Waldo McNutt.
Question: Were all of the persons you named known to you as members of the Young Communist League?
Goff: That is true.
Question: Did you have caucus meetings of that group?
Goff: Yes, sir.
Question: To determine—
Goff: Both before the Congress and after. We met in caucus, and we were told in the caucus to choose whom we wanted on the slate for the candidates for the National Congress.
Question: Was Joseph Cadden at that time chairman?
Goff: No, Hinckley was.
Question: Was Cadden secretary?
Goff: He was secretary.
Question: Did you receive as a member of that group any special instructions to the effect that you and others were not, under any circumstances, to address Cadden and Hinckley in such a way as to disclose their party membership?
Goff: That is true. I was warned by Leon Kaplan, who was counsel for the W.O.L. at Milwaukee, and also a member of the National Committee, and Kling, a National Board member, arrived there a week before the meeting to warn us of that, and also this Carl Ross, a member of the National Board.
Question: Who is Carl Ross?
Goff: He is secretary of the Young Communist League.

Question: He is one of the leaders, and Herndon is president. . . . You also had connections with the American Student Union?

Goff: Yes, that is right.

Question: You know that the Young Communist League held caucuses to determine the policies of that organization?

Goff: Yes. We adopted the policy of changing off from the Oxford pledge to the policy of collective security. That was determined by the party caucus.

Goff was a member of the National Committee of the Young Communist League. In this capacity, he received copies of the minutes of the National Resident Board of the Young Communist League. Mr. Goff turned the originals of these official minutes over to the Special Committee on Un-American Activities. At the upper left-hand corner of each set of these minutes appeared the words "Please destroy after reading."

The relationship of the Young Communist League to the Southern Negro Youth Congress is illustrated in the minutes of April 9, 1938. "Our major objectives were secured," declared the minutes. "The congress movement showed an advanced political note on almost every point," was one of the observations made in the minutes. Edward Strong, member of the administrative committee of the American Youth Congress, is chairman of the Southern Negro Youth Congress.

The minutes of June 11, 1938, gave a picture of how the Young Communist League was working behind the scenes to guide the policies of the World Youth Congress which was convened at Poughkeepsie, N. Y., in August, 1938.

In the minutes of July 9, 1938, Gil Green, head of the Young Communist League in the United States, discussed the work of the American Youth Congress and the World

Youth Congress in a manner which threw a good deal of light on the communist control of both of these bodies. Green also discussed the World Youth Congress in the minutes of July 23rd.

At the annual Communist Party picnic in Baltimore, the section organizer of the Communist Party and the Baltimore delegate of the American Youth Congress were the speakers.

At the Second American Youth Congress held in Detroit in 1935, Clarence Hathaway, leading American Communist and editor of the *Daily Worker*, was one of the principal speakers. There was "prolonged applause" from the delegates for Hathaway's blunt and emphatic communist pronouncement in which he declared:

I am sure that the American youth, guided and led by the American Youth Congress will be a force working for the defense of the Soviet Union, our Socialist Fatherland, and for the defeat of our own robber imperialist government and for the victory of the American toiling masses (Prolonged applause).

In his book, *Communism in the United States*, Earl Browder pointed to the collaboration of the Young People's Socialist League and the Young Communist League in the American Youth Congress, and attributed that successful collaboration to the work of the Youth Section of the American League Against War and Fascism. Browder further declared that, in the American Youth Congress, "the political center of gravity is the work of our Y.C.L." He added: "Practically all the basic proposals and policy came from us or from those influenced by us."

The Eastern Pennsylvania Youth Congress, affiliated with the American Youth Congress, adopted a program which bears the distinct marks of the Communist Party "line," including "Support of the Soviet Union's Proposals for Total Disarmament."

Writing in his pamphlet, *Young Communists and the Unity of Youth,* Gil Green declared that the young Communists took the lead in seeing to it that non-Communists played the important role in determining the language of the "Declaration of Rights of American Youth." Green observed: "By working in this manner, we did not weaken the prestige of the Young Communist League, but strengthened it."

In his Report on the Sixth World Congress of the Young Communist International, held in Moscow in 1935, Gil Green showed how the American Youth Congress represented a part of the People's Front which the Communist International had ordered Communists throughout the world to set about building.

In his book, *From Bryan to Stalin,* William Z. Foster said of the Communist Party: "It is playing an important part in the American Youth Congress."

Speaking of the American Youth Congress in his book, *The People's Front,* Earl Browder wrote: "We Communists are proud that our party, and especially our Young Communist League, has good working relations with these organizations of young people."

The official organ of the Young Communist League, *West Coast Young Worker,* asked: "Why does the Young Communist League put all its energies behind building a successful American Youth Congress?"

When Carl Ross, national secretary of the Young Communist League, testified before the Committee on Education and Labor of the United States Senate, it was the American Youth Congress which gave out a formal press release concerning his testimony.

Finally, in July 1939, after the American Youth Congress had been charged with domination by the Communists for several years, the organization, meeting in its annual session, adopted a resolution which condemned "all forms of dictatorship, regardless of whether they be communist, fascist, nazi or any other type."

This resolution was clearly an evasion. It did not condemn communism. When he appeared before the Special Committee on Un-American Activities, Mr. Hinckley stated that the young Communists "voted for that resolution."

On July 8, 1939, the *Daily Worker* explained why the young Communists voted for the resolution. "There is no such thing as 'communist dictatorship,'" said the *Daily Worker*, "so that they did not take a stand against something in which they believe."

In recent years, the Communist Party has had three distinct phases of policy with respect to the present administration at Washington. These phases have been as follows: (1) pronounced hostility toward the Administration, 1933 to 1935-6; (2) a period in which the Communist Party made great efforts to ingratiate itself with the Administration, 1936 to August, 1939; and (3) the present period in which the Communist Party again bitterly attacks the Administration. The published statements of the Communist Party and of the American Youth Congress over the past six years show that both organizations have gone through these three phases, and with both organizations the changes from one phase to another have been simultaneous.

In 1935, Browder wrote: "Roosevelt is carrying out more thoroughly, more brutally than Hoover, the capitalist attack against the living standards of the masses and the sharpest national chauvinism in foreign relations." In the same year, the American Youth Congress took a similar position.

In 1938, Browder wrote: "Only the courageous implementing of the policy laid down by President Roosevelt in Chicago can save our country, and all the capitalist world, from unparalleled reaction and catastrophe." In the same year, the American Youth Congress supported whole-heartedly the foreign policy of the Administration. "In this regard, the delegates welcomed the good neighbor policy inaugurated by President Roosevelt and would welcome even further cooperation for its fuller application," said the official report of the World Youth Congress which was convened at Poughkeepsie, N. Y., in August, 1938. The World Youth Congress, in its report, also stated: "Most delegates were agreed on the necessity for discriminating in the treatment of the aggressor and his victim, for the organization of deterrents to aggression and for quarantining the war makers."

In 1940, Browder said: "When Roosevelt assumed the leadership of the war party, he inevitably assumed the leadership of domestic reaction." In a letter to the President, the Maryland Youth Congress wrote: "Last Friday you spoke for those aggressors against the American people." The New York Youth Congress, at its session on May 25, 1940, adopted a resolution which "unequivocally condemned the armament program of the National Government." Out of the one thousand delegates, only twelve dissented from this resolution.

The highest Communist leaders, in both New York and Moscow, have declared repeatedly in one way or another that they took over the American Youth Congress in its infancy, that they have been the guiding force in its policies ever since, and that they propose to use the organization for ends which are clearly un-American. If the leaders of the American Youth Congress believe these Communist claims to be untrue, they have only to issue a denial of them. If they believe that the prestige of the American Youth Congress has been damaged by these Communist claims, it is a simple matter for them to issue an unequivocal condemnation of communism and the Communist Party. But, in the six years of its existence, the American Youth Congress has declined, by overwhelming votes, again and again, to go on record in condemnation of communism, the Communist Party, the Soviet Union, or Stalin's wars of conquest upon small nations.

CHAPTER VI

A TROJAN HORSE AS AN INSURANCE AGENT

ONE of the largest and most influential organizations set up and controlled by the Communists is the International Workers Order.

At its recent annual convention, William Weiner was re-elected president of the I.W.O. Weiner has been financial secretary of the Communist Party for a number of years. Last year he was convicted for obtaining an American passport by fraud. When he appeared as a witness before the Special Committee on Un-American Activities, Weiner stated under oath that he was born in Atlantic City. The jury before which he was subsequently tried found that he had been born in Russia and that his real name is Welwel Warzower.

The general secretary of the International Workers Order is Max Bedacht, a German-born Communist functionary and one-time secretary of the Communist Party of the United States He came to the United States in 1908, and has lived in New York, Detroit, San Francisco, Philadelphia, and Chicago. He has been a barber, a factory worker, and an editor. He was naturalized in the Superior Court of San Francisco, in April, 1915. He was a charter member of the Communist Party, and, since its beginning, has held important posts in the Party. He served as the Party's propaganda director for a period of two years, and edited the *Communist* for a while. He was acting secretary of the Party in 1929 and has served as district organizer. He has been a candidate on the Communist ticket for United States Senator in both New York and Illinois. At one time, he was a member of the national executive committee of the American League for Peace and Democracy. He was also a member of the national committee of the International Labor Defense. He has been the general secretary of the International Workers Order since 1933.

Bedacht admitted that he had made four or five trips to Russia since 1919; and that he was once a member of the executive committee of the Communist International. He refused to say whether he had traveled to Moscow on an illegal passport, on the ground that his answer might incriminate him. He refused to say whether he would support the United States in the event of a war with Russia; but he did state emphatically that he approved the Soviet-Nazi Pact.

The records of the State Department show that the first American passport ever issued to Max Bedacht was dated May 10, 1933; so that, for a period of twelve to fifteen years, while he was traveling back and forth between this country and Russia, he did not have an American passport in his real name.

The national executive secretary of the I.W.O. is Herbert Benjamin who until recently was general secretary-treasurer of the Workers Alliance. According to the testimony of Earl Browder, Benjamin is an alternate (known as a "candidate" in Party language) on the national committee of the Communist Party. Benjamin's shift from the Workers Alliance to the I.W.O. is a good illustration of the way the Party moves its functionaries from one organization to another.

One of the vice-presidents elected at the convention of the I.W.O. this year was Louise Thompson, long an outstanding Negro woman member of the Communist Party. Miss Thompson's record of affiliations is an interesting one with which to illustrate the interlocking personnel of the Communist Trojan Horse organizations. Her record in addition to being vice-president of the I.W.O. is as follows: member of the Women's Commission of the Communist Party; member of the editorial board of the *New Pioneer*, Communist Party publication for children; contributor to the *Party Organizer*, an official Party publication; contributor to the *Working Woman*, another official Party magazine; one of the editors of the *Woman Today*, a front magazine of the Party; member of the Committee of Professional Groups for Browder and Ford, an election campaign group; member of the Non-Partisan Committee for the Reelection of Congressman Vito Marcantonio, a group made up almost exclusively of Party members and fellow travelers; speaker at the annual gatherings of the National Negro Congress; member of the Arrangements Committee for the United States Congress Against War, out of which grew the American League for Peace and Democracy; member of the National Scottsboro Committee of Action; member of the National Committee for the Defense of Political Prisoners; member of the National Committee for People's Rights; member of the National Committee of the International Labor Defense; and sponsor of the League of Women Shoppers.

Another of the recently elected vice-presidents of the International Workers Order is Rockwell Kent, the well-known artist. In his own person, Kent is a study in red. His record of affiliation with communist-controlled organizations is matched by very few Americans. Only such persons as Robert Morss Lovett, secretary of the Virgin Islands, Roger Baldwin, director of the American Civil Liberties

Union, Malcolm Cowley, editor of the *New Republic*, Donald Ogden Stewart, Hollywood writer, Vito Marcantonio, member of Congress, and Leane Zugsmith, writer, have records that compare in volume with that of Rockwell Kent.

Kent has denied that he is a Communist. Nevertheless, he wrote in the *New Masses:* "I joined the American Artists' Congress because I . . . hope that an artists' union would serve the only worthwhile political cause of today: Communism." In the minds of most people, that is enough to justify one in describing Kent as a Communist. But even if we did not have his own statement that Communism is the "only worthwhile political cause of today," we have his record of Communist affiliations which is even more conclusive in its implications.

In the last presidential election, Kent was chairman of the Committee of Professional Groups for Browder and Ford. Unless we are to indulge in meaningless quibble, we must assume that anyone who campaigns for the candidates of the Communist Party is not an opponent of Communism. In the last congressional elections, Kent was a member of the Citizens Committee for Amter. Israel Amter, long an outstanding leader of the Communist Party, was running for Congress on the Communist Party ticket.

Four years ago, Kent was a member of the Non-Partisan Committee for the re-election of Congressman Vito Marcantonio.

In recent years, the magazine *Soviet Russia Today* has published two "open letters" signed by numerous Communist Party members and fellow travelers. One of these letters urged "closer cooperation with the Soviet Union." The other was a defense of the Moscow purge trials. Both letters were signed by Rockwell Kent.

Kent has been a contributor to the Communist weekly, *New Masses*. Last year he was a member of the United May Day Provisional Committee which had charge of the May Day demonstration of the Communist Party. He is a member of the National Committee of the International Labor Defense (see Chapter VIII). He has been a contributing artist for *Soviet Russia Today*.

Kent was a member of the National Committee of the now-defunct American League for Peace and Democracy. As has already been pointed out, he has been a sponsor for the League's New York successor, the New York Peace Association.

Kent was chairman of the National Committee for the Defense of Political Prisoners, and is now chairman of the National Committee for People's Rights. He is affiliated with the National Emergency Conference for Democratic Rights, also with the American Committee for Democracy and Intellectual Freedom.

The Conference on Pan American Democracy listed Kent as one of its sponsors along with a select group of Party members and fellow travelers. He has been affiliated with the communist-controlled League of American Writers, and is a sponsor of the Motion Picture Artists' Committee which is made up largely of the communist-inclined members of the screen world. Frontier Films lists him on its Advisory Board. He signed the Call to the First Congress of the Mexican and Spanish American Peoples of the United States, an organization which was planned in the secret councils of the Communist Party of Texas.

Kent was a member of the Medical Bureau and North American Committee to Aid Spanish Democracy. When that was transformed into the Spanish Refugee Relief Campaign, under the honorary chairmanship of Harold L. Ickes,

Kent became a sponsor of the new organization. When the Communists lost control of the Spanish Refugee Relief Campaign by the narrow margin of one vote, they abandoned the organization and set up in its place the United American Spanish Aid Committee. Kent became a sponsor of that. He was affiliated with the Washington Committee to Lift the Spanish Embargo, and was a sponsor for the Refugee Scholarship and Peace Campaign. His sponsoring has also included the American Committee for Non-Participation in Japanese Aggression.

In New York, the Communist control what is known as the Progressive Committee to Rebuild the American Labor Party. Kent is a member of its Executive Committee.

Kent himself has told why he joined the American Artists' Congress. He expected it to serve the cause of Communism. Recently, there were important defections from the Artists' Congress by artists who had become weary of its domination by the Communists. Kent is honorary president of the Artists Union of Philadelphia.

It is obvious, of course, that no man who does not give his whole life to it can possibly know what is going on in so many organizations as these with which Rockwell Kent is affiliated in one way or another. He represents the application of the Communist tactic of using prominent persons as sponsors for their front organizations. The supply of these sponsors is distinctly limited, and it is necessary, therefore, for the Communist Party to use it over and over again. By so doing, however, they provide a very definite clue to the identification of their Trojan Horses.

Now, in addition to all the positions which we have enumerated, Kent assumes the position of vice-president of the International Workers Order.

In his book, *Communism in the United States,* Earl

Browder has the following to say about the International Workers Order:

> Since the Seventh Convention we have made another important addition to the list of mass revolutionary organizations; this is the Mutual Benefit Society, International Workers' Order. The International Workers' Order has before it the problem of how to consolidate and further extend its mass membership, without lowering its previous high standard of revolutionary activity, of political education of its members, especially through involving them more directly in the class struggle.

In a pamphlet issued by the campaign committee of the International Workers Order, is found the following statement:

> For these reasons, we propose to the members and to the friends of the International Workers' Order to support the platform, to vote for the candidates and to help in the election campaign of the Communist Party. . . . Of all the parties in the field, we find the Communist Party to be the only one that concerns itself with the welfare and interest of the masses.

In the *Daily Worker* for August 4, 1936, is a front page story announcing that the "nationally known leaders of the International Workers Order yesterday pledged $50,000 of the $250,000 People's Chest against reaction which is being raised by the election campaign committee of the Communist Party."

The International Workers Order was formed in 1930. It is incorporated under the laws of the State of New York, with a total membership of 165,000. It has 21,000 junior members and 1,900 lodges in 20 States of the Union. It claims to be a mutual benefit society, insuring its members in amounts from $100 to $3,000. Every member must carry mortuary benefits, but other benefits are optional.

Bedacht testified that the organization is growing very fast; and that the present monthly income from dues and premiums is about $110,000, or a total of more than $1,000,000 a year. It engages in social and political activities and, according to Bedacht, cooperates with anti-fascist movements and efforts to oppose anti-Semitic propaganda. It raised $40,000 to assist the Loyalist cause in Spain. It has formed committees to raise funds for the *Daily Worker*. It publishes a monthly magazine called *The Fraternal Outlook*, which has a circulation of 91,000. About a year and a half ago, the I.W.O. organized a full-time leaders' training school in New York.

The I.W.O. was affiliated with the American League for Peace and Democracy and contributed $100 every month to the League.

The International Workers Order will not permit a member of the police force to be a member.

From 1937 to 1939, the I.W.O. paid the *Daily Worker* the sum of $26,799.50 for publicity and advertisements.

In an article written by Max Bedacht for the *Daily Worker*, is found the following statement:

In this article, our main concern is how our proletarian fraternal organization, the International Workers' Order, can make the workers class-conscious. We will, therefore, deal here only with the third task, above mentioned, the problem of making the workers class-conscious. This problem is of the greatest importance. It is the major problem of Communist leadership in a non-party mass organization . . . Very seldom we make serious efforts of combining our revolutionary activities in such organizations with avowed purposes. For instance, the efforts to revolutionize the members of our mutual benefit society, of the I.W.O., must have something to do with the solution of the problem which brings the workers into the ranks of the I.W.O. . . . There is practically no limit to the degree of class consciousness which the I.W.O. can develop among its membership. . . . It is an organization that allows Communist leadership to drive its roots into the unchartered depths of the American working masses, where class consciousness has not yet penetrated. . . . The building of the I.W.O. is, therefore, one of the most important tasks of the mass work of the Communist Party. . . . The International Workers Order remains what it set out to be, an active proletarian mutual benefit society. The development of its members into militant trade unionists or into Communists thus becomes a natural result of a correct functioning of the I.W.O. as an active workers' mutual benefit society.

In another article written by Max Bedacht, under the heading "Bosses Know This," is found the following statement:

The capitalists spend a good deal of time and energy on the fraternal movement. Is it not also worth time and energy on the part of the revolutionary movement to work in this field, to counteract this capitalist activity and influence? Is it not also worth while for the revolutionary workers to take the absence of social insurance, and the need for mutual insurance as the starting point of a broad workers' mass movement?

Bedacht has declared his personal allegiance to the Communist International. In a statement which appeared in the *Daily Worker* and was identified by him as his statement, Bedacht said:

The decision of the Communist International has been made. Though some members of the United States delegation have opposed the decision of the Comintern, I emphatically believe that the decision of the Communist International must be executed loyally.

In his testimony, Mr. Bedacht agreed that if the Communist Party of the United States, or any other country, does not follow the Comintern "line," it has to get out.

At the Chicago convention of the International Workers Order, Earl Browder was one of the speakers. The *Daily Worker* of June 20, 1933, reported as follows:

> The huge audience in the Coliseum rose to its feet, singing the "Internationale," as it acclaimed Earl Browder, secretary of the Communist Party, who lashed away at President Roosevelt.

In the magazine *Communist* of August, 1933, there appears an article over the signature of Earl Browder containing the following statement:

> We must promote the use of every means of concentration; every feature of our work must carry through the principle of concentration. Party organizations, unemployed councils, I.W.O., I.L.D.—all of these are tremendous instruments for us.

The proof of complete Communist control of the International Workers Order is established out of the mouths of the organization's own leaders. Bedacht could not possibly have made that proof stronger than he has by his writings over a period of years. Despite this proof, we find that John L. Lewis, chairman of the C.I.O., and James B. Carey, secretary of the C.I.O., have put the seal of their endorsement upon the organization.

On the stationery of the United Mine Workers of America, John L. Lewis wrote the following letter:

April 5, 1938

Mr. William Weiner, *President,*
Mr. Max Bedacht, *General Secretary,*
International Workers Order,
80 Fifth Avenue,
New York, New York.

Dear Sirs:

Thanks greatly for the telegram on April 1st. It was most thoughtful of you to send it and I greatly appreciate the sentiments which you expressed. I send you thanks also on behalf of the membership of the United Mine Workers of America.

I wish you would extend to the members of your organization the greetings and good wishes of the United Mine Workers of America.

Sincerely yours,
John L. Lewis.

James B. Carey wrote the following letter to the I.W.O.:

International Workers Order,
80 Fifth Avenue,
New York City.

Dear Sirs and Brothers:

I have heard of the work performed by the International Workers Order during the great organizational drive in Steel. Our own International Union has from time to time received assistance from this progressive and fraternal organization.

We are glad to see that the I.W.O. continues to grow and know that its increasing strength will add to the strength of the American labor movement.

Fraternally yours,
James B. Carey,
General President,
United Electrical, Radio and Machine Workers of America.

When the two leading figures in an American labor movement which numbers several million members add the prestige of their names to the support of one of Stalin's most obvious Trojan Horses, it is clear that a menacing situation exists, one which requires the fullest exposure. John L. Lewis can hardly claim to be ignorant of the fact that William Weiner and Max Bedacht to whom he addressed his letter have been nationally prominent Communists for many years. James B. Carey can hardly plead ignorance in describing a Communist organization as "progressive," or in confusing subversive activity with progress. If ignorance it was which accounted for these two letters, it is a type of ignorance which disqualifies these two labor leaders from leading the workmen of America in a period when national defense is so closely bound up with the problem of stamping out the "fifth column."

CHAPTER VII

A TROJAN HORSE FOR THE UNEMPLOYED

So FAR as actual membership is concerned, the Workers Alliance is the largest Trojan Horse ever to come from Moscow's stable. At the peak of its influence some months ago, the Alliance had a membership of 600,000. Unlike the American Youth Congress and American League for Peace and Democracy which counted their millions by the simple process of totalling the aggregate of members in their affiliated organizations, the Workers Alliance actually enrolled more than a half million of our unemployed on its own membership books.

The complete history of the Workers Alliance would serve, all by itself, to illustrate most of the workings of Stalin's Trojan Horse technique. The present organization was formed through a merger of three already existing groups of the unemployed: the National Unemployment Councils, the National Unemployed Leagues, and the Workers Alliance (the last-named not to be confused with the organization after the merger). The merger of the three groups was effected in April, 1936.

The National Unemployed Leagues and the original Workers Alliance may, for our present purposes, be dismissed with a paragraph. The former organization was led by one Arnold Johnson who is this year the Communist Party's candidate for the governorship of Ohio. Unlike most of the members of the Communist Party (many of whom keep their membership secret), Johnson entered the

Party's ranks with a public declaration. It read, in part, as follows:

> We stand with the Soviet Union. We hail its socialist success and declare it to be the shining hope of the workers of the world ... We, as true Communists, call upon all comrades who believe likewise to forget their self-righteous sectarianism and oppositionism and to accept and work for the realistic program of the Communist Party of the U.S.A. and of the Communist International.

That made Johnson's position perfectly clear, and it is a pity that all Communists, especially those from the professional, literary, and office-holding strata of our society, have not possessed like courage and forthrightness in stating their convictions. Johnson brought his National Unemployed League into the present Workers Alliance. As for the original Workers Alliance, it may be observed that it was largely Socialist (as distinct from Communist) in its political affiliations. It was led by David Lasser, who became national president of the merger of the unemployed groups.

The organization known as the National Unemployment Councils was rigidly controlled by the Communist Party. At the time of the formation of the larger Workers Alliance, Herbert Benjamin was the Communist Party's national leader among the unemployed. He became the general secretary-treasurer of the new Workers Alliance in 1936. (As has been pointed out in an earlier chapter, Benjamin has now been transferred by the Communist Party to the position of national executive secretary of the International Workers Order.) It will be readily seen that Benjamin's position as general secretary-treasurer of the Workers Alliance was the key position in the organization. Furthermore, his completely Party-controlled National Unemployment Councils gave the new organization its political complexion. Even Lasser, having broken with the Communist Party's leaders, now concedes that the Workers Alliance which he headed for four years up until June, 1940, is under the complete domination of the Communist Party.

Let us go back to the origins of the National Unemployment Councils. These groups of the unemployed were set up on explicit instructions from Moscow. In their very inception, they gained a great deal of national publicity through a series of riots and disorders which they staged in many American cities on March 6, 1930. The *Daily Worker*, official newspaper of the Communist Party, announced in an eight-column headline on February 17th of that year: "World Unemployment Day Advanced to March 6." The story in the *Daily Worker* read, in part, as follows:

> The Executive Committee of the Communist International has decided to postpone the International Day for struggle against Unemployment. The date previously decided for International Unemployment Day was February 26th. To enable our Parties to prepare thoroughly real mass demonstrations and to carry on a broader preparation campaign the E.C.C.I. has decided to postpone it until March 6th. The Communist Party of the United States of America must utilize the added eight days for a most energetic campaign and organizational preparation so that great masses will be mobilized. The committees of action must be organized everywhere to guarantee the best cooperation between employed and unemployed workers. The Trade Union Unity League must receive every assistance by the Party forces in organizing the Unemployment Councils . . .

The foregoing statement, which is only one of thousands of its kind, should settle once and for all the question of whether or not the Communist Party receives instructions from Moscow. In obedience to Moscow's instructions, the demonstrations were held on March 6th. In New York, Detroit, Los Angeles, and elsewhere, they were turned into large-scale riots. Under the incitement of provocative speeches by William Z. Foster, Robert Minor, Israel Amter, Herbert Benjamin, Pat Toohey, James W. Ford, Rose Wortis, Jack Johnstone, Fred Biedenkapp, Norman Talentire, and others, the demonstration in New York was turned into a pitched battle against the police. Foster and some of the others were tried and convicted for their part in the rioting, and subsequently served prison sentences. Such was the real birth of the National Unemployment Councils.

The Communist Party press capitalized upon the violence which its leaders had incited on March 6th. Ten years later, on March 6, 1940, the Party celebrated the anniversary of its rioting. The *Daily Worker* editorially, called it "a date emblazoned on the pages of American history." Two whole pages of this official Party newspaper were devoted to the reminiscences of Foster, Amter, and Benjamin, and to other discussions of the incidents which marked the large-scale launching of the National Unemployment Councils.

Without exception, the leaders of the National Unemployment Councils—both national and local—were Communists. No attempt was made to hide the face of the Party in those days.

In December, 1931, the Communist Party, through its Unemployment Councils, staged "a hunger march" on Washington. The march was led by Herbert Benjamin. A document obtained from the files of Mr. Benjamin had the following to say with respect to the political significance of the National Hunger March: "It has been one of the greatest national mobilizations of workers carried out under the leadership of the Party." In discussing the future of the Unemployment Councils, the document went on to say:

> The struggle for immediate relief, for these immediate demands, must by no means be slackened but it must be tied up with a fight against the bourgeois political parties, bourgeois politicians and with an incessant exposure of the stand of the A.F. of L. officials and the Socialist Party, thereby raising the political consciousness of the unemployed masses and developing the struggle toward a higher level.

The instructions which were sent from Moscow for the holding of the March 6th demonstrations and the building of the Unemployment Councils came, as a rule, through the Red International of Labor Unions at Moscow (usually called the R.I.L.U.) to the Trade Union Unity League (usually known as the T.U.U.L.) to the leaders of the communist unemployed work. Many of these original instructions are in the possession of the Special Committee on Un-American Activities. One such set of instructions, or directives as they were customarily called, threatened Communist leaders with "removal" in case they did not carry out orders. This same document commands the T.U.U.L. leaders in the United States to "decide upon two or three large scale factories for direct communication with the R.I.L.U. (the sending of minutes, reports, and other materials)." In other words, these local factory nuclei of the Communist Party were to set up a system of reporting directly to the R.I.L.U. in Moscow.

A few days after the transmission of the foregoing directives to the United States, the R.I.L.U. sent a supplementary document of directives to William Z. Foster in which the following statement appeared: "Transform the factories into fortresses of the revolutionary trade union movement."

Still a few days later, the R.I.L.U. instructed its affiliated sections, including that in the United States, to begin a series of articles in the Party press dealing, among other things, with "work among the unemployed and linking it up with the work and struggle of the workers in industry."

Yet another set of directives from the R.I.L.U. to the T.U.U.L. in the United States called the attention of the Intercoms (International Committees) to the importance of the work among the unemployed. The document stated:

> The Intercoms should pay more attention to the unemployed movement, to their organization according to various industries and to the establishment of contact between the unemployed and workers on the job, in order to help the R.I.L.U. sections in the organization and extension of the struggle of the unemployed and in the linking up of their struggle with that of the workers on the job.

Immediately after the national hunger march led by the Communist Party and immediately following the receipt of the several sets of directives from the R.I.L.U., the T.U.U.L. issued its own directives on the subject of work among the unemployed. These directives stated that "the struggle for state social insurance" was one of the two central problems before the revolutionary trade union movement in the United States. They added:

> It is, therefore, the duty of the T.U.U.L. and all class-conscious workers . . . to propagate the necessity of the class struggle, of mass action, as the only method of struggle for the demands of the workers and unemployed.

A document entitled "Draft Resolution and Directives of the T.U.U.L. on the Work of the Revolutionary Unions,

Leagues and Minorities in the Struggles and Movement of the Unemployed" elaborated through eight pages the responsibility of the T.U.U.L. in the work of organizing the unemployed. The document definitely stated: "The T.U.U.L. fractions are responsible for the organization in every unemployed committee and councils of subcommittees for trade-union work."

A document from the Polburo (political bureau) of the Central Committee of the Communist Party of the United States stated:

Our work among the unemployed is a key to all our mass work and in this sense—in our opinion—must be the central task of the Party and of the entire revolutionary movement in the present moment.

This document further declared:

In every headquarters city of the district there shall be selected a comrade to lead the work among the unemployed. To form a committee similar to the CC (Central Committee), one from the T.U.U.L., one from the Party Sect to be in charge of coordinating the work in the entire district.

The foregoing statement shows precisely the degree and nature of the control of the National Unemployment Councils by the Communist Party.

The minutes of the bureau of the National Unemployment Councils for September 7, 1932, definitely linked the Councils with the Communist Party through support of its candidates for president and vice-president. The minutes state: "Official launching of march to take place thru huge mass meeting, this to serve as national rally for our candidates (Foster and Ford)."

The minutes of the bureau of the Unemployment Councils for December 13, 1932, stated that one of the methods for "combating the enemy" was by "penetrating them."

The minutes for the Unemployment Councils of December 27, 1932, showed the relation between the Pioneer Bureau (children's organization of the Communist Party), the Anti-War Conference in Latin America, the Trade Union Unity League, the Marine Workers Industrial Union, and the Workers International Relief on the one hand, and the National Unemployment Councils on the other hand.

The foregoing sets of minutes of the National Unemployment Councils list the persons present. All of them were outstanding members of the Communist Party, such as Benjamin, Winter, Sullivan, Girsch, Stachel, Jackson, Shepard, Weissman (Wiseman in later days), Amter, Todes, Wagenknecht, and Reddin. These were the national leaders of the National Unemployment Councils. All of them are listed on official documents of the Communist Party in the possession of the Special Committee on Un-American Activities as Party members.

Early in 1932, the Communists in the United States launched a campaign to collect 2,000,000 individual signatures and 1,000,000 on collective endorsements for an unemployment insurance bill.

This signature campaign was launched at a conference of the R.I.L.U. held in Prague, Czechoslovakia, in August, 1931. A document from Benjamin's files stated that "the resolution of the Prague Conference published in the *Communist* of this month offers further enlightenment of the forms of organization which you must apply." Investigation discloses that such a resolution was actually published in the *Communist* for December, 1931, and that it elaborated in great detail the manner in which the unemployment councils were to be set up in all countries. In other words, the Communist Party in the United States, functioning through the T.U.U.L., was simply carrying out the directives of the Moscow-controlled R.I.L.U. when the Communist Party here threw its energies into the building of the Unemployment Councils and the launching of the signature campaign for unemployment insurance.

In its mimeographed instructions on how to launch the signature campaign, the National Unemployment Councils stated: "All our Press shall be required to run a special column under the head, 'The Fight for Unemployment Insurance.'"

It is significant to observe that the National Unemployment Councils were in a position to say that "our press shall be required, etc." Investigation has shown that the *Daily Worker* began immediately to run a special column under the head which was specified by the National Unemployment Councils.

The directives for the signature campaign stated that "workers, especially foreign born workers, must be assured that the signatures will not be actually turned over to the government." This assurance was obviously for the purpose of shielding the signatories from identification by government agencies, and could only have meant that the Communist Party understood very well that government agencies knew the National Unemployment Councils to be a Communist Party organization.

These directives stated further that the "revolutionary unions of the T.U.U.L. shall send out individual and collective signature blanks, etc." Again, it is apparent that the National Unemployment Councils exercised authority not only over the Communist Party press but also over the T.U.U.L. as well. This is not strange when it is remembered that the Unemployment Councils were simply the

Trade Union Unity League and the Communist Party in a different guise.

The pyramiding of Trojan Horse organizations is one of the distinctive features of the Communist strategy. A new Trojan Horse is built out of a number of previously existing Trojan Horses. For example, when the American League Against War and Fascism was first launched, there were forty-nine organizations listed as its constituent bodies, each of the forty nine being entitled to equal representation in the new Trojan Horse. Out of the forty nine supporting groups, thirty four were already existing Communist Trojan Horses. The same pyramiding of communist-controlled organizations was used to advance the work of the National Unemployment Councils. From 1934 down to the time of the formation of the Workers Alliance in 1936, numerous communist-controlled or communist-sympathizing groups appeared in the field of the Party's work among the unemployed. An enumeration of some of these will show how they were used to feed the Moscow-directed movement.

The Veterans National Liaison Committee had its headquarters in Washington, D. C., under the chairmanship of George D. Brady. In a letter to Israel Amter who was acting as national secretary of the Unemployment Councils at the time, Brady wrote pledging the cooperation of his veterans organization.

The Trade Union Conference for United Action was one of the Trojan Horse organizations which was controlled by the Communist Party. At its Cleveland convention, the organization began the agitation which eventually enabled the communists to capture the organized movement of the unemployed. In its "Call to Action," the Trade Union Conference for United Action listed as one of its major objectives the following: "Build up the mass organizations of unemployed workers; promote the unification of all mass organizations of the unemployed, locally, statewide, and nationally." James W. Ford, vice-presidential candidate on the Communist Party ticket, was vice-chairman of the Cleveland convention. Louis Weinstock, leader in local No. 9 of the Painters Union and closely identified with the Communist Party for many years, was secretary of the arrangements committee for the convention. Louis Budenz, now president of the *Daily Worker*, was treasurer. Among the signers of the "Call to Action" were the following avowed members of the Communist Party: I. Amter, Frank Borich, Philip Frankfeld, Ben Gold, Ernest Kornfeld, Andrew Overgaard, Carl Winter, Herbert Benjamin, Earl Browder, James W. Ford, Clarence Hathaway, John Meldon, Philip Raymond, Joe Weber, Fred Biedenkapp, Ann Burlak, William Z. Foster, Roy Hudson, Andrew Onda, and Jack Stachel.

The Interprofessional Association for Social Insurance was distinctly communist-inclined in its sympathies. Mary van Kleeck of the Russel Sage Foundation was president of the organization, and Jacob Fisher was secretary. In a letter to Arnold Johnson, Miss van Kleeck and Mr. Fisher proposed the formation of a provisional national council for their newly-formed Interprofessional Association. They invited Johnson to become a member of this provisional national council and assured him that the National Unemployment Councils and the Trade Union Unity League were also being invited to name members. In a memorandum dated March 28, 1934, Miss van Kleeck gave the names of the members of the executive committee of the New York Chapter of the Interprofessional Association. Among them were persons who had had many connections with organizations controlled by the Communist Party, such as Kyle Crichton who wrote a weekly page for the *New Masses* under the alias of Robert Forsythe, Maxwell Stewart who is on the editorial board of *Soviet Russia Today*, and Jules Korchien who is now with the newspaper *PM* and has been with the Federal Housing Administration. The dominant element on the executive committee of Miss van Kleeck's organization was a group of well-known fellow travelers of the Communist Party. A need was felt for a new respectable professional lot of window dressing for the "social insurance" campaign of the National Unemployment Councils.

The National Congress for Unemployment and Social Insurance grew out of Miss van Kleeck's efforts. On September 12, 1934, Miss van Kleeck again wrote to Arnold Johnson, this time asking him to become a member of the organizing committee for the proposed National Congress. When the National Congress for Unemployment and Social Insurance materialized early in January, 1935, its sponsoring committee which Miss van Kleeck had initiated included the following avowed members of the Communist Party: Herbert Benjamin, Max Bedacht, William Z. Foster, Granville Hicks, Lem Harris, Israel Amter, Earl Browder, Ben Gold, Roy Hudson, Elmer Johnson, Fred Biedenkapp, Ben Davis, Jr., Harold Hickerson, and Grace Hutchins. Most of the remaining members of the sponsoring committee were prominent fellow travelers. Herbert Benjamin was its executive secretary. The committee's headquarters were at 799 Broadway, New York, a building which we have already pointed out has housed so many Communist Party groups.

The International Juridical Association next came into this intricate picture. Shortly after the sessions of the National Congress for Unemployment and Social Insurance, Leo J. Linder wrote to Israel Amter offering the services of the International Juridical Association in the drafting of a social insurance bill. Mr. Amter appeared to be occupying some authoritative position in the National Congress for Unemployment and Social Insurance, although the records in the possession of the Special Committee on Un-American Activities do not indicate that Mr. Amter held any official position in the organization. Later in the year, in a letter dated September 25, 1935, Leo J. Linder wrote Herbert Benjamin that Dorothy Douglas and Katherine Lumpkin, professors at Smith College, had drafted some notes and suggestions for a social insurance bill. It appeared that these two Smith College professors were working for the movement through the International Juridical Association.

The International Juridical Association is still functioning as a communist-controlled legal group. Among the Communist Party members on its national committee, are the following: David J. Bentall, candidate for attorney-general of Illinois on the Communist ticket in 1928; Leo Gallagher, candidate for secretary of state of California on the Communist ticket in 1938; Yetta Land, candidate for county prosecutor of Cleveland, Ohio, on the Communist ticket in 1936; and Isaac E. Ferguson, a charter member of the Communist Party. Employees of the federal government who are on the national committee of the International Juridical Association include the following: Henry T. Hunt, Department of the Interior; Nathan Witt, National Labor Relations Board; and David K. Niles, Department of Commerce.

During the period preliminary to the formation of the Workers Alliance in April, 1936, the Communist Party conducted its most energetic national campaign around the social insurance bill which was known as H. R. 2827 or the Lundeen Bill. In the *Communist* for November, 1936, William Z. Foster wrote, as follows:

Here I can mention only a few of the Communist Party's chief current activities: At the present time it has mobilized the support of at least 5,000,000 workers and others in support of the Workers Unemployment Insurance Bill (H.R. 2827).

The Communists were in direct touch with Representative Ernest Lundeen, later a United States Senator, who introduced their social insurance bill. On July 25, 1935, Congressman Lundeen wrote to Herbert Benjamin asking for a speech which Benjamin had apparently promised to prepare for him. It should be noted that this letter from Congressman Lundeen to Benjamin was addressed to the latter as secretary of the National Joint Action Committee. This Committee will be discussed later.

On July 22, 1935, Congressman Lundeen wrote to Benjamin concerning the organization of support for H.R. 2827, this time addressing Benjamin as organizer for the National Unemployment Councils.

On August 15, 1935, Congressman Lundeen wrote to Benjamin on the subject of "a new alignment in the country" which the Congressman declared to be "of extreme importance."

On August 17, 1935, Benjamin replied to Congressman Lundeen's letter of July 25th, promising to forward copies of the requested speech within a few days.

The Project Workers Council for Joint Action was an organization which had a tie-up with such well-known communist-controlled organizations as the Unemployment Councils, the Office Workers Union (affiliate of the Trade

Union Unity League), and the Federation of Architects, Engineers, Chemists, and Technicians.

The National Emergency Conference Against the Government Wage Program was convened in Washington, D. C., in June, 1935. The leaders of the gathering were prominent Communist Party members. Frank Mozer, candidate for public office in Philadelphia on the Communist ticket, was elected chairman unanimously. Herbert Benjamin gave the "general report." Philip Frankfeld, now secretary of the Communist Party in Boston, was elected secretary of the continuations committee. Merrill C. Work and Sam Wiseman, avowed Communist Party members from New York, were among the leaders. The Conference adopted a resolution in favor of the Lundeen Bill, H.R. 2827.

In the summer of 1935, one of the many "front" organizations of the Communist Party working among the unemployed was known as the United Committee of Action. This organization's headquarters were located at 799 Broadway, New York, N. Y., where so many other communist-controlled groups have had their headquarters for many years. The United Committee of Action was "sponsored by the American League of Ex-Servicemen."

The American League of Ex-Servicemen also had its headquarters at 799 Broadway, New York, N. Y. A letter from the organization, dated October 19, 1935, is signed by P. V. Cacchione. Cacchione is an outstanding Communist Party leader and communist candidate for office in New York City.

It has already been shown that Herbert Benjamin was addressed in a letter from Congressman Lundeen as secretary of the National Joint Action Committee for Genuine Social Insurance. The secretary of this organization was Morris J. Angel who is now affiliated with the New York

Peace Association. In a communication dated April 9, 1935, Morris J. Angel wrote as secretary of the New York Joint Action Committee to one Steinberg. The matter dealt with in this communication seems to pertain to "inactivity" in Section 20. In the files of the Special Committee on Un-American Activities, there is a document which identifies one Steinberg as the District Representative of Section 20 of the Communist Party of New York. Steinberg's first name is Max. In addition to his being District Representative of Section 20 of the Communist Party, District No. 2, Steinberg is listed as responsible for the Party's "concentration" work in the metal industries.

In the minutes of the New York Joint Action Committee, May 6, 1935, the names of the persons present were listed. These included J. Landy (one-time organizer in New Jersey for the International Workers Order), M. Stone (one-time communist candidate for State Assembly in New York), and M. J. Angel.

The minutes of the New York Joint Action Committee, May 22, 1935, list the following additional Communists as present: Helen Lynch (Communist Party member deceased), and Sam Wiseman (communist candidate for State Assembly in New York in 1936), now head of the Workers Alliance for New York.

On April 8, 1935, the New York Joint Action Committee held an "emergency conference" for H.R. 2827 (Lundeen Bill). Almost all of the organizations listed as having representatives present were well-known communist groups.

The minutes of the New York Joint Action Committee for December 7, 1935, show that Norman Tallentire, long an outstanding member of the Communist Party, was present.

In a letter dated June 25, 1935, J. Landy, acting secretary

of the New York Joint Action Committee addressed Sam Weissman as "Dear Comrade" and signed with the greeting "Comradely yours."

Early in 1936, Pauline Rogers was secretary of the New York Joint Action Committee. Miss Rogers was communist candidate for State Assembly in New York in 1936. She has held many posts in communist Trojan Horse groups.

Herbert Benjamin was executive secretary of the National Joint Action Committee for Genuine Social Insurance. Its principal function seems to have been to support the campaign which the Communist Party was conducting for the Lundeen Bill.

In November, 1935, J. Landy signed a communication on the letterhead of the National Joint Action Committee. Mary van Kleeck was listed on the letterhead as a member of the Committee, and F. Elmer Brown, active leader of the Communists in the typographical union in New York, was listed as chairman.

In October, 1935, Joseph Landy addressed a letter to Sam Wiseman (name sometimes spelled Weissman) on the letterhead of the Fraternal Federation for Social Insurance. The letter read as follows:

Oct. 16, 1935

SAM WISEMAN,
11 W. 18 St.,
N.Y.

Dear Comrade Wiseman:

Referring to your letter of the 15th inst., there seems to be a misunderstanding on your part about the entire matter. This is of course due to the fact that you have only heard from Comrade Angel.

When the sub-committee of the district met to discuss the

TROJAN HORSE FOR THE UNEMPLOYED

HR 2827 some weeks ago we decided that we would devote most of our attention to the reviving of the Fraternal Federation and the Trade unions. This was done because the Joint Action committee was and had been for quite a long while almost non-existent. I was made responsible for the Fraternal Fed. and the Joint Action Committee. I state this merely to clarify the situation.

When Angel and I discussed the election campaign some weeks ago we decided to propose a distribution of 100,000 leaflets, in addition to circularizing all the candidates for office. We at that time roughly figured that the entire cost of this *particular* campaign would raise the cost of the leaflets, plus letters, postage, labor etc. to $2.00 per thousand. At the meeting on Sept. 23 I made the motion accordingly, and it was thus accepted.

Upon going over the figures a few days ago I found that the total actual cost of this election campaign would only cost $1.25 per thousand. I therefore proposed to Angel that we reduce the price. He of course refuses to do this because he wants the Joint Action Committee to have a reserve of money for use after the election campaign. This is something that is entirely contrary to the motion I made, and also to the general decision of the district sub-committee.

I propose that instead of giving the Joint Action Committee, an organization that is almost non-existent, and that we had decided will be pushed into the background for a while, $50.00 to play with, that we instead reduce the cost of the leaflets and thus distribute more of them. I do not think it is correct to bleed the A.F. of L. committee and my organization for money that we both need for immediate action in connection with the Bill.

An instance; The Artists Union only took 1000 leaflets because of the cost. Sam Nessin informed me that were it not for the fact that the leaflets had already been printed he would only have taken 10,000. He has to charge the locals $2.00. Could he not distribute more at a lower price?

As a matter of fact Nessin only paid $1.25 per thousand thus far. And I know that he will not pay anymore because he does not have the money. You have only paid $5.00 thus far. The C.P. has not paid any at all. The local action committees in so far as I know have not paid any money at all.

In so far as the charges that I am hindering the campaign. Angel is to put it mildly cockeyed. I am only three weeks on a new assignment. You can of course visualize the amount of work I have, to put it in order to familiarize myself with the work and to organize it. Yet, I have put in at least three full days rushing from printer to organization, etc. in order to get the work done. Angel seems to think that because I am a fulltime functionary all I have to do with my time is run errands and seal envelopes. I left him a note yesterday asking him to fold some letters and to deliver some leaflets. He does not do it, but tells me that since he is working it is my job to do it. Nonesense.

Comrade Angel of course is too quick to place "charges" etc. Instead of accepting my proposal to meet with the committee, he ran off with the threat that he would tell Amter that I am hindering etc.

Comrade Shaffer agrees with me.

I have incidently already spent $24.00 on the leaflets. I will spend up to $1.25 per thousand and no more until a committee decides otherwise.

Comradely yours,
Joseph Landy.

The contents of this letter are most important as showing the manner in which the Communist Party handled some of its "front" organizations. The chairman of the Fraternal Federation of Social Insurance was one G. Primoff, candidate on the communist ticket for Congressman from New York in 1931 and also in 1936. In this letter, Landy clearly identified himself, Wiseman, and Morris J. Angel as members of the Communist Party.

To recapitulate briefly, evidence has already been presented to show that the National Unemployed Leagues were under communist leadership at the time of their entrance into the Workers Alliance in April, 1936. Arnold Johnson, their national leader, had openly taken a stand in support of the Communist International. In the newly-formed Workers Alliance, forty-eight of the affiliates were from the National Unemployed Leagues.

Sixty-seven of the affiliates in the new organization were from the National Unemployment Councils which were completely communist in their leadership and to a very large extent in their membership as well.

The Workers Alliance had specified that all organizations which affiliated with it must do so on the basis of a "class struggle" program. On March 3, 1935, at its convention in Washington, D. C., the Workers Alliance of America adopted a unity resolution in which point No. 6 read as follows:

That we favor such unity on the basis of a class struggle policy and that no organizations willing to support such a policy and to enter a united organization shall be excluded.

For several years prior to the consummation of the unity which was achieved in the Workers Alliance in April, 1936, the Communist Party had been pressing energetically for such a merger. It should be remembered that the National Unemployment Councils, in typical communist fashion, never hesitated to urge all kinds of "united fronts" with those individuals and groups which were looked upon as enemies of the proletariat.

In the *Daily Worker* for July 10, 1935, the National Unemployment Councils proposed a unity of organizations working among the unemployed on the basis of a tri-partite representation from the National Unemployment Councils, the National Unemployment Leagues, and the Workers Alliance (the already existing organization which was under the leadership of David Lasser).

In his book, *The People's Front*, Earl Browder wrote of the role of the Communist Party in the formation of the Workers Alliance, as follows:

> Later we helped unite all organizations of the unemployed into one united national organization of the unemployed—the Workers Alliance of America.

Numerous leaders of the Workers Alliance (as it is presently constituted) are avowed members of the Communist Party. With respect to many others, there is ground for belief that they, too, are members of the Communist Party although belonging to that large group of undercover members of whom the official publications of the Party sometimes speak. One by one let us note the open Party members who are on the small National Executive Board of the Alliance.

Arnold Johnson, a member of the National Executive Board of the Workers Alliance, urged acceptance of the program of the Communist Party and of the Communist International, and during the current political campaign is communist candidate for the governorship of Ohio.

Russell Watson, a member of the National Executive Board, was communist candidate for magistrate in Philadelphia in the elections of 1937.

Harold P. Brockway, a member of the National Executive Board, was communist candidate for governor in Washington in 1936. He was also on the ballot as a presidential elector in the same year.

Alex Noral, a member of the National Executive Board,

was communist candidate for United States Senator from the State of Washington in 1932. Noral was also communist candidate for presidential elector for the State of California in 1936.

Wallace Talbot, a member of the National Executive Board, was communist candidate for governor of Utah in 1936.

Emma Tenayuca, a member of the National Executive Board, was associated with the American League for Peace and Democracy in Texas, and is the state chairman of the Communist Party of Texas.

J. Austin Beasley, a member of the National Executive Board, is international organizer for the United Cannery, Agricultural, Packing, and Allied Workers of America, a C.I.O. affiliate which the Special Committee on Un-American Activities found unanimously to have an entrenched communist leadership. Donald Henderson, avowed member of the Communist Party, is head of this union of which J. Austin Beasley is international organizer.

Sam Wiseman, a member of the National Executive Board, was candidate on the Communist Party ticket for State Assembly in New York in 1936. Wiseman is also state organizer of the Workers Alliance in New York.

Frankie Duty, a member of the National Executive Board, has been praised as a communist leader in the *Party Organizer* and in the *Communist*.

M. Dean Weiner, a member of the National Executive Board, signed the communist nominating petitions in Pennsylvania in 1940. M. Dean Weiner was until recently secretary of the Workers Alliance in the State of Pennsylvania. He was taken from that position and made secretary of the Communist Party of Pennsylvania.

Hilliard Bernstein, a member of the National Executive

Board, was a member of the Abraham Lincoln Battalion in Spain—a fighting unit which Earl Browder declared to be made up predominantly of Communist Party members.

James H. Dolsen admitted on the stand before the Special Committee on Un-American Activities that he was an official of the Workers Alliance in Pittsburgh.

In an official press release, the Workers Alliance of Greater New York publicized its endorsement of the Communist Party's candidates for the City Council in New York.

The handbills of the Workers Alliance and of temporary federated groups in which the Workers Alliance is included show a preponderance of communist-controlled organizations in such associations. For example, Local No. 453 and Local No. 5 of the American Federation of Teachers, District Council No. 9 of the Painters Union, the National Maritime Union, the American Communications Association, the Fur Workers International Union, the International Workers Order, the Progressive Women's Council, the Transport Workers Union, the Artists Union, the American Newspaper Guild (WPA Section), and the Federation of Architects, Engineers, Chemists, and Technicians naturally associate themselves together in demonstrations and federated committees on the obvious basis of their common communist proclivities.

Helen Lynch was one of the most active Communist Party members among the women of New York City. When she died about two years ago, the *Daily Worker* had much to say about her active service for the Party. Near the second anniversary of her death, the New York County Workers Alliance held a Helen Lynch Memorial at which Sam Wiseman, Communist Party member and Workers Alliance official, was the principal speaker. The Workers

Alliance has named one of its centers in honor of Helen Lynch.

The Workers Alliance has regularly participated in the May Day Parades which have been managed by the Communist Party. Despite the fact that the Communists themselves describe these events as united fronts which are not under their control, trade unions and other organizations, which understand left-wing political matters and oppose the Communist Party, refrain from participation in the parades which are controlled by the Communist Party, and if they parade at all on May Day they do so under non-communist auspices.

The politically initiated will have no difficulty in following the zigzags of the "line" of the Communist Party and in detecting the ready response with which communist-controlled groups accept every important change in the Party's "line." The Workers Alliance from the time of its formation in April, 1936, down to the present, has followed faithfully the "line" of the Communist Party regardless of the sudden and complete changes which have taken place in the Party's policies.

The Communist Party describes the present war in Europe as an "imperialist war" and accuses "Wall Street" of working to bring about the entrance of the United States in that War. The Workers Alliance views the war in the same manner and makes the same accusation against "Wall Street."

The Workers Alliance has adopted the communist-originated slogan of The Yanks Are Not Coming.

During the period, 1936-1939, when the Communist Party was putting forth great effort to ingratiate itself into the favor of the Roosevelt Administration, the Workers Alliance was following the identical "line." Now that the

Communist Party has entered an entirely new phase in its attitude toward the Administration, the Workers Alliance follows suit obediently.

One of the less important indications of any organization's closeness to the Communist Party is the use of the Party's printing establishment, the Prompt Press, for the printing of its handbills, leaflets, and pamphlets. This has been discussed at some length in connection with the American Youth Congress and the Transport Workers Alliance. Many samples of Workers Alliance literature in the possession of the Special Committee on Un-American Activities show the use of printers' union label No. 209. Label No. 209 is leased by the Prompt Press.

Left-wingers are far more expert in detecting the identity and operations of each other than is the general public. Socialists know Communists and vice versa, with an almost infallible sense. Both wings of the socialist movement have publicly charged the Workers Alliance as at present constituted with complete domination by the Communist Party. The socialist group under the leadership of Norman Thomas has made such a charge. Likewise the socialist faction known as the Social-Democratic Federation which split from the Norman Thomas group.

For several reasons it has seemed necessary to present at length the bare factual evidence concerning the Communist domination of the Workers Alliance. It has been the largest of the communist Trojan Horses in recent years. It has had an intricate history of growth from beginnings which go straight back to Moscow. Until quite recently, it represented a powerful lobby in Washington. Members of the House of Representatives and of the United States Senate —scores of them— have felt impelled to accept invitations from the Workers Alliance to appear on its programs. Cabinet officers have likewise placed themselves at its disposal. The American people stand to gain by the internal dissension which has at last overtaken the Alliance and appears to lessen its influence greatly over the unemployed as well as over official Washington.

CHAPTER VIII

A TROJAN HORSE IN THE COURTS

THE International Labor Defense is the Trojan Horse in which the Communist Party is concealed when it appears in court. Of course, neither the I.L.D. nor the Party admits this fact. In the Trojan Horse era of Stalin's operations here, such admissions are not made, certainly not as a rule.

Testifying before the Special Committee on Un-American Activities on October 17, 1939, Vito Marcantonio, member of Congress and president of the International Labor Defense, answered questions of the Committee's counsel, as follows:

> Mr. Marcantonio. I also did definitely ascertain for myself whether or not the International Labor Defense, which was convened here in 1937, was connected with the Communist Party, and I ascertained that it was definitely not connected with the Communist Party.
> Mr. Whitley. And you were thoroughly satisfied that the International Labor Defense, in its origin and activities, has not ever been subject to Communist control or influence.
> Mr. Marcantonio. That is correct.
> Mr. Whitley. Congressman, in checking up on the organization before you accepted the position as national chairman, did you determine whether the International Labor Defense was ever, at any time, affiliated with, or check up on, the International Red Aid, with headquarters at Moscow?
> Mr. Marcantonio. I never knew the International Labor Defense to be anything of the sort.

A TROJAN HORSE IN THE COURTS 107

Anna Damon, an avowed member of the Communist Party for many years and also national secretary of the International Labor Defense, likewise denied under oath that the organization is affiliated with either the International Red Aid or the Communist Party.

The facts pertaining to the origin and subsequent connections of the International Labor Defense are matters of record. Let us consider the testimony of the organization's president and secretary in the light of these facts.

In the first place, let us sketch the organizational biography of the president of the I.L.D., Congressman Vito Marcantonio.

The International Labor Defense is not the only organization in which the Communists have utilized the name and prestige of Mr. Marcantonio. His many outstanding services to a vast array of communist front groups serve to explain why the Communists selected him to head their defense organization. It is impossible to go into all of his many communist connections in this discussion, but a partial account of them will illustrate, once more, how the Communists use a willing helper over and over again.

The *New Masses* is an out-and-out Communist Party publication, no matter what its charter or incorporation papers may appear to show. In fact, even the Communist International in Moscow dips its fingers into the policies of the publication. A former editor of the *New Masses*, Joseph Freeman, was dropped from the publication recently because the Communist International, through the medium of its own official magazine, found the writings of Freeman to be tainted with "petty bourgeois" deviations. A glance at any issue of the *New Masses* will establish the fact of its complete subservience to the Communist Party. Its editors are members of the Communist Party. Its articles, editorials, and other writings follow the Party "line" as faithfully as if the publication were edited by Joseph Stalin himself. In the light of the foregoing facts, we must consider the enthusiastic praise which Mr. Marcantonio bestowed upon the paper in a testimonial which he wrote for it. Under his own name, as president of the International Labor Defense, there appeared in the *New Masses* of April 12, 1938, the following statement:

> No other magazine can possibly take its place. It is not just another liberal magazine. There is no other weekly in the country that can be depended upon for consistency and political acumen in its comment on events. There is no other magazine in which the facts behind the political and economic scene can be found as accurately and readily. I do not know how anyone in the progressive movement can afford to be without it, if they have the price.

The only "consistency" which characterizes the comments of the *New Masses* is its consistent support of the policies of Joseph Stalin in all their weird shifts.

When Stanley M. Isaacs, Borough President of Manhattan, appointed Simon W. Gerson, an avowed member of the Communist Party, to the position of assistant Borough President, Congressman Marcantonio was one of those who publicly endorsed the appointment.

The full significance of Mr. Marcantonio's testimonial for the *New Masses* and of his endorsement of Gerson's appointment may be better grasped if we try to imagine what the Congressman himself would have to say about any individual who endorsed Fritz Kuhn's publication, *Weckruf*, or what he would have to say about Kuhn's appointment to the position of assistant Borough President of Manhattan.

Mr. Marcantonio has not only praised the *New Masses;* he has written articles for it frequently.

Other communist-controlled groups with which Congressman Marcantonio has been affiliated in one way or another include the following: the American League Against War and Fascism, the American League for Peace and Democracy, the New York Peace Association, the Brooklyn Community Peace Congress, the Emergency Peace Mobilization Committee, the Refugee Scholarship and Peace Campaign, the American Friends of Spanish Democracy, the North American Committee to Aid Spanish Democracy, the Lawyers Committee on American Relations with Spain, the Washington Committee for Democratic Action, the Coordinating Committee Against Profiteering, the United Action Against Fascism and Anti-Semitism, the Jewish People's Committee, the American Friends of the Chinese People, the International Workers Order, the Descendants of the American Revolution, the Conference on Constitutional Liberties in America, the First Congress of the Mexican and Spanish American Peoples of the United States, the American Committee for Anti-Nazi Literature, the German-American League for Culture, the League of American Writers, the Artists Union, the American Student Union, the American Youth Congress, the National People's Committee Against Hearst, the National Negro Congress, the Unemployment Councils, the New York Joint Action Committee for Genuine Social Insurance, the Workers Alliance, the American Committee for the Protection of the Foreign Born, the New York Conference for Inalienable Rights, the Theatre Arts Committee, Consumers Union, the magazine *Champion,* the Golden Book of American Friendship with the Soviet Union, the Budenz-Patterson-Wirtz Defense Committee, and the National

Committee for People's Rights. The connections of Congressman Marcantonio with all of the foregoing organizations are matters of documentary evidence.

The International Labor Defense was established as a result of a decision of the Fourth Congress of the Communist International held in Moscow, November 7 to December 3, 1922, which instructed "all the Communist Parties to establish an organization to render material and moral aid to the imprisoned victims of capitalism." At the time when this decision of the Communist International was promulgated, the American Communist Party was very much torn by internal dissension, and it was not until two and a half years later, in 1925, that it got around to the setting up of its I.L.D.

On the ninth anniversary of the International Labor Defense, in 1934, the Communist Party published an account of its own origin and that of the parent body, the I.R.A., including the following comment:

> The International Red Aid, with connections in most European countries, had been formed in 1922 and was already coordinating the defense work on an international scale, making available to all countries the collective experiences of the world proletariat. The I.R.A. was formed under the leadership of the Communist International."

The international affiliates of the I.R.A. took different names in the various countries, such as Secours Rouge International in France, El Secorro Rojo International in Spain, Rote Hilfe in Austria, International Rote Hilfe in Germany, MOPR in Russia, and the International Labor Defense in the United States.

Ostensibly, the initiative for this international movement came from the Society of Old Bolsheviks and the Association of Former Political Prisoners in Moscow which called the first congress of the International Red Aid to meet in Moscow, July 14, 1924. But these two organizations were merely a convenient cover under which the orders of the Communist International were carried out—the orders which had been given in 1922 and which resulted in the organization of the I.R.A. in the same year.

The Communist Party of Great Britain, like the communist parties everywhere else, knew of the formal connection between the International Red Aid and the American International Labor Defense and published the following statement concerning the I.L.D.:

> The International Labor Defense is the American section of the International Red Aid. It publishes a monthly organ, the *Labor Defender*, with a circulation of 16,000. It is a broad organization in which communists take a leading part.

The *Labor Defender*, official monthly of the International Labor Defense, in its issue of December, 1929, contained the following statement:

> There is little wonder in the fact that the idea of a world organization for workers' defense has originated in the Soviet Union, and that our section of the International Labor Defense (MOPR) is the strongest and largest of all sections of the world I.L.D. organization.

The pamphlet, *Ten Years of Labor Defense*, by Sascha Small, published officially by the International Labor Defense, states that "the I.L.D. in 1927 became affiliated with the International Red Aid as its American Section."

Another official pamphlet of the organization—*What Is the I.L.D.?*—has the following to say:

The I.L.D. became a member of the only international working class defense organization, the International Red Aid ... The Soviet Russian section of this organization, the MOPR, has several millions of members.

One may ask, pertinently, what the MOPR in the Soviet Union has done to defend the imprisoned victims of Stalin's regime, but the question is, of course, as rhetorical as it is pertinent.

All of the early publications and other official statements of Congressman Marcantonio's own organization refute his testimony. Some of the I.L.D.'s later official statements, after the Congressman's assumption of its presidency, do likewise.

Following the adoption of the new Trojan Horse tactics by the Communists, after the Seventh World Congress of the Communist International and the introduction of People's Front movements in ostensible support of democracy throughout the world, there was an evident attempt to conceal the international affiliations of the I.L.D. Where they had formerly boasted about it, the leaders of the organization began to deny its affiliation with the I.R.A. The conclusion may safely be drawn, however, that this affiliation has not changed basically, and there is ample evidence to support that conclusion. Why, for example, does the International Labor Defense still retain the word "international" in its name? More often than not, Communists change the names of their organizations when they revise their "line." Why, likewise, do the affiliates of the International Red Aid in other countries still use their original names? And why do the highest authorities in Moscow still speak and write of the I.L.D. as a world movement?

In June, 1937, when Mr. Marcantonio was a member of the Legal Advisory Committee of the I.L.D. and Miss

A TROJAN HORSE IN THE COURTS 113

Damon was its acting national secretary, the *Labor Defender* (their own organ) published a letter sent from Spain and signed "L.", which reads, in part, as follows:

Dear Sasha: The first person I met when I reached Spain was a representative of El Secorro Rojo Internacional, the I.L.D. of Spain . . . All over the world the I.L.D. has helped us in Spain. Money, medical supplies, clothing, food—all from the workers of America, France, England, Mexico and the Soviet Union. Everywhere the I.L.D. has organized aid to our people.

The foregoing letter was addressed to Sascha Small who was editor of the *Labor Defender* and also a well-known member of the Communist Party. The author of the letter apparently did not know that he was supposed to keep the I.L.D.'s international connections a secret, and the editor of the *Labor Defender* likewise committed a deviation from the new Party "line" in publishing a letter which so frankly followed the old "line."

When James H. Dolsen was a witness before the Special Committee on Un-American Activities, he stated under oath that the International Labor Defense is the American section of the International Red Aid in Moscow. Dolsen certainly should know about such connections, for he was an international agent of the Moscow organization for many years. He was, however, apparently unaware of Mr. Marcantonio's and Miss Damon's testimony to the contrary.

In the *Daily Worker* for August 11, 1940, we read of a meeting of the I.L.D. in Moscow at which "Wilhelm Pieck delivered the report on the work of the International Labor Defense and the tasks confronting it."

In a volume entitled *The United Front* by Georgi Dimitroff, published by the International Publishers in 1938, when Mr. Marcantonio and Miss Damon were both holding office in the I.L.D., we find the following statement:

Under present conditions, when bourgeois reaction is growing, when fascism is raging and the class struggle is becoming more acute, the role of the I.L.D. is increasing immensely. The task now before the I.L.D. is to become a genuine mass organization of the toilers in all capitalist countries . . . The Communists and revolutionary workers who are active in the I.L.D. organizations must realize at every step the enormous responsibility they bear before the working class *and the Communist International* for the successful fulfillment of the role and tasks of the I.L.D.

In a foreword to Dimitroff's book, it is stated that the material included covers "all important international developments since 1935 . . . Taken together these papers represent the development of the political line of the Communist International over this period."

In greeting the Soviet Union on the occasion of the seventeenth anniversary of the Bolshevik revolution, the *Labor Defender* published a statement which reads, in part, as follows:

Here we wish to convey the greetings of the 200,000 members and affiliates of the International Labor Defense to the soviet workers and peasants, and to pledge defense to the only land that is an asylum for the oppressed and persecuted of all nations.

Despite all denials, the evidence is clear that the International Labor Defense has, from its very earliest years, been affiliated with the International Red Aid in Moscow and, further, that its sympathies are wholly with the Soviet Union and contrary to the interests of the United States. The close connections of the I.L.D. with the Communist Party are just as well established by documentary evidence as is the affiliation of the I.L.D. with Moscow's International Red Aid.

A TROJAN HORSE IN THE COURTS

Before 1935, Earl Browder was proud to declare the fact of the closeness of the I.L.D. to the Communist Party. In the *Daily Worker* of June 23, 1934, there is an article by Browder entitled "The Party Must Support and Build the I.L.D." The following is an excerpt from the article:

At the most crucial point of the Scottsboro case, for example, financial collapse was only averted by the I.L.D. calling directly upon the Communist Party and borrowing several thousand dollars out of the party's meager funds which were vitally needed elsewhere. The same condition exists more or less in other cases in every locality.

In a statement by the well-known Negro Communist, William L. Patterson, vice-president of the I.L.D., we read:

Also it will, of course, be necessary to deal with past events in such a manner as to show the inseparable relation of the growth and development of the I.L.D. to that of the revolutionary movement as a whole, particularly to that of the leadership of the revolutionary movement, the Communist Party . . . Their work interlocks, like the fingers of clasped hands. The policies of the I.L.D. are based upon the class struggle, and its program is a program of class against class. It must be obvious that only the vanguard of the working class, the Communist Party, which guides and coordinates the activities of the class struggle organizations, guarantees consistency to such a policy and such a program."

Benjamin Gitlow, former communist candidate for the vice-presidency, former secretary of the Communist Party, former member of its executive committee, one of the founders of the International Labor Defense and a member of its national executive committee for five years, has given testimony, backed by official minutes of the Communist Party, which shows how the I.L.D. was established and the part which the Communist Party played in its establishment. His testimony reads, in part, as follows:

It is the legal defense organization of the Communist Party and of the Communist International in this country, and serves, also, as a highly political and propagandist communist organization. The International Labor Defense from its very inception has been consciously used by the Communist Party to enable the party to gain a foothold in all kinds of organizations, particularly in trade unions, and it has been one of the most effective recruiting organizations for the Communist Party . . . Now, I have here the minutes of the executive council of the Communist Party of June 26, 1925. That was the period in which the I.L.D. was organized. The question under consideration was the International Labor Defense, and Comrade Cannon submitted copies of the resolutions to be introduced at the International Labor Defense Conference, which were approved, together with the reports of the various resolutions . . . A copy of the constitution as approved by the subcommittee was also submitted . . . The steering committee, decided upon by the subcommittee, consisting of Dunne, Gitlow, and Cannon, was approved, and the executive committee recommended that Comrade Cannon be chairman of the conference . . . The Committee reported that Comrade Cannon be elected secretary of the International Labor Defense, and Comrade Cannon submitted the recommendation that the national committee consist of a clear majority of party members. Comrade Cannon, who became secretary of the International Labor Defense, and who was there as a Communist Party member; submitted the following slate of candidates for the national committee of the International Labor Defense: Nonparty members—Debs, Nearing, Robert W. Dunn, R. W. Whitaker, Bishop M. Brown, Wentworth, Howat, A. S. Blackwell, Ellen Hayes, McNamara, Meitzen, Ralph Chaplin, and Fred Mann. In this nonparty list there are included as nonparty members and secret party members, the following: Robert W. Dunn, a party member; Meitzen, a party member; Bishop M. Brown, a party member; and Ralph Chaplin, a party member. The party members to be elected to the national committee of the I.L.D. were to include the following names: Dolla, Cannon, Maurer, Dunne, Cora Meyer, Wm. Mollenhauer, Robt. Minor, Harrison George, Foster, Karsner, Ruthenberg, Gitlow, Dan W. Stevens, Fred Merrick, Rose Baron, and Fred Biedenkapp.

In Chapter II of the present volume, eighteen criteria for the identification of a communist Trojan Horse were suggested. The International Labor Defense is one of the very few agencies of Stalin in this country which qualifies as a communist Trojan Horse by the test of every one of these eighteen criteria. It qualifies, in other words, as the *standard* Trojan Horse.

CHAPTER IX

A TROJAN HORSE FOR NEGROES

Moscow has long considered the Negroes of the United States as excellent potential recruits for the Communist Party. It has envisaged an unusual opportunity to create racial hatred between the white and Negro citizens of the United States. It has hoped and worked for the Negro to play a very important role in the communization of America.

It is certain that the Negroes in the United States enjoy more liberties and a higher standard of living than the Negroes in any other country, and that communist success in this country would plunge the Negro race into slavery. The thinking Negroes of our country realize this, and they are successfully combating the insidious wiles of Moscow's influence.

Under our free institutions, the Negro has made great progress in the United States. Despite propaganda and misrepresentation, he lives in peace with the white people of the South. Lynching has practically disappeared. The white and the Negro understand each other through long years of association. There are, of course, some in both races who are exceptions to this rule, but upon the whole there is no other country on the face of the earth where two distinct races enjoy such friendly relationships. This can only be broken by the success of misguided reformists and foreign agents who seek to capitalize upon prejudice in order to promote the interests of their foreign masters. It means nothing to them that the success of their program would bring about the enslavement of the Negro race in America, and the loss of the great gains he has made in the past century. All that these emissaries of Stalin are concerned with is the use of the Negro for Stalin's purposes.

Communists believe that an appeal to racial prejudice and an exaggeration of grievances will gradually separate the two races into hostile camps and that the resulting clash will be a sort of auxiliary to the class struggle and civil war. Hence, no pains have been spared to condition the Negro people for revolutionary doctrines and plans. Elaborate maps have been made in Moscow showing that in many sections of the South the Negro population predominates. This was the foundation for the Communist Party's slogan, "Self-determination for the Black Belt." Negro publications are encouraged to attack the white race; and communist publications, pamphlets, and throw-aways are distributed on a large scale among the Negro citizens of the United States.

The Negro is told that he is persecuted and maltreated; that his lot in the United States is unbearably hard; and that he is, in fact, a peon or slave of his white masters. He is told that the only country which recognizes his rights is Soviet Russia, and that the only political party which will battle for his emancipation is the Communist Party of the United States.

The Special Committee on Un-American Activities received evidence of numerous instances where Negroes have been brought from the South to participate in meetings of communist organizations in other sections of the country. At these meetings the Negro has been given a taste of "social equality." For instance, witnesses have testified that dances have been arranged so that Negro men could dance with white partners. And, in fact, communist girls have been sent among Negroes to practice "social equality." Thus, by profession and practice, the Communists encourage the Negro to demand "social equality" with the whites.

Negroes have been given free trips to Moscow where they have been entertained royally and on the basis of complete "social equality." These Negroes have then returned to the United States to relate their experiences to other Negroes and thereby increase the prestige and influence of the Communist Party.

Much of the communist work among the Negroes of the South is carried on with attempted secrecy, with the result that few people realize the extent to which the Communists carry their program of race hatred.

Communist Negroes are placed in strategic positions in organizations so that they may carry on the work of the Party under the guise of social and economic programs. These Negro leaders conceal the fact that they are affiliated with the Communist Party. But they are systematically preparing the way for bolder efforts in the future. They constantly hammer home to the Negro members of their organizations that the Negro is mistreated and that he must demand his social and economic rights.

The Negro is fundamentally religious, and the church plays an important part in his life. His loyalty to the church is an outstanding trait in his character, hence the Communists have sought to infiltrate the Negro church with communist preachers and lay leaders. The Special Committee on Un-American Activities had one example of a prominent Negro clergyman who regularly praised the Soviet Union in his sermons as the land of equality and model government. The Committee inspected some of these sermons and found throughout them the familiar communist "line." Of course, the Communists take great pains to conceal from the Negroes the fact that Communism is materialistic and atheistic and opposed in principle and practice to Christianity. The Negro is told that Communism is the application of Christian teachings, and that he can embrace Communism without sacrificing his religion.

In the Negro schools and colleges, a special effort has been made to "bore from within," and to indoctrinate Negro youth with communist beliefs. To some extent, the communist program, with reference to the penetration of the educational field, has been successful.

One of the familiar methods of the Communists is to publish Negro papers which feature popular Negro slogans. In these papers, special stress is laid upon the economic plight of the Negro. But throughout the publications are interspersed communist doctrines and an occasional commendation of the Soviet Union. The whole thing is done so cleverly that only those familiar with communist techniques are able to detect it.

How much money Russia and the Communist Party of the United States have spent upon their Negro program, no one can estimate, but from available evidence, it appears to be a very large sum. Moscow realizes that it can never revolutionize the United States unless the Negro can be won over to the communist cause. We find, therefore, that district and branch organizations of the Communist Party have been established in all the Southern States. In most instances, these organizations are financed by the Communist Party's national office. The records of the Party and the admissions of communist leaders have established this fact before the Special Committee on Un-American Activities.

In each of the Party's districts, there are paid agents of

Stalin who concentrate their attention upon the Negro population. At first, the program of these paid agitators consists of creating and stimulating race hatred. Gradually the Negro is taken up the mountain of communist promises, and finally, on the summit, he is shown Utopia. In this final stage of communist propaganda, the Negro is promised absolute domination over the white race in the South. He is told that the South is to be divided into regions or districts, where Negro rule will be established.

Apart from James W. Ford and two or three other Negro leaders in the Party, the Communists' principal authority in matters that pertain to Negroes is James S. Allen whose real name is Sol Auerbach. In a Communist Party pamphlet entitled *Negroes in a Soviet America*, in which James W. Ford and James S. Allen collaborated as authors, we find the doctrine of violence which Communists have advocated among Negroes. "We emphasize," say the authors, "that capitalism cannot be done away with by the ballot . . . Anyone who tells you to depend upon the ballot and civil rights for your defense is betraying you."

Have the Communists succeeded to any considerable extent in winning the Negro to the cause of "Red" dictatorship? It is a tribute to the patriotism, loyalty, and religion of the Negro that the answer to this question is in the negative. While some progress has been made among Negroes, the fact remains that the program has not succeeded to the extent expected by communist leadership. This is especially significant in view of the fact that the Communist Party has given Negroes representation on the Party's national committee out of all proportion to their numbers in the Party or the population.

Nevertheless it is undoubtedly true that much misunderstanding has been brought about by communist propaganda

A TROJAN HORSE FOR NEGROES

and activity among the Negroes. We cannot view with unconcern the future consequences of this destructive program of Moscow. At the same time, we must acknowledge with gratitude the refusal of the great majority of Negroes to be duped by the agents and ideologists of the ruthless dictator, Stalin.

The evidence before the Special Committee on Un-American Activities shows that the Communist International has long been active in its efforts to organize special Trojan Horses for the Negroes of the United States. In 1930, the Executive Committee of the Communist International adopted and transmitted to the American Communist Party its instructions on the Negro question. This resolution stated very definitely that it would be the policy of the Communist Party to organize the Negro people of the South on the basis of self-determination, that is, setting up a separate state and government in the South, the purpose of which would be a two-fold one in the course of publicizing and agitating for the immediate demands for poor farmers in the South.

In an article, "The Negro Question in the United States," taken from the *Communist International*, volume 12, number 9, the program with reference to the Negro in the United States was set forth in the following language:

> First of all, true right to self-determination means that the Negro majority and not the white minority in the entire territory of the administratively united Black Belt exercises the right of administering governmental, legislative, and judicial authority. At the present time, all this power is concentrated in the hands of the white bourgeoisie and landlords. It is they who appoint all officials, it is they who dispose of public property, it is they who determine the taxes, it is they who govern and make the laws. Therefore, the overthrow of this class rule

in the Black Belt is unconditionally necessary in the struggle for the Negroes' right of self-determination. This, however, means at the same time the overthrow of the yoke of American imperialism in the Black Belt on which the forces of the local white bourgeoisie depend. Only in this way, only if the Negro population of the Black Belt wins its freedom from American imperialism, even to the point of deciding itself the relations between its country and other governments, especially the United States, will it win real and complete self-determination.

The Communists first organized the American Negro Labor Congress. In 1929 or 1930, this organization was changed to the League of Struggle for Negro Rights at the St. Louis convention of the American Negro Labor Congress. On the national council of this organization were such well-known Communists as Clarence Hathaway, editor of the *Daily Worker*, William Z. Foster, chairman of the Communist Party, Robert W. Dunn, Israel Amter, Earl Browder, and Gil Green.

By the middle of 1930, the American Negro Congress had almost 3,000 members in Detroit alone. In addition to their actual membership, they influenced more than 5,000 Negro people through their Unemployment Councils, Tenants' League, and other organizations set up by the Party to work among the Negro population.

Out of the American Negro Congress and the League of Struggle for Negro Rights there grew the present National Negro Congress. The National Negro Congress is a continuation and modification of the Party's strategy and program in line with the change of communist policy which took place in 1935.

William Nowell testified that the National Negro Congress is nothing more than a new and modified version of the Communist International's "line" on the subject of Negroes in the United States. Howell said:

The purpose of the present organization is essentially that of the old organizations. The only thing that has happened is what is true of the communist policy in general; it is due to the change in international conditions, and in line with the whole situation of the communist bureaucracy and communist dictatorship, everything is sacrificed. . . .

So, therefore, the policy of the National Negro Congress is essentially not different from that of the two older organizations out of which that has been developed. That is, it is for the self-determination of the Negroes in the South, to utilize the movement it creates and to unite it with the movement of the working people in the North, the industrial workers in the South, the intellectuals, the professionals and so forth, to eventually bring about an overthrow of the capitalistic system, using communist terminology and the establishment of the dictatorship of the proletariat.

With reference to the national leaders of the National Negro Congress, William Nowell testified as follows:

The best known among the national leaders to me is John P. Davis, who together with me acted as a member of the Communist Party fraction, Davis from the national fraction and myself the Detroit chapter of the organization. Of course, there are others that I know just through reading of them. I know Philip Randolph, but I never worked with him; and I know such local leaders as Ed Williams and Merrill Work, who were members of the Communist Party fraction with me in the conduct of the local work of the Detroit chapter. . . . In fact, we had received instructions from the central office of the Communist Party to begin to organize the Detroit chapter of the National Negro Congress. Davis was to be sent along later to consolidate, and not to be known as a Communist. Our job was to get certain things done, and Davis was to come along and contact liberals and so on, and get them all together. The fraction would be a driving force, of course, and the chapter would be organized, and it would be a good front. . . .

Well, it wasn't more than a week, I believe, that Davis was there. We worked together. I communicated with him and heard indirectly from him through the district office of the party. I had been removed as a means of political discipline at that time and was doing what is called mass work or fractional work. . . . We received communications from the Central Committee of the Communist Party to establish a branch of the National Negro Congress. . . . William Weinstone, who was district secretary of the Communist Party, handed over the letter to me. I was head of the city fraction, that Negro fraction, and organized the work in colored organizations. So we began to work, Ed Williams and myself, Lyonie Williams, Paul Kirk, and several others. We organized a good big fraction, and when we had the ground prepared, it was understood through the local fraction and the national fraction that Davis would be sent in, and he was sent in. And, of course, we had contacted people, other party people, and when the ground was prepared, Davis was sent in, of course, to speak to them and to officially set up the chapter.

John P. Davis is the executive secretary of the National Negro Congress and as such holds the highest position of real authority in the body, despite the fact that the title of president is nominally of a higher rank. The record of Davis and his affiliations with communist-controlled organizations is a long one. Even if we did not have the sworn testimony concerning his membership in the Communist Party, his other communist connections would be more than enough to indicate that he is an important figure in the field of Moscow's Trojan Horses. Inasmuch as Communists very rarely use the services of one of their functionaries in one organization only, Davis' record of many communist

A TROJAN HORSE FOR NEGROES 127

organizational connections is a part of the evidence that the National Negro Congress is simply one more of Stalin's Trojan Horse devices for revolution.

Davis is a member of the national committee of the International Labor Defense and also a member of that organization's legal advisory committee. He is a member of the national committee of the International Juridical Association, an organization whose connections with the Communist Party were set forth in an earlier chapter. He was a speaker at the fourth annual convention of the International Workers Order. The American Youth Congress used him as one of the signers for its convention call in 1939. Until the time of its sudden suicide, Davis was a member of the national committee of the American League for Peace and Democracy. In August, 1940, he was a speaker at the fifth national convention of the Workers Alliance, after the president of that organization, David Lasser, had denounced it as completely communist-controlled and handed in his resignation. In June, 1940, Davis was a sponsor and speaker for the Conference on Constitutional Liberties in America, sharing the platform with the well-known Communist woman, Elizabeth Gurley Flynn. He is a sponsor of the United American Spanish Aid Committee, an organization run by an old-time Communist Party member, Fred Biedenkapp, and which is this month's edition of the Communist Party's Trojan Horse for Spanish affairs. He was also a sponsor of one of the earlier editions, the Washington Friends of Spanish Democracy which was headed by Leon Henderson, a member of the President's National Advisory Defense Commission. Earlier still he was a member of the Lawyers' Committee on American Relations with Spain. He was a sponsor of the China Aid Council, an organization whose representative in China was personally selected by Earl

Browder according to the latter's own public declaration. Davis is now sponsoring the Washington Committee for Democratic Action, the national capital's successor to the American League for Peace and Democracy.

Since its formation, the National Negro Congress has had two presidents, A. Philip Randolph and Max Yergan. Each of these men has a long record of affiliation with communist-controlled groups.

Randolph's record of such affiliations includes the following organizations: The International Labor Defense, the American Youth Congress, the American Relief Ship for Spain, the Medical Bureau and North American Committee to Aid Spanish Democracy, the Spanish Refugee Relief Campaign, the American League Against War and Fascism, the American League for Peace and Democracy, the China Aid Council, the Conference on Pan American Democracy, the League for Mutual Aid, Consumers Union, the Milk Consumers Protective Committee, the Consumer-Farmer Milk Cooperative, and the Consumers National Federation.

Yergan's record of affiliations with communist-controlled groups surpasses in number those of both Davis and Randolph. In fact, his record makes him one of the principal sponsors of communist Trojan Horses in the country. He succeeded Randolph in the presidency of the National Negro Congress this year. Merely listing Yergan's other connections, we find the following: the Communist Party's weekly *New Masses*, the American League for Peace and Democracy, the China Aid Council, the American Youth Congress, the American Student Union, the International Labor Defense, the American Committee for Democracy and Intellectual Freedom, the International Committee on African Affairs, the United American Spanish Aid Com-

A TROJAN HORSE FOR NEGROES

mittee, the Refugee Scholarship and Peace Campaign, the Union of Concerted Peace Efforts, the Conference on Constitutional Liberties in America, the New York Conference for Inalienable Rights, the National Emergency Conference for Democratic Rights, the National Committee for People's Rights, the Conference on Pan American Democracy, and the magazine *Equality*.

The National Negro Congress was formed in line with the united front policy adopted by the Communist International in 1935. From the official proceedings of the Second National Negro Congress held October 15 to 17, 1937, we learn that the Congress represented in "true spirit" the "united front." The National Negro Congress has also followed the Communist "line" in denouncing Japan, Germany, Italy, and the Franco forces in Spain, but it has refused to condemn Russia and Communism.

Among those sending greetings to the Second National Negro Congress were John L. Lewis of the C.I.O., Tom Mooney, from San Quentin Prison, Ben Gold (Communist), general president of the International Fur Workers Union, Elmer Benson of Minnesota, and President Roosevelt.

James W. Ford, Communist Negro leader and the perennial candiate for vice-president of the United States on the Communist Party ticket, was the keynote speaker of the Congress.

In the case of the National Negro Congress, we find Stalin using the identical motive that Hitler has exploited so successfully, namely, that of racial hatred. The red and brown Fuehrers will apparently make their Trojan Horses wallow in any kind of mire.

CHAPTER X

COMMUNIST THEORY OF LABOR UNIONS

BEFORE discussing the extent to which Communists have penetrated the labor unions of the United States, it is important that we take a look at the Communist theory which underlies all of the Party's activities in unions. There is nothing hit-or-miss about Communist activity in unions; it is all based upon a carefully considered theory of action. The application of that theory changes from time to time, but its essence remains the same. On no other subject have Communists written so voluminously, from the days of Karl Marx down to the present time.

It would be hard to imagine a more colossal pretense than that which holds that the Communist theory of trade unions on the one hand and the congressional theory of collective bargaining embodied in the National Labor Relations Act on the other hand are one and the same thing. Despite the Trojan Horse efforts of the Communist Party to make these two theories appear identical, whenever they have occasion to appeal for aid to the National Labor Relations Act, the two theories are, in fact, fundamentally contradictory. The administrators of the National Labor Relations Act who have assumed or maintained that Communist trade unionists are just like any other trade unionists have done so in plainest violation of the facts about the matter.

The Communist theory of trade unions rests upon the premise of "the subordination of the economic struggle to the political struggle of the working class." In other words, to put the matter bluntly, the Communists hold that a good trade union ("the economic struggle") should be an appendage to their Party ("the political struggle"). A. Lozovsky, head of the Red International of Labor Unions, is the author of a book entitled *Marx and the Trade Unions* which is the principal textbook in use at the Communist Party's Workers' School. In his book, Lozovsky observed correctly that "Marx always stressed the primacy of politics over economics." According to Lozovsky, Marx attached "tremendous significance to the economic struggle of the proletariat and the trade unions," but at the same time "he placed the political all-class tasks of the trade unions higher than the private corporative tasks." The phrase, "private corporative tasks," is the Communist's way of describing collective bargaining over wages, hours, and working conditions. These matters of collective bargaining, according to Marx and all Communists after him, are simply means to a political end.

It cannot be assumed for one minute that the congressional intent embodied in the National Labor Relations Act was to "place the political all-class tasks of the trade unions higher than the private corporative tasks." On the contrary, it must be assumed that the interest of Congress was limited to the establishment of collective bargaining over wages, hours, and working conditions. Congress did not intend to build trade unions which would become the basis for a Communist revolution.

All Marxists, whether Communist or Socialist, hold that trade unions are the chief class-struggle instrument for building a political movement with which to destroy free, private, and competitive enterprise. In a context which clearly showed adverse criticism of the A. F. of L., Norman

Thomas—mild and gentlemanly Socialist though he may be —observed that "A. F. of L. unions are primarily concerned with establishing the principle and working the machinery of collective bargaining." With what else, one may properly ask, should they be concerned, primarily or secondarily? Certainly no one will contend that Congress was interested in anything else when it enacted the National Labor Relations Act.

For many years, Marxists have held the A. F. of L. guilty of "reformism" or "business unionism," by which they have meant to say that the A. F. of L. was not concerned with building the Socialist Party or the Communist Party.

In the literature of the Communist Party, trade union "reformism" has been customarily associated with the leadership of Samuel Gompers in the American Federation of Labor. A. Lozovsky, for example, has set Marxism over against Gompersism, as follows:

> The Marxian spirit can be sensed in demonstrations, in bloody strikes and hunger marches of the unemployed in the U.S.A. Revolutionary Marxism is winning one position after another . . . In whose favor is history working? Evidently in favor of revolutionary Marxism and not Gompersism.

Communists would like to have the general public believe that they are interested in the advancement of trade unions as they are commonly understood by the American People and by the legislators who passed the Wagner Labor Relations Act. They have, however, filled their literature with the opposite theory, namely, that trade unions are bad, counter-revolutionary, class-collaborators, Fascist, and deserving of destruction unless they are, in Lenin's own words, "a useful auxiliary to the political, agitational and revolutionary organizations."

Because the A. F. of L. steadfastly refused to allow itself to become "a useful auxiliary to the political, agitational and revolutionary organizations," the Communist bosses in Moscow ordered their American agents, Browder and company, to destroy the A. F. of L. Such an order was literally transmitted from Moscow to the United States. While it has its humorous aspect, in the thought of a small group like Browder's destroying an established labor organization with millions of members, it also has its serious aspect, in that it reveals clearly the trade union theory of the Communist Party. In the *R.I.L.U. Magazine*, official organ of Moscow's world-wide labor union set-up, A. Lozovsky wrote of the destruction of the A. F. of L., as follows:

There is no need to shout from the house-tops "destroy the unions" as was done in Germany. But that we want to break up the reformist trade unions, that we want to weaken them, that we want to explode their discipline, that we want to wrest them from the workers, that we want to explode the trade union apparatus and to destroy it—of that there cannot be the slightest doubt.

Lozovsky, as we have already noted, is head of the Red International of Labor Unions, sometimes known as the Profintern. William Z. Foster was the head of its American section, the Trade Union Unity League, until it was disbanded in order to send all Communist trade unionists into the A. F. of L. for disruptive purposes. Writing in the *Communist*, Foster acknowledged that the American Communist Party received its "line" on trade unionism direct from Moscow. In an article entitled "The Decline of the A. F. of L.," Foster wrote, as follows: "Events are proving the correctness of the Comintern and Profintern line for the building of new unions in the United States."

It is a settled principle of Communist theory that all of the Party's activity must contribute directly or indirectly, immediately or ultimately, to the growth of the revolutionary movement which is under its leadership. Karl Marx said that "the trade unions are schools of Communism." Communist leaders have reiterated that view over and over again. In a letter dated February 18, 1865, Marx wrote to Engels that "the working class is revolutionary or it is nothing." With reference to this latter statement of Marx, Lozovsky observed: "This is what defines the line of action of Karl Marx." It also defines the line of action of Communists today. If it were not for that line of action, the Communist Party would have small interest in trade unions.

Roger Baldwin, who has run the American Civil Liberties Union ever since its beginning, stated the Marxist position as it is generally understood by Communists when he said: "Trade-unionism alone furnishes a class base of revolutionary power for the exploited masses." Baldwin further declared:

> I would rather see violent revolution than none at all ... Even the terrible cost of bloody revolution is a cheaper price to humanity than the continued exploitation and wreck of human life under the settled violence of the present system.

Communists have been just as blunt in stating their theory of labor strikes as they have been in discussing their theory of trade unions in general. Lozovsky put the matter clearly when he wrote: "It means that the revolutionary Marxists have their own strike tactics—differing radically from the strike tactics of the anarchists and reformists." What these special Marxist strike tactics are, which differ so radically from those of the reformists, Lozovsky explained, as follows:

We have already seen that Marx and Engels referred to strikes as "social war," as "economic revolt," "real civil war," "guerilla war," "school of war," "advance guard collisions."

Communists, as we shall show in a later chapter, envision the eventual overthrow of capitalism and the bourgeois state through civil war. It is only natural, therefore, that they should attach great importance to the small-scale rehearsals of civil war which they find possible in labor strikes. Let Marx, Engels, and Lenin refute the officers of the National Labor Relations Board who assert that Communist leadership in a trade union or in a strike is wholly irrelevant to the issues which come before them in labor disputes. Concerning strikes, Marx wrote, as follows:

In this struggle—a veritable civil war—are united and developed all these elements necessary for a future battle; once having reached this point, association takes on a political character.

Note the emphasis on training for a future battle and the frank admission that strikes are political in character, as far as the Communists are concerned. From the pen of Marx's associate, Engels, we have the following illuminating evaluation of strikes:

They are the school of war of the workingmen in which they prepare themselves for the great struggle which cannot be avoided . . . And as schools of war they are unexcelled.

The master teacher of them all, Lenin, summed up his discussion of strikes in these words:

Here we have the program and the tactics of the economic struggle and the trade union movement for several decades to come, for the whole long period in which the workers are preparing for a "future battle."

Aside from training the working class in the art of civil war, strikes also serve other subsidiary purposes. They constitute, for example, an important method of sabotaging the whole capitalist system. With respect to this Communist purpose in strikes, Lozovsky wrote:

> Marx knew that the economic strike was an important weapon in the hands of the proletariat against the bourgeoisie, since everything that deals a blow to the capitalists deals a blow also to the capitalist system.

Again, strikes are, from the standpoint of the Communist Party, indispensable for developing class consciousness in the minds of workers. Lozovsky explained that Marx proved "the vast significance of strikes for turning the proletariat into a class."

Committed as they are to the view that strikes are unexcelled as schools of civil war, it would be the height of folly to allege that Communists exert themselves to keep picketing within peaceful bounds. Of course, no such thing is true. On the contrary, the Communist tactic in strikes is invariably to provoke violence from the side of the management and the police. This is so elementary in Communist practice that it borders on the ridiculous to offer proof for it. All the proof needed is to be found in the Marxist theory of trade unions and labor strikes which we have cited. Nevertheless, Mrs. George Soule, who has written a pamphlet for the Communist Party's International Labor Defense, declared: "I have been in many strikes, and I have never seen any trouble started by any labor groups." That is an incredible statement to come from one who has been so close to the Communist Party, but its meaning is simple to anyone who understands the unique logic of Communists. The trouble is always *started* by employers if they

COMMUNIST THEORY OF LABOR UNIONS 137

do not promptly comply with whatever demands the Communist union leaders present to them. In Communist circles, it is reckoned a "provocative" thing for an employer to be slow in yielding to even the most absurd and impossible demands. The non-provocative employer—the one who *starts* no trouble—is one who turns over his plant to Communists to do with it as they will, one who takes no measures whatever for the defense of his constitutional rights to life and property, and one who otherwise recognizes that a Soviet America would be vastly superior to what we have now. An employer's refusal to do any one of these things will brand him, among Communists and those who are hoodwinked by them, as having *started* the trouble. Of course, after such an employer has *started* the trouble by his stubbornness in refusing to see the Communist light, the Communists are then free to keep the trouble going—free to demolish automobiles and buildings, to stone or beat the employer and non-striking employees, and to inflict whatever other damage they choose to inflict. If, in doing these things, Communists come into conflict with officers of the law who, like the employers, are stubborn in refusing to see the Communist light, it becomes the function of the American Civil Liberties Union and the International Labor Defense to see that the Communists incur no penalties for having *continued* the trouble which the employer *started*, and it has been the standard practice of the National Labor Relations Board to prosecute employers for failing to yield to the Communists' demands.

In the outline for its course on trade unionism at the Workers' School, the Communist Party lists three concepts of trade unions: (a) Reformist, (b) Anarcho-Syndicalist, and (c) Marxist. According to the outline, reformist trade unions are those which accept the idea of class collaboration and "arbitration as a means of settling labor disputes." The Communists oppose such unions. The anarcho-syndicalist unions are those which hold the "theory that the union is the primary organ to wage the class struggle" and proceed to a "repudiation of the need for a workers' political party." The Communists also oppose these unions. The Marxist unions are those which have the structure of "industrial unionism" and which are based upon the theory that trade unions are "schools of Socialism."

In the light of all the foregoing authoritative statements of the Communist or Marxist theory of unions, it is apparent that nothing could be more relevant, in the interests of employees, employers, and the general public alike, for a government agency such as the National Labor Relations Board to ascertain the extent to which any particular trade union is under the leadership of Communists. A trade union under Communist leadership is not a trade union at all in the sense which Congress must have intended in its enactment of the Wagner Act. Such a labor organization is a "school of Socialism" conducted under the guise of trade unionism. It is a Trojan Horse useful only to Stalin and inimical to all American interests, especially to the interests of the workingmen of America. A strike under Communist leadership is likewise not a strike at all; it is "an advance guard collision . . . in which the workers are preparing for a future battle." Did Congress set up an agency for the promotion of schools of Socialism and for training workers, as Marx said, in real civil war? The question answers itself.

The *New Republic*, often a protagonist of things Communist, has dismissed the menace of Communism in the trade unions with the assertion that Communists are in the C.I.O. unions in "about the same proportions as they exist in the communities from which their membership is drawn." This statement is, of course, completely evasive of the real issue, which is one that concerns the nature and purpose of the activities of Communists in the unions. Who would think of trying to dismiss the question of gangsters and racketeers in trade unions with the cavalier observation that they are in the unions in "about the same proportions as they exist in the communities from which their membership is drawn"? If, as is clear to all, gangsters and racketeers operate in trade unions for the purpose of collecting the swag, of exploiting workers mercilessly, and of maintaining policies which are at variance with the purposes of unions as these are commonly understood, then all who are genuinely interested in unions will strive for the elimination of the gangsters and racketeers regardless of the nicety of their proportional representation in the unions. Communists are not gangsters in any ordinary sense of the word, but they are even more dangerous than gangsters wherever they are able to maneuver themselves into positions of trade union leadership. Communists are publicly on record with respect to their determination to destroy the so-called reformist trade unions, and have frankly declared their policy of turning the unions which they control into schools of Communism and training schools for real civil war.

The *New Republic* has offered the equally disingenuous argument that union membership is made up of Catholics, Jews, Protestants, Republicans, and Democrats, as well as of "a mere sprinkling of Socialists, Communists, Trotskyites and Lovestoneites." Everyone knows that an employee's religion is irrelevant to his trade union membership for the simple reason that there is no special trade union "line" held by Catholics, Jews, or Methodists as such. The churches do not send their members into trade unions with rigid instructions to carry out a specific policy. The Communist Party, on the other hand, not only requires its members to join whatever unions they may be eligible to join, but it also charges them, on pain of Party discipline, with the responsibility for executing carefully drawn plans for work in the trade unions. These things are as well known to the editors of the *New Republic* as they are to anyone else.

John Brophy, erstwhile director of the C.I.O., is the author of yet another disingenuous argument with respect to Communists in trade unions. Addressing the National Council of Catholic Women, Brophy said:

> After all Communism is the outgrowth of the denial of workers' rights, a thing that has grown out of the soil of repression and oppression. Labor unions have to take the workers that the employers have brought together. We don't question a man about his political beliefs.

It is equally true that gangsterism is believed by many to grow out of the soil of undesirable social conditions. Should gangsterism in a trade union, therefore, be tolerated simply because it is a natural growth from the soil of poverty and psychological maladjustment? Again, the question answers itself. In fact, the argument of Brophy and also that of the editors of the *New Republic* spring from a clearly recognizable soil—the soil of their own congeniality to the presence of Communists both in our communities and in the trade unions.

John L. Lewis has been quoted in the press as saying the employers hire Communists. At the time the statement was made, there was the plain implication that unions must, therefore, tolerate Communist leadership. Lewis' implication was at complete variance with the constitutional provision of his own union which bars Communists.

To sum up the basic theory of the Communist Party, the Communist-led labor union is the best and oldest of the Trojan Horses with which the Communist Party hopes to get its revolutionary troops into the very heart of the country's economic life. It goes without saying that no real trade unionism exists in the Soviet Union any more than it does in Hitler's Third Reich or in Mussolini's Corporative State. Any independent labor action, expressing itself in a strike, would be met in the Soviet Union with Stalin's bullets. Communism liquidates trade unionism as completely as it does free enterprise. The very suggestion of labor's collective bargaining in the Soviet Union is a grim joke. The truthful slogan would be: workers of the world unite under Stalin; you have nothing to lose but your freedom!

CHAPTER XI

COMMUNISM IN THE LABOR UNIONS

AMERICAN labor has borne the brunt of the Communist Party's effort to pursue its penetration of mass organizations; and to a degree that effort has been successful. American labor has a task of great seriousness and importance on its hands. The serious factor in the situation, from the standpoint of the nation as a whole, lies not only in the economic views which the Communist members of labor organizations may hold; but also in the foreign control over Communist Party members, which leads to sabotage and espionage, and in the Communist "rule or ruin" policy so disruptive to the labor organizations themselves.

Up until the year 1934, the Communist Party pursued the policy of dual unionism, setting up rival labor organizations in the same industries as were organized by the affiliates of the American Federation of Labor. During this period, the Trade Union Unity League, with affiliations in Moscow, was established in this country. All of the Communist labor unions in the United States were affiliated with the Trade Union Unity League.

There are no accurate figures as to the total membership of these Communist unions during the time of their separate existence. While the membership never compared with that of their rival unions in the legitimate trade union field, it is undoubtedly true that some ten or fifteen thousand Communists belonged to these unions and received their training in class warfare through them. As an adjunct to the unions, the Communist Party maintained workers schools in the larger industrial cities of the country. At one time, the total enrollment in these workers schools was approximately 10,000. While relatively small in membership, these Communist unions were responsible for many strikes which were characterized by unusual violence, such as the one at Gastonia, North Carolina.

The Special Committee on Un-American Activities heard the testimony of Joseph Zack who was in charge of the labor activities of the Communist Party in the United States from 1919 to 1934. He was the national trade union secretary and was the trade union director in the New York district of the Communist Party. At one time, he was secretary of the Trade Union Unity League in the eastern district. He served as a member of the national committee of the Communist Party upon three different occasions. He was sent to Russia in 1930 at the expense of the Communist International to study in the Lenin Institute and to represent the Foster faction of the Communist Party in the Communist International. Some of the information received by the Committee with reference to Communist labor organizations and their leadership came from Zack. The Committee also received valuable information from Benjamin Gitlow who was a former secretary of the Communist Party of the United States.

But more important than the verbal testimony of these witnesses, and many others, were the original minutes of the Communist Party covering a considerable period of time. In these minutes is the whole story of Communist strategy and aims in the trade union field. These minutes mention the names of present labor leaders, such as John Brophy, until recently director of the C.I.O., and Powers Hapgood, an official in the C.I.O.

The Special Committee on Un-American Activities had access to the records of certain C.I.O. labor unions, which reveal the extent of Communist penetration and control. From all of these sources of information, a very definite picture is obtained of Communist activities among the workers in the great industries of this country.

Sometime in 1934, the Communist Party of the United States received instructions from Moscow to abandon its policy of maintaining separate trade unions and to penetrate the American Federation of Labor. As a result of this new policy, the Communists dissolved their own T.U.U.L. unions and joined those affiliated with the American Federation of Labor for the purpose of "boring from within."

In obedience to these orders from Moscow, the central committee of the Communist Party in the United States adopted a lengthy and detailed resolution in January 1935, covering the immediate tasks of the Communist Party, its units and members. That resolution read, in part, as follows:

The influx of hundreds of thousands of new workers from basic industries and mass production plants into the American Federation of Labor unions, and the growing radicalization of the main mass of its membership make the American Federation of Labor unions more militant and mass unions in character, opening up new and greater possibilities of revolutionary mass work within them.

In view of this, the main task of the party in the sphere of trade-union work should be the work in the American Federation of Labor unions so as to energetically and tirelessly mobilize the masses of their members and the trade unions as a whole for the defense of the everyday interests of the workers, the leadership of strikes, carrying out the policy of the class struggle in the trade unions . . .

The party fractions must win the revolutionary unions for a struggle for trade-union unity by methods which correspond to the concrete conditions in each industry. The existing revolutionary trade unions and their locals join the American Federation of Labor or its unions wherever there exists parallel mass American Federation of Labor trade unions, or the "red" trade unions can join the American Federation of Labor directly.

When the rift between William Green and John L. Lewis and their respective followers developed, the Communists in the A. F. of L. were instructed to do everything within their power to bring about a definite split. From the evidence presented before the Special Committee on Un-American Activities, it is very clear that the Communists played an important role in bringing about the withdrawal of the C.I.O. unions from the A. F. of L. and the formation of the C.I.O.

When Lewis and his followers established the C.I.O., they were immediately confronted with a problem growing out of the scarcity of trained and experienced organizers. Their immediate task was to organize the workers in the heavy industries. They wanted to accomplish this as quickly as possible, in line with the wishes of the Administration that these workers be organized.

There is no question but that the President regarded it as a necessary part of his program to have these workers organized for purposes of collective bargaining. The President felt that no recovery could be brought about until this was accomplished. There is reliable information that the President sent for William Green and asked him to organize the workers in the heavy industries on a mass scale, but that Mr. Green informed the President it was impossible to do this as quickly as the President wanted it done.

After Green had rejected his proposal, the President sent for John L. Lewis and made the same request of him.

Lewis was quick to seize upon this opportunity, and, with the approval of the Administration and the valuable aid given him by the National Labor Relations Board, he set about to organize all the workers in the mass production industries. There was one thing lacking—trained organizers and leaders. But the Communist Party was ready to meet this need. It had five or ten thousand Communists who had received training in the workers schools and in the Communist labor unions. These Communists had received instruction in the theories and tactics of class warfare. In addition, they had practical experience gained in Communist-controlled strikes.

It is clear from the mass of information which the Special Committee on Un-American Activities has received, that Lewis decided to utilize these trained Communists to help him build up his industrial union organizations as quickly as possible. He might have thought that he could get rid of them when their services were no longer required. At any rate, hundreds of Communist organizers were employed by the C.I.O. to organize the workers into industrial unions, according to much testimony before the Committee.

The Committee received and published the names of about 300 of these Communist organizers. Labors Non-Partisan League was invited to appear before the Committee and deny the testimony with reference to these Communist organizers who were employed by the C.I.O.; but the League did not see fit to accept the invitation.

With the aid of these Communist organizers, and with the cooperation of the National Labor Relations Board, the C.I.O. was able, in a very short period of time, to organize millions of workers into industrial union organizations. The Communist organizers proved their ability to recruit workers into these organizations. But, having accomplished this purpose, they set about to use the unions for their own revolutionary purposes. In the first place, they got themselves elected or appointed to strategic positions in the unions. This was comparatively easy, because the great majority of the new recruits were ignorant of Communist tactics and their parliamentary procedures. Let us illustrate the manner in which these Communist organizers entrenched themselves in positions of leadership in these unions.

There was considerable evidence before the Special Committee on Un-American Activities that thousands of new recruits were added to the rolls each week and that so much money was taken in from dues that the organizers and officials carried the money in their pockets. A local of the heavy industries, such as automobiles or steel, would have as many as 15,000 members; but the average attendance at union meetings would not exceed three or four hundred. The failure to attend these meetings was in line with the American custom of joining everything, but rarely attending anything.

In each local, there would be a Communist fraction composed of the Communist members of the local. The fraction always met in advance of the scheduled meeting of the local. At this advance meeting the Communists outlined the program which they agreed to put through at the regular union meeting. For instance, they would agree that a certain Communist was to introduce a resolution pledging the union to support the *Daily Worker's* campaign for funds, or to contribute money out of the treasury for some other Communist purpose. It might also be agreed that a certain Communist would be nominated and supported as secretary of the local or named to some other strategic position. Having agreed upon their program, every Communist member of the local would be present at the meeting and remain until the meeting was adjourned.

When the meeting began, the fraction of Communists found it comparatively easy to control every important action taken by the local. In the first place, the non-Communists in the local did not always know who the Communists were. In the second place, the non-Communists, with very few exceptions, were unskilled in parliamentary procedure and wholly lacking in any definite program. Immediately after the meeting was called to order, the Communists would move that one of their comrades be elected chairman of the meeting and that another comrade be elected secretary.

With Communists occupying the temporary offices in the local, the rest of the Communist program went through without a hitch. The Communist members were scattered throughout the house, and naturally they were recognized by the chairman in preference to non-Communists who sought to speak. By their united action, they created the appearance of unanimity on the part of the great majority of those present at the meeting. This would not have been possible in a meeting of experienced trade unionists who were familiar with Communists strategy. The members of the American Federation of Labor are experienced trade unionists, and the Communists have found it impossible to make headway in many such unions. Hence, the Communists appreciated the great opportunity which the new industrial unionism afforded them, and they were quick to take advantage of it. The C.I.O. was the answer to their prayer.

Instance after instance of this Communist strategy has come before the Special Committee on Un-American Activities. For example, in one of the large industrial unions in the automobile industry, Communists, although a minority, completely ran the organization. This particular local had thousands of members who had been recruited hastily into the union; but very few of them attended the regular meetings of the local. So strongly entrenched was Communist leadership in this local that two Communist lecturers were employed by the local and paid, out of the local's funds, to lecture to the members of the local and their friends on Marxism. These two lecturers used the visual lecture charts put out by the Communist Party. The Communist officials in this union engineered the meetings so that funds were voted out of the treasury for Communist purposes upon many occasions.

In another union in Chicago, the books revealed the control which the Communists had over the union. For instance, thousands of copies of the *Daily Worker* were purchased with union funds and distributed free of cost to members of the union. If a careful and systematic audit of the books of many of the unions affiliated with the C.I.O. were made, it would reveal that thousands of dollars were voted out of the treasuries of these unions to finance the Communist program in the United States.

To illustrate the tactics which the Communists use to control labor unions, let us quote briefly from the testimony of Zygmund Dobrzynski who was national director of the organizing committee of the United Automobile Workers of America Ford drive. It was his function to supervise the organization of the workers in the Ford plant. There were approximately 4,000 members in his local. Mr.

Dobrzynski described the strategy of the Communists as follows:

> During the first organizational days, when the U.A.W. was first formed, and the men were beginning to recognize that unionism was the thing they needed, they came in by the hundreds; the automobile industry was made up of men, primarily, who had never been in any union before, and who were completely inexperienced, not knowing even how to make a motion on the floor . . . These members of the Communist Party knew how to speak; some of them had extensive soap-box experience, and experience in other organizations, and they took advantage of this fact. It is very simple for a man who understands public speaking and the parliamentary rules to control a meeting of uninitiated people.

In explaining how Communists were able to control Plymouth Local 51, which had 10,000 members, Felix J. McCartney, a member of that union, said:

> The good people that have attended these meetings have become so discouraged by the action of these Communists in prolonging any discussion about any action that would be of any benefit to the workers—that is, a motion or a resolution would be put on the floor looking to the benefit of the workers, and these people would get up and talk against it so long, and prolong the meeting so these people would get so discouraged, the good people, that they would leave the meeting.

This witness testified that the average attendance at meetings of this union was from 100 to 300; and that the same situation prevailed in other locals in the automobile industry.

In explanation of the Communist tactics, Richard Eager, who was plant chairman and chairman of the bargaining committee at the Ternstedt manufacturing division of General Motors, and also a member of Local 174 of the United Automobile Workers which had a membership of 32,000, said:

> They [the Communists] first contact whoever is the plant chairman, and, after they make the motion, he is supposed to recognize only those people who will speak in favor of the motion. Secondly, they will have one of their group to move the previous question. That shuts off debate. They will wrangle over the question before they call the previous question. They will talk a long time and the people will get tired of listening, so that when the previous question comes up, they usually accomplish their purposes in the vote, while nobody in the opposition has an opportunity to speak.

This witness further stated: "The policies in our local and in our plants are controlled by the Communist Party."

Homer Martin, who was head of the United Automobile Workers, testified before the Special Committee on Un-American Activities that the Communists, by reason of having a tightly organized minority, were able to seize the strategic positions in the unions.

Joseph Zack testified that at the time the C.I.O. was formed eleven unions controlled by Communists were taken out of the A. F. of L. and affiliated with the C.I.O.

Zack testified that Wyndham Mortimer, a leader in the United Automobile Workers and a national director of the C.I.O., joined the Communist Party in 1933, and that he, Joseph Zack, endorsed his application to join the Communist Party.

Zack also testified that Joseph Curran, general secretary of the National Maritime Union of the C.I.O. and a member of the board of directors of the C.I.O., was a member of the Communist Party.

Zack said that John Brophy, until recently director of the C.I.O., worked very closely with the Communist Party between 1925 and 1928, and, in this connection, he testified: "At that time, there was an internal fight in the United Mine Workers, and the Comintern invested tremendous amounts of funds to put John L. Lewis out. At one time Brophy was running for president against John L. Lewis. His campaign was organized entirely and directed by the Communist Party."

Zack testified that Michael Obermeier, secretary of Local 6 of the International Alliance of Hotel Workers and Bartenders, has been a member of the Communist Party since the party was formed.

According to Zack, Lewis Weinstock of the Painters Union was a charter member of the Communist Party. Zack testified that the same is true of J. Ruben, president of the New York Hotel Trades Council; and that Ben Gold, president of the Furriers Union, has been a member of the Communist Party since it was formed.

Zack identified other officials and leaders of unions affiliated with the C.I.O. as members of the Communist Party.

The Special Committee on Un-American Activities received the sworn testimony of witnesses who identified more than half of the directors of the C.I.O. as either members of the Communist Party, or former members of the Party, or as fellow travelers who follow the Communist Party line.

Earl Browder, general secretary of the Communist Party, testified that about 50,000 members of the Communist Party are active in trade unions; and, of this number, that two-thirds are active in the C.I.O. and one-third in the A. F. of L. Browder testified that hundreds of these Communists occupy positions of leadership in these unions.

COMMUNISM IN THE LABOR UNIONS 153

The evidence which shows the extent of Communist penetration of the trade union movement consists of the testimony of officials in trade unions, former members of the Communist Party, minutes of the Communist Party, and records of certain locals.

Jack Stachel, high functionary of the Communist Party, sent directions to the districts of the Communist Party on November 16, 1935, in which, among other things, he said:

> The districts must set themselves the tasks of forging working united fronts with all progressive officials—and those officials who for whatever reason show leftward and (or) progressive tendencies—regardless of their past record—on the following main issues:
> 1. Labor Party.
> 2. Industrial form of organization.
>
> At the same time, the struggle to win over the rank and file —united front from below—must become the main task of the fractions.

In these instructions, Stachel bitterly attacked the conservative leadership of the American Federation of Labor.

The resolution adopted by the central committee of the Communist Party, January 15 to 18, 1935, in New York City, and which is found on pages 180 to 186 of the record of the Hearings of the Special Committee on Un-American Activities, corroborates these instructions issued by Jack Stachel as to the manner in which Communists should infiltrate trade unions and seize control of strategic positions.

In discussing the role of the Communist Party in the organization of the C.I.O., William Z. Foster, chairman of the Communist Party of the United States, wrote in the *Daily Worker*, January 13, 1937, as follows:

> The Communist Party heartily supports the C.I.O. organiz-

ing campaigns in steel, automobile, rubber, glass, textile, etc., and it mobilizes all its forces to assist in this work. It extends this aid for the same reason that it supports every forward movement of the workers wherever it may originate or whatever form it may take, whether it be a strike, an organization campaign, the carrying on of independent working class political activity, or what not.

After the Communist Party had transferred a great majority of its members from the American Federation of Labor to the C.I.O., orders came from Moscow to introduce the sit-down strike technique as a vital part of class warfare. The sit-down strike technique had been used by the Communists in France and other foreign countries, and they regarded it as an effective weapon to produce chaotic and revolutionary conditions in an industry.

The Communist leadership in Russia had been induced to believe that, on account of the economic depression in the United States, the time was ripe for a revolution. Plans were carefully laid to bring about this revolution in the basic industries located in the East and on the West Coast. To this end, the Communists planned first to create chaotic conditions in these industries through a series of paralyzing strikes. As a preliminary campaign to these strikes, the grievances of the workers, whether real or imaginary, were exaggerated in the Communist press and by Communist speakers in the unions. The sit-down strike was pictured as the only effective weapon that the working class could use to better its conditions.

The sit-down strikes spread through American industry and practically paralyzed industry in Michigan and on the West Coast. The Special Committee on Un-American Activities received evidence that the cost of the sit-down strikes to the workers and to industry ran into billions of dollars.

When these strikes were at their height, I delivered a speech on the floor of the House denouncing this method as revolutionary and illegal. Some of the members of the House hissed my speech and when my resolution to investigate sit-down strikes came before the House, it was overwhelmingly defeated.

This showed the power wielded by the Communists and their fellow travelers during that period. Few members of the House believed that the sit-down strike was defensible or advisable; but the Communist Trojan Horse in America had become so influential that few members dared to antagonize it. Public officials like Secretary Perkins openly condoned the sit-down strike, and no action was taken by the Government to prosecute the sit-down offenders. It was this attitude on the part of Congress which convinced me that subversive propaganda and activities should be investigated and exposed.

As an illustration of the prominent part played by the Communist Party in the United States in instigating and promoting the sit-down strikes, let us quote excerpts from a book by William Weinstone, called *The Great Sit-Down Strike*. Weinstone was the district organizer of district No. 7 of the Communist Party, Detroit, Michigan. He was born in Russia, joined the Socialist Party in this country in 1915, and was one of the first members of the executive committee of the Communist Party. When the central committee was created, he became one of the Communist leaders in the United States. In connection with his report on the automobile organizing campaign and the automobile strike, Weinstone wrote, as follows:

In the first place must be mentioned the work of the Communist members of the union as well as the work of the Communist Party itself.

What were the activities of the Communists? The Communists and the Communist Party gave the most loyal backing and support to the strike, to the aims, policies, and activities of the union and the C.I.O. The Communists worked ardently and earnestly in helping to build up the union and tried in every way possible to properly prepare the strike so that it would rest upon a strong foundation. In the strike itself, the Communists sought to imbue the strikers and the workers generally with the greatest discipline, organization, and perseverance. There is no doubt that where the Communists were active and took an outstanding part, particularly at the most decisive points of the struggle, there the strike was strongest, and this made for the success of the whole battle.

The existence of the groups of Communists within the shops was undoubtedly of great help, because thereby a corps of experienced people were in the shops to help in the solution of the new problems connected with the sit-down. The shop form of organization, the shop groups [units], has more than justified itself. Where the party organization paid attention to these units, there the efforts of many years of work were fully rewarded.

In conclusion, the strike of the automobile workers reveals the new forces that are at work within the country, forces which are driving toward an extension and strengthening of the labor movement and which are welding also the unity of the working class and of all progressive-minded people, a process which is giving rise to the growth of a real people's movement—a real people's united front—a movement which will embrace also the most aggressive revolutionary-minded section of the working class—the Communists and the Communist Party.

It is the attitude of John L. Lewis with reference to Communism which is so puzzling. In 1924, Lewis posed as the outstanding opponent of Communism in the United States. At that time, he had already become president of the United Mine Workers of America. His organization prepared and published an exposé entitled "Attempt by Communists to Seize the American Labor Movement." This exposé was presented to the United States Senate by Senator Henry Cabot Lodge and ordered to be printed at government expense. The pamphlet states that "these articles are the result of an independent searching investigation on the part of the United Mine Workers of America which led directly to original sources."

The first article states that the United Mine Workers "desires to reveal and make known the sinister and destructive groups and elements attempting to 'bore from within' its own ranks and membership and to seize possession of the organization, and, through such seizure, to later gain possession of all legitimate trade-unions." It further says that "the Communist organization on the American continent is composed of more than six thousand active leaders and lieutenants, and approximately one million members, adherents, and sympathizers, scattered in every state and province of the United States and Canada, and who are actively or tacitly promoting the scheme to import Bolshevism and Sovietism to this side of the Atlantic."

After outlining the general objectives of the Communist conspiracy in America, the pamphlet of the United Mine Workers enumerates the following major points in the revolutionary program of the Communists as aimed against its organization and other legitimate trade-unions:

Seizure of all labor unions through a process of "boring from within" them, and utilizing them as a strategic instrument in fulfillment of their revolutionary designs upon organized and constitutional government.

Invasion of the United Mine Workers of America, with the ouster of its present officials and leaders and the substitution of a leadership of Communists, that it may be used as an instrumentality for seizing the other labor unions of America, and for eventually taking possession of the country.

A well-organized movement is being promoted within the four railroad brotherhoods and sixteen railroad trade-unions to amalgamate all railroad workers into "one departmentalized industrial union," controlled by a single leader of Communist principle and affiliation, and owing allegiance to the Communist organization.

Seizure of the American Federation of Labor, with the ouster of its officials, and through such seizure gaining control of all its affiliated units and trade-unions.

Conversion of all craft trade-unions into single units of workers within an industry known as "industrial unions," with coordination under a super-Soviet union owing allegiance to, and accepting the mandates of, the Communist International and its subsidiary, the Red Trade Union International, at Moscow.

Through conquest and subjugation of the labor unions, and conversion and mobilization of farmers and other related groups, the overthrow of existing institutions, and the creation of a condition similar to that which now prevails in Russia.

We have Lewis' own statement, made in 1926 at the convention of the American Federation of Labor, when he said:

We are fundamentally concerned, however, when that interest which now exerts a dictatorship over 130,000,000 people in Russia systematically and persistently attempts to impose their philosophy and impose their theories of government and impose their own particular machinery and their own specific ideas upon the workers of all the other countries of the civilized world . . . For years past, our union has been subject to their deceitful attacks, to their intrigues and to their conspir-

COMMUNISM IN THE LABOR UNIONS 159

acy. Many of you will remember that 3 or 4 years ago the United Mine Workers of America published a résumé of communist activities in America.

Now compare the attitude of Lewis in 1924 and 1926 with his present attitude. In 1926, the Communist Party was weak in comparison with its present strength. Its greatest growth occurred between 1934 and 1939 after its perfection of the Trojan Horse policy. If Lewis considered the Communist threat serious in 1926 when the party was numerically weak, what is his attitude on this question today?

Before the Special Committee on Un-American Activities began its Hearings, I discussed this subject with John L. Lewis in his office in Washington. I conferred with him upon the suggestion of Harvey Fremming, who was at that time president of one of the large unions affiliated with the C.I.O. Lee Pressman, his chief lieutenant, was present at this conference. I told Lewis that information had come to me that the Communists had made considerable progress in the C.I.O. and that naturally I was anxious to get the truth. He assured me that my information was inaccurate and that the charge of Communism in the C.I.O. was inspired by selfish interests which were seeking to discredit the C.I.O. He said that there were few Communists in the ranks of the C.I.O., and that he was seeking to combat Communism by improving the wages and working conditions of laboring people.

I was not satisfied with his answer and immediately wrote him a letter inviting him to appear before the Special Committee on Un-American Activities to give us any information he might have on Communism, Fascism, and Nazism. He did not accept this invitation. In the meantime, I received detail information showing that Communist organizers had been employed by the C.I.O., and that some of the leaders in some of the unions affiliated with the C.I.O. were Communists.

After I determined to receive in evidence the testimonies of witnesses showing these facts, the C.I.O. adopted a belligerent attitude toward the Special Committee on Un-American Activities. Through their publications, they assailed the Committee as red-baiters and foes of organized labor.

Assuming that Lewis was sincere in his belief that there were few Communists in his organization, the exposure of the true situation before the Special Committee on Un-American Activities should have convinced him that he was mistaken, or at least it should have aroused his curiosity on the subject. The natural course for one who had been so bitterly opposed to Communism in 1926 would have been to investigate these charges and the sworn testimony of witnesses before the Committee. If this testimony was false, Lewis should have availed himself of the opportunity to disprove it, or at least to deny it. But Lewis did no such thing; he chose instead to denounce the Committee.

No one can read the Hearings of the Special Committee on Un-American Activities without being convinced that Communists are entrenched in positions of leadership in some of the important unions affiliated with the C.I.O. The very fact that the Committee unanimously found this to be true is a strong indication of the conclusive nature of the evidence. At least, this fact imposed a duty upon Lewis and the responsible leaders of his organization to conduct an independent investigation of their own for the purpose of finding out the true situation.

The truth is that the evidence received by the Special Committee on Un-American Activities of Communist infiltration of the C.I.O. is conclusive. It comes from nearly every source from which reliable information can be obtained. It does not depend upon the statements of disgruntled and ousted officials of the C.I.O. It is based upon testimony and documentary evidence which would be received in any court of the land; and it shows that what John L. Lewis predicted in 1924 and 1926 has actually happened.

It is, of course, impossible to deal with all of the unions where Communists are entrenched in positions of leadership; but it is important to discuss certain unions which control basic industries that are vital to our national defense. In two chapters which follow, some of the evidence received by the Special Committee on Un-American Activities is presented in order to establish beyond any question that the unions which control communications, transportation, and shipping are headed by Communists.

CHAPTER XII

WHEELS AND THE REVOLUTION

THE world has seen what disaster can befall a nation when a few strategically-placed fifth columnists are at work in its transportation and communication system. We have direct reports to the effect that a single individual in the air transport system of Holland did more effective work for the invading Nazi army than did thousands of Nazi troops themselves. We are also in possession of private information that an operator in the railway system at the important junction of San Quentin, France, completely confused and disrupted the movements of the French army at the most critical moment of Hitler's break-through at Sedan.

Modern industrial civilization lives on wheels. The endless movement of men and supplies is so elaborate and at the same time so delicate in the degree and nature of its organization that even a moment's reflection on its amazing detail will almost stagger our imaginations. Let that ceaseless movement of the wheels of transportation which our civilization requires be halted for more than a few minutes, and a veritable paralytic stroke would turn civilization into chaos. Well might the turning wheel be the foremost symbol of an ordered physical existence in our kind of civilization. A modern industrial people could spare the political machinery of its government for a much longer period than it could spare its system of turning wheels.

The Communists know all this. They understand its implications far better than the average citizen does. They

WHEELS AND THE REVOLUTION

know where the physical controls of our industrially organized society are to be found. The Communists would far rather elect a half dozen of their able members to the Transport Workers Union in New York than to put the same men into the United States Senate.

As a matter of fact, Communists who hold leading positions in the Transport Workers Union have set it down in print, where all may read, that they regard the control of our wheels of transport as vital to the success of their revolution. John Santo, who is now the general secretary-treasurer of the Transport Workers Union, wrote in the *Daily Worker,* as follows:

> The building of this new union is of the greatest importance to all other trade unions as well as to the whole working class. First of all it is a key industry, without which all other industries would be paralyzed.

Santo, who has been identified again and again by both oral and documentary evidence as a member of the Communist Party, was one of the original organizers of the union of transport workers in New York. His article in the *Daily Worker* was written during the early organization efforts which the Communist Party made among transport workers in New York.

In a secret document of the Communist Party, John Santo was listed as district representative for Section 22 of the Communist Party in New York. Our Committee has a full record of Santo's past. His real name is not Santo.

Inasmuch as the purpose of the Communists in organizing transport workers is what it is, it is an almost incredible thing that a man like Santo has been permitted to obtain a strategic position in an organization which holds such vast power over the life of our greatest city. It is a question of the gravest national concern whether America, like France, will awake too late to the menace of the communist grip upon some of our basic industries.

Discussing the strategic character of the union of transport workers in the *Daily Worker*, one of the secretaries of the transport union which is headed by Michael Quill, John Santo, and Austin Hogan pointed out that "if the transit workers of New York should strike for six hours only, the life of the whole city would be upside down," and further that there would be "a gigantic battle of New York transit workers against the Wall Street bankers; a battle the like of which New York has never seen, and which would knock a number of bricks off the capitalist structure."

The Transport Workers Union was first organized in New York in 1934. Since then it has become an international union with locals in various parts of the United States, Canada, and Alaska. Its main strength, however, remains in New York. Its total dues-paying membership, according to official claims, is about 90,000. The union is at present affiliated with the C.I.O.

The Transport Workers Union was in the beginning an independent body. In 1935, its leaders sought affiliation with the Amalgamated Association of Street, Electric Railway and Motor Coach Employees of America, but the latter union suspected Quill, Hogan, and Santo of being Communists, and their request for affiliation was rejected.

Concerning the next effort of the Transport Workers Union to find an affiliation, the bulletin of the Amalgamated Association of Street, Electric Railway and Motor Coach Employees had the following to say:

Next the Transport Workers commissars tried to affiliate with the New York lodge of the International Association of

Machinists. Apparently the New York Machinists knew too much about the set-up, for they turned Quill down.

Later, Quill and his associates were able to obtain a charter for affiliation from the International Association of Machinists in Washington and thus to enter the ranks of the American Federation of Labor.

Among the principal officials of the Transport Workers Union, almost from the time of its formation, were Michael J. Quill, Austin Hogan, John Santo, and Thomas H. O'Shea. These four made a trip to Detroit in 1935 for the purpose of seeking affiliation with the Amalgamated Association of Street, Electric Railway and Motor Coach Employees.

On their way to Detroit, they stopped at the Communist camp Nitgedaigat to solicit funds for their new union. They were assisted in this fund-raising by the Negro Communist, Angelo Herndon.

The first president of the Transport Workers Union was one Thomas H. O'Shea. In April, 1940, O'Shea appeared as a witness before the Special Committee on Un-American Activities. He testified that he had been a member of the Communist Party, having joined at the time the Transport Workers Union was being formed. According to O'Shea, he was appointed to the presidency of the union by the Communist Party and was not elected by the membership of the organization. When Michael J. Quill was a witness before the Special Committee on Un-American Activities, he testified that O'Shea had been his predecessor in the presidency of the union but that he, Quill, was the first *elected* president of the organization.

O'Shea testified that he had been asked to step out of the presidency of the union by the Communist Party in order that Quill might be elected in his place. This was partially confirmed by Quill who declared that he had been unopposed for the office at the time of his election in December, 1935.

The new weekly magazine, *Friday*, which made its first appearance on March 15, 1940, leans strongly toward the Communist Party "line." This fact is evidenced by the magazine's announcement that two of its cartoonists of whom it is "pretty proud" are Fred Ellis and Bill Gropper. Both Ellis and Gropper have been well known as communist cartoonists for many years. Their work has appeared regularly in the *Daily Worker*, the *New Masses*, and other Communist Party publications. Ruth McKenney, one of the editors of the *New Masses*, contributed a eulogistic article on Michael Quill and the Transport Workers Union in the March 22nd issue of *Friday*. Among other things, Miss McKenney wrote: "Michael Joseph Quill, first and only president of the Transport Workers Union, etc. etc." The complete refutation of Miss McKenney's characterization of Quill as the "first and only president of the Transport Workers Union" is to be found not only in the fact that O'Shea's name appears as president of the union on the membership books of 1935 but also in the bulletins of the union. In the Transport Workers *Bulletin*, a picture of O'Shea was published with the following characterization: "Tom O'Shea, fighting president of the TWU."

In the *Daily Worker* for April 24, 1940, officials of the Transport Workers Union in New York are quoted as saying of O'Shea that: "the company stooge was defeated when he ran for reelection" as president of the union. Quill himself has since stated under oath that O'Shea did not run for reelection against him in December, 1935. Furthermore, it is clear that O'Shea was not repudiated by his union at that time inasmuch as his name appeared subsequently as one of the union's business agents in the Transport Workers *Bulletin.*

In short, the record clearly establishes O'Shea's competence as a witness concerning the communist control of the Transport Workers Union.

In 1936, Austin Hogan was general secretary of the Transport Workers Lodge, International Association of Machinists. Today, he is the president of the New York local of the Transport Workers Union, the local which comprises the larger part of the entire membership of the union. Hogan's name was originally Gustav Dilloughry.

Hogan has been identified as a member of the Communist Party by John J. Murphy, and Thomas H. O'Shea.

In the *Daily Worker* for June 1, 1934, there appeared an article which was sub-captioned "1,000 Workers Bid Irish Communist Leader Adieu." Among the participants on the program of this farewell meeting for the Irish communist leader were Earl Browder, James W. Ford, Charles Krumbein, Mike Gold, and Austin Hogan. Browder, Ford, Krumbein, and Gold are among the outstanding communist leaders in the United States.

Michael Quill was elected president of the Transport Workers Union in December, 1935, after O'Shea had been instructed by the Communist Party leaders to withdraw in order that Quill might be chosen head of the union without opposition. Quill has remained in the presidency of the union until the present time.

John J. Murphy testified before the Special Committee on Un-American Activities, as follows:

I sat in unit 19-S meetings of the Communist Party with Mr. Michael Quill, and knew him for years before as station agent on the lines of the Interborough Rapid Transit Co.

Edward Maguire's testimony before the Special Committee on Un-American Activities included the following with reference to Michael Quill:

Mr. Starnes: Have you collected dues from all those you have called here?
Mr. Maguire: Yes, sir.
Mr. Starnes: Were they members of your unit?
Mr. Maguire: Yes, sir; of the unit known as 19-S.
Mr. Thomas: Then do I understand you collected dues from Michael J. Quill?
Mr. Maguire: Yes, sir.
Mr. Starnes: You say you were secretary-treasurer of that unit?
Mr. Maguire: The unit known as 19-S.

Michael Kelly testified that Michael Quill asked him to join the Communist Party and to attend the Communist Party's Workers School at 50 East 13th Street, New York, N. Y.

Michael J. M'Carthy also testified that Quill had solicited him for membership in the Communist Party.

Thomas H. O'Shea likewise testified that he had personally known Michael Quill to be a member of the Communist Party.

Michael Quill's connections with various Communist-controlled organizations have been numerous.

Quill contributed an article to the December, 1937, issue of *Champion*. *Champion* was a publication of the Young Communist League and of the International Workers Order.

At a mass meeting under the sponsorship of the Greater New York Committee for Employment, in May, 1938, Quill was one of the speakers. According to the *Daily Worker's* account of this meeting, the following communist-controlled organizations were represented: American League for Peace and Democracy, Workers Alliance, National Negro Congress, and Harlem Division of the Communist Party.

In June, 1939, an organization known as the Associated Blind, Inc., held its annual dance in the hall of the Transport Workers Union. The *Daily Worker* listed Quill among the sponsors of the event, together with such well-known Communists and Communist fellow travelers as Max Bedacht, Granville Hicks, Donald Ogden Stewart, and Jerome Davis.

In April, 1939, Quill was a speaker at a mass meeting of the Manhattan Citizens Committee. A. Phillip Randolph, president of the National Negro Congress, and Ben Gold, avowed Communist head of the International Fur Workers Union, were also among the speakers. The American League for Peace and Democracy, the National Negro Congress, and the Jewish People's Committee were listed in the *Daily Worker* as organizations supporting the meeting. At the time Ben Gold and William Weiner, both nationally prominent members of the Communist Party, were president and secretary, respectively, of the Jewish People's Committee.

In December, 1938, Quill wrote the International Labor Defense, as follows:

Aware of the very necessary and able work done by the International Labor Defense in behalf of organized labor throughout the past and preceding years, I am happy to join with you in your annual Christmas Drive for labor's Neediest Cases. I am urging all in our union and our affiliate organizations in the labor movement, and I am asking all my friends personally to support the Christmas drive. I feel confident that whatever goal you have set for yourselves will be achieved and that funds collected will go as have always been the case in the ILD, to very worthy fighters for the workers of America.

In December, 1938, Quill was a sponsor for a New Year's Eve Ball of the Non-Sectarian Committee for Political Refugees. Associated with him in the sponsorship of the Ball were Marc Blitzstein, Millen Brand, Malcolm Cowley, Lillian Hellman, Granville Hicks, Genevieve Taggard, and Richard Wright. These seven persons were also among the signers of a publicly-released statement "in support of the verdicts of the recent Moscow trials of the Trotskyite-Buckharinite traitors." Their Communist connections have been numerous.

In November, 1938, Quill was a speaker at a mass meeting "to protest Nazi atrocities." The meeting was held in Pittsburgh under the auspices of the League for the Protection of Minority Rights and the American League for Peace and Democracy. Ben Gold was also a speaker at the meeting.

In June, 1938, Quill was a speaker at a meeting under the auspices of the American Friends of the Mexican People. The principal speaker of the occasion was V. Lombardo Toledano, general secretary of the Confederation of Mexican Workers. In the Mexican labor movement, Toledano is known as a Stalinist.

Quill is a sponsor of the Consumer-Farmer Milk Cooperative, Inc., together with Max Bedacht of the International Workers Order and A. Phillip Randolph of the National Negro Congress. Rose Nelson is a director of the organization. Miss Nelson is now an official of the International Workers Order and has been a section organizer of the Communist Party.

The *Daily Worker* for December 20, 1938, announced

that Quill would be a speaker at a meeting under the auspices of the Progressive Women's Council and the American League for Peace and Democracy. The Jewish People's Committee was also represented by a speaker at the meeting. The Progressive Women's Council, of which Rose Nelson was once the head, has now merged with the International Workers Order.

Quill is a member of the Labor Advisory Committee of Consumers Union of U.S., Inc. Ben Gold and Louis Weinstock, both well-known Communists, are also members of this committee.

The American Labor Party, which Quill once represented on the Council of the City of New York, withdrew its endorsement of Quill on the ground that he refused to follow the policy of the American Labor Party in its stand on the Soviet-Nazi Pact.

Quill has been identified with the so-called Communist wing of the American Labor Party. He addressed a mass rally at which Bernhard J. Stern was also a speaker. Stern, as we have pointed out, uses the alias of Bennett Stevens in his work for the Communist Party. The so-called Communist wing of the American Labor Party is known as the Progressive Committee to Rebuild the American Labor Party. Among Quill's associates on this Committee are Joseph Curran, Lillian Hellman, Charles Hendley, Rockwell Kent, and Mervyn Rathborne.

The Ladies Auxiliary of the Transport Workers Union is affiliated with the League of Women Shoppers. In records which the Special Committee on Un-American Activities obtained at the headquarters of the Communist Party in Philadelphia, the League of Women Shoppers was designated as a "Party organization."

The Ladies Auxiliary of the T.W.U. was also affiliated

with the Progressive Women's Council prior to the time the latter organization was merged with the International Workers Order. Rose Nelson, who was secretary of the Progressive Women's Council, was organizer of Section 15 of the Communist Party in New York in 1934. In this latter capacity, Miss Nelson was active in support of the taxicab drivers' strike out of which there was one of the beginnings of the Transport Workers Union.

When the Progressive Women's Council merged with the International Workers Order in March, 1939, Rose Nelson became an official of the latter organization as head of the I.W.O. City Women's Department.

The completely Communist control of the Progressive Women's Council is reflected not only in Miss Nelson's leadership of the organization but also in the fact that it merged with another Communist-controlled group, the International Workers Order. Elsewhere, the completely documented account of the Communist control of the International Workers Order will be presented. At this place, evidence on that point is confined to an article by Max Bedacht. Bedacht's article, which appeared in the *Daily Worker* for May 21, 1934, is headed "Organize Workers' Children, Or the Priests Will Get Them." Bedacht stated that children in the International Workers Order who were over nine years of age received the *New Pioneer* Magazine free of charge. The *New Pioneer* Magazine for May, 1934, taken merely as a sample of its general propaganda, had the following to say:

> Then, one fine day, you will chase out the bosses, the cops, and the landlords. Like your comrades in the Soviet Union ... With them you will make a World Soviet Republic!

One of the leaders of the Ladies Auxiliary of the Transport Workers Union is Isobel Walker Soule. She was co-author of the Union's *Guide for Ladies Auxiliaries*.

Isobel Walker Soule was listed in the *Daily Worker* as one of the prominent guests present at a meeting in honor of Ella Reeve Bloor. The article in the *Daily Worker* was captioned "Women C. P. Leaders Honor Mother Bloor."

Harry Sacher is counsel for the Transport Workers Union. Mr. Sacher has been listed as a lecturer at the Communist Party's Workers School in New York.

In July, 1933, the Communist Party of the United States adopted a trade union policy known as "concentration." This policy was set forth in a document called "An Open Letter to All Party Members." It was published in the *Daily Worker* for July 13, 1933, in a special supplement.

The policy of concentration meant simply that the Communist Party decided to specialize in the larger industrial areas of the United States rather than to carry on work generally throughout the country. Excerpts from the "Open Letter" will serve to elucidate the policy of concentration:

> The entire work of the Party and the best forces of the Party were to be directed first of all to building up and consolidating the Party and revolutionary trade union movement in the most important industrial centers of the country . . .
>
> Talk about defense of the Soviet Union and struggle against imperialist war is nothing but empty phrases unless systematic work is carried out in the war industry plants and in the ports . . .
>
> Concentration of our work on the most important factories . . .
>
> But the Party cannot carry out this task successfully unless at the same time it establishes its base in the decisive big factories . . .

Thomas H. O'Shea testified before the Special Committee on Un-American Activities that the communist work of organizing the transit workers in New York grew out of the policy of concentration enunciated in the "Open Letter."

F. Brown, alleged by witnesses before the Committee to be an American representative from the Communist International, wrote in the *Communist* for September, 1933, that Pittsburgh, Cleveland, Detroit, Chicago, and New York were concentration points in the strategy of the Communist Party.

Also in the September, 1933, issue of the *Communist*, J. Peters wrote that

The five concentration districts, Chicago, Detroit, Cleveland, Pittsburgh, and New York were assigned the special task of concentrating on altogether about 50 factories . . .

Writing in the *Party Organizer* for March, 1935, Louis Sass said:

After our Extraordinary Party Conference, we seriously undertook to carry through the Open Letter and its central principle: concentration. One of the concentration points assigned to us by the District is the city traction, an industry where thousands of American workers, hitherto untouched by our movement, are organized into company unions on the I.R.T. and B.M.T. systems.

Shortly after the publication of the "Open Letter," Charles Krumbein, now state secretary of the Communist Party in New York, wrote in the *Party Organizer*, as follows:

Another point I think we should consider for concentration is city transport. Transport in all big cities plays a very important political role. I think it is a field that we must concentrate on.

By March, 1936, the Communist Party was prepared to claim that a transport workers union had been built and led by its members.

Inasmuch as a very large number of the transit employees in New York City are of Irish extraction, the Communist Party, according to its own claims, began early to devise a special approach to these Irish workers.

Both the *Daily Worker* and the Transport Workers *Bulletin* have featured the life story of the Irish revolutionist, James Connolly. According to the testimony of Thomas H. O'Shea, this was calculated to overcome the anti-communist sentiments which were prevalent among the Irish transit workers.

The Transport Workers Union has regularly participated in the May Day parades under the control of the Communist Party. One of the tests for determining the fact of Communist control in the trade unions and other organizations is participation in these parades which are under the direction of the Communist Party.

According to a recent issue of the Transport Workers *Bulletin*, the Union has a "closed shop" for "everything on wheels" in Alaska. O'Shea testified that the Union has a special interest in Alaska because of its potential importance for air bases in proximity to the Soviet Union. Since the time of O'Shea's testimony, it has been established that the Soviet government is extraordinarily active in military preparations in its territory which is nearest to Alaska.

CHAPTER XIII

AN AUSTRALIAN COMMUNIST CONTROLS AMERICAN SHIPPING

IT WOULD be hard to exaggerate the strategic importance of the shipping industry in any program for national defense. Whether or not those who operate our ships and man all their auxiliary services are unqualifiedly loyal to the United States is a question of paramount importance. Seamen, longshoremen, radio and telegraph operators, and all others who make up the personnel of the maritime trades must, without exception, be Americans of undivided loyalty, if we are to be invulnerable in any possible crisis.

Are the leaders in the unions which control labor in the shipping industry Communists or sympathetic toward Communism? It would seem that no more important question could confront those who have the safety of the nation at heart. What is the answer? What do the unchallengeable facts show?

Let us examine the situation in three of the labor unions that affect the shipping industry: the International Longshoremen's and Warehousemen's Union, the National Maritime Union, and the American Communications Association. These unions are headed by Harry Bridges, Joseph Curran, and Mervyn Rathborne, respectively. All three men are members of the national executive board of the C.I.O. Witnesses have repeatedly identified all three as Communists. All three deny the accusation with vehemence.

If we assume, for the moment, that those accusations which are made without substantiating documentary evidence cancel the denials or vice versa, have we anything left which constitutes indisputable proof? Let us look at the facts.

In December, 1936, a mass meeting was held in Madison Square Garden in New York. A flyer announcing the meeting called for a "quick strike victory." The meeting was ostensibly under the auspices of the Joint Strike Committee, or so the flyer stated. The Joint Strike Committee included representatives from the American Radio Telegraphists' Association (Mervyn Rathborne's union which is now known as the American Communications Association), the Marine Firemen, Oilers' and Watertenders' Union, and the Eastern and Gulf Sailors' Association. The speakers who were featured at the meeting were Harry Bridges and Joseph Curran. Only they were announced on the flyer. The all-important fact about this meeting—a fact which was not announced publicly—was that the Communist Party paid the bill for the use of Madison Square Garden that night. A letter from the president of the Madison Square Garden Corporation states that "the rental of $3500 was paid by certified check drawn by D. Leeds." There is no mystery about the identity of D. Leeds. The *Daily Worker* for August 20, 1936, describes David Leeds as "treasurer of the New York State Committee of the Communist Party." We know that Leeds held some such position from the fact that he had a New York bank account with an annual turnover of more than $1,000,000 which he transferred last year to William E. Browder, brother of Earl. This unassailable documentary evidence establishes the important fact that the Communist Party paid for the public appearance of Harry Bridges and Joseph Curran as well as for a meeting in which Mervyn Rathborne's union participated. Incidentally, Leeds' real name is Amriglio, and for years he has managed the May Day parades which have been conducted under the control of the Communist Party in New York—parades in which documentary evidence shows that Curran's and Rathborne's unions have taken prominent parts.

For several years, the Communist Party has been eminently satisfied with the leadership of Bridges, Curran, and Rathborne in their respective unions. Through the pages of the *Daily Worker*, the *New Masses*, and the *Communist*, the Party has given them top-ranking publicity and equally high approval—things that are accorded only rarely to non-Party members and never to those who fail to follow the Party "line."

A great public debate has raged around the question of Harry Bridges' membership in the Communist Party. Bridges is by far the most powerful of the labor leaders in the shipping industry. An Australian by birth and citizenship, he exerts a power over American shipping that long ago became intolerable from any rational standpoint. In no other country than the United States could such a situation exist.

Bridges was the leader of the general strike in San Francisco in 1934. That strike was organized by the Communists. Its opponents so charge, and the Communists have admitted it with great pride. That gives us one point on which there is unanimity of opinion. The subject of the San Francisco general strike of 1934 was discussed at length by Jack Stachel in the *Communist* of November, 1934. For many years, Stachel was the Communist Party's generalissimo on all trade union matters in the United States, and the *Communist* is the official monthly organ of the Party in this country. More recently, Stachel has been executive secretary of the Communist Party of the United States, having been succeeded in that position during the past year by Roy Hudson. But let us see what Stachel wrote in the *Communist* on the subject of the San Francisco general strike. "The San Francisco strike proves," he said, "that it is not only possible for the Communists to organize and lead struggles in the A. F. of L. unions but that it is possible to win the struggles." Was it Bridges or was it the Communist Party that led the San Francisco general strike? Or was it both? Concerning Bridges' role in the strike, Stachel wrote in the *Communist*, as follows: "What will happen . . . if the workers elect not only one Bridges, but hundreds of Bridges in the section and district leadership, not to speak of national leadership? There will be big struggles. The workers will become revolutionized." It would be difficult to think of a more explicit manner in which the Communist Party might announce that Bridges is a Communist. Stachel's words can have no other meaning. Bridges' leadership is eminently satisfactory to the Communist Party because under that leadership the "workers will become revolutionized." And, Stachel might have added, when the workers become revolutionized in any degree that is acceptable to the Communists, American institutions will be in grave danger.

We have already noted in a previous chapter that District Council No. 2 of the Maritime Federation of the Pacific, which is entirely under the control of Harry Bridges, has taken the initiative, as far as appearances go, in the Communist Party's "anti-war" drive which is organized around the slogan, the Yanks Are Not Coming. Such an intimate connection between the Communist Party on the one hand and the Maritime Federation of the Pacific on the other hand could not possibly exist without the fullest approval of Harry Bridges.

In July, 1939, Bridges sent personal greetings to the annual convention of the International Labor Defense, an organization which, as we have shown, was set up as the result of specific instructions from Moscow.

In February, 1937, we find Bridges sending personal greetings to another Communist Party Trojan Horse, the International Workers Order. In the *New Order,* official organ of the I.W.O., Bridges' greetings appeared along with those of Earl Browder, general secretary of the Communist Party, Paul M. Reid, executive secretary of the American League for Peace and Democracy, and Herman F. Reissig, executive secretary of the North American Committee to Aid Spanish Democracy.

In January, 1935, Bridges appeared as a member of the Sponsoring Committee for the National Congress for Unemployment and Social Insurance—an out-and-out Communist Party affair with which we have dealt previously. His co-sponsors in that organization included such prominent Communist Party members as Israel Amter, Fred Biedenkapp, Max Bedacht, Herbert Benjamin, Earl Browder, Ben Davis, Jr., William Z. Foster, Ben Gold, Granville Hicks, Roy Hudson, Grace Hutchins, Elmer Johnson, Waldo McNutt, and George Primoff. With such a list of outstanding Communist Party members predominating in the National Congress for Unemployment and Social Insurance, with such a demonstrable background of Communist Party history as the organization was shown to have in our discussion of it in an earlier chapter, and with a Communist executive secretary in the person of Herbert Benjamin, it should be as clear as it is possible for anything to be clear that the group was subsidiary to the Communist

Party. Bridges' membership in the group certainly constituted "affiliation" with the Communist Party within the meaning of the several statutes and judicial interpretations that bear upon the subject. In commenting on these statutes and judicial interpretations, James M. Landis made the following observation in his *Findings and Conclusions* "In the Matter of Harry R. Bridges": "Also it seems evident that membership in another organization which in turn is subsidiary to or allied with the proscribed organization would constitute affiliation." The "proscribed organization" was the Communist Party. Its "subsidiary" organization was the Sponsoring Committee of the National Congress for Unemployment and Social Insurance, of which Harry R. Bridges was publicly a member. Bridges was, therefore, "affiliated" with the Communist Party, according to Dean Landis' own understanding of the statutes and their judicial interpretations. The law which makes the deportation of alien Communists mandatory specifically declares that affiliation with, as well as membership in, the Communist Party is sufficient ground for deportation. "The statute proscribes affiliation equally with membership," according to Dean Landis.

It is clear from the record of the hearings before Dean Landis that the Department of Labor failed to obtain and present much evidence pertinent to the question of Bridges' affiliation with or membership in the Communist Party. On the other hand, a great deal of Bridges' own testimony before Dean Landis went far toward establishing his affiliation with the Party. Bridges' testimony made credible the statements of witnesses who declared that they had known him as a member of the Communist Party.

Bridges testified, for example, that he had "encouraged seamen to join the Marine Workers' Industrial Union."

Dean Landis greatly understates the case when he says that "the communist membership was stronger" in the Marine Workers' Industrial Union than in any other of the maritime groups. The fact of the matter is that the Marine Workers' Industrial Union was completely under the control of the Communist Party. In every sense of the word, it was subsidiary to the Communist Party. It was one of the unions affiliated with the Trade Union Unity League which was in turn affiliated with the Red International of Labor Unions whose headquarters were in Moscow. The Marine Workers' Industrial Union was no more a bona fide trade union than the Communist Party is a bona fide political party. Even the most elementary knowledge of the facts about the Communist Party's work would have been sufficient to prove the Party's absolute control over the Marine Workers' Industrial Union.

Bridges further testified before Dean Landis that he "was active in getting the strike committee" of his union to accept as its own paper the *Western Worker,* official newspaper of the Communist Party on the Pacific Coast. He admitted that he "encouraged subscriptions to the paper," and that he gave it some financial aid through the method of advertising in its columns.

According to Bridges' own testimony, he had known the following Communist Party members as "associates and friends": Earl Browder, Sam Darcy, Harry Jackson, Morris Rapport, John Davis, Miles G. Humphreys, William Schneiderman, James Branch, Ida Rothstein, Minnie Carson, Alexander Noral, Elaine Black, Lawrence Ross, Elmer Hanoff, Walter Stack, Walter Lambert, Rudy Lambert, Betty Gannet, Sam Telford, Roy Hudson, John Shoemaker, and Pettis Perry.

Regarding Bridges' "attitude toward Communism,"

Dean Landis makes the following illuminating comment: "Bridges' views on Communism would put him in direct opposition to those who believe that Communism is in itself a danger to the democratic method. Communists, he claimed, were normally good trade-unionists. He failed to accord with the viewpoint that regarded the Communist Party as a true revolutionary party bent upon bringing about the overthrow of the Government by resort to force and violence." If such was the fashion in which Bridges declared his attitude toward the Communist Party when he testified before Dean Landis, it is clear that Earl Browder himself could not have served the interests of Moscow better if he had substituted for Bridges on the witness stand. It must be assumed that Bridges is gifted with at least a normal adult intelligence and that his wide experience in trade union activity for almost a decade has placed him in possession of some basic information about the Communist Party. Granted these assumptions, it is unthinkable, except on the theory that he was deliberately trying to shield the Communist Party, that Bridges would declare (1) that Communism is not a danger to the democratic method, (2) that Communists are normally good trade unionists, and (3) that the Communist Party does not aim ultimately to bring about the overthrow of the Government by force and violence. If such pretense about the nature and aims of the Communist Party were allowed to stand, there is hardly any limit to the permission which we would have to accord Communist Fifth Columnists to operate against the safety of the country.

In 1934, when the mother of Tom Mooney died, Harry Bridges together with the avowed Communist, Leo Gallagher, led the funeral procession. Behind them marched the Young Communist League in uniform.

Now that the Bureau of Immigration and Naturalization has been transferred from the Department of Labor to the Department of Justice, it is time that the case of Harry R. Bridges be re-opened.

The evidence of Curran's closeness to the Communist Party is very substantial. Like Bridges' leadership, Curran's is altogether satisfactory to the Party.

One of the witnesses who appeared before the Special Committee on Un-American Activities and brought with him a very large amount of original documentary evidence to support his verbal testimony was Kenneth Goff. We have already noted Goff's testimony concerning the Communist control of the American Youth Congress. Goff testified that Curran autographed his delegate's card when Goff was in New York attending the 8th National Convention of the Young Communist League. He produced the card bearing Curran's signature. The signature has been checked and found authentic. Of course, this does not prove that Curran himself is a member of the Communist Party, but it does prove that he was sufficiently sympathetic toward the Young Communist League to put his signature on a card which showed plainly enough what its uses were.

If Curran had autographed a delegate's card belonging to a member of the German-American Bund, there would be no hesitation to classify him as a Nazi sympathizer.

While we are on the subject of autographs, we may note another one of Curran's expressions of sympathy with Communism. Almost three years ago, the Communists celebrated the 20th anniversary of the Soviet Union. All over the United States, they collected signatures of friends of the Soviet Union and then published part of them in their magazine *Soviet Russia Today*. The collection as a whole

COMMUNIST CONTROLS SHIPPING 185

was known as the *Golden Book of Friendship with the Soviet Union*. Among the signers of the *Golden Book* was Joseph Curran. His signature there matches that on Goff's delegate's card perfectly. Among Curran's co-signers of the *Golden Book* were the following: Robert Morss Lovett, Ben Gold, William Gropper, Malcolm Cowley, Granville Hicks, John Howard Lawson, Lynd Ward, Paul de Kruif, Josephine Herbst—all distinguished by their pronounced pro-Soviet ideas and some of them open members of the Communist Party.

If Curran had sent greetings to the German people on some anniversary of the establishment of Hitler's Third Reich, there would be no doubt in any mind about his pro-Nazi inclinations.

Pursuing Curran's record of Communist affiliations further, we find that he has been a speaker for the American Youth Congress, appearing on the same program which featured Harry F. Ward, national chairman of the American League for Peace and Democracy, and Max Yergan, president of the National Negro Congress.

In September, 1938, Curran contributed an article to the magazine *Champion* which, as has been shown, was a publication of the Young Communist League and of the International Workers Order. He has also written for the magazine *Fight*, official publication of the American League for Peace and Democracy, and for the magazine *Fraternal Outlook*, official organ of the International Workers Order.

The *Daily Worker*, for April 26, 1940, featured photographs of Curran and William Weiner as they addressed a mass meeting of the International Workers Order. Weiner, it may be pointed out again and again in order to clarify these matters as much as possible, is the Communist who was recently convicted for fraudulently representing himself as an American citizen.

Curran is a member of the Progressive Committee to Rebuild the American Labor Party, the Communist-dominated branch of the A.L.P. The Progressive Committee includes, in addition to Curran, such well-known fellow travelers (who are sometimes secret Party members) as Morris Watson, Eugene P. Connolly, Bella V. Dodd, Lillian Hellman, Rockwell Kent, Michael J. Quill, Marvyn Rathborne, Herman Shumlin, and Robert K. Speer. The Progressive Committee to Rebuild the American Labor Party has named Curran as a candidate for Congress.

In June, 1940, Joseph Curran was one of the speakers at the Conference on Constitutional Liberties in America, a gathering which convened in Washington, D. C., and out of which came a permanent organization known as the National Federation for Constitutional Liberties. Laudable as the name of the gathering appeared, it was simply one of the latest of the Trojan Horse affairs of the Communist Party. It represented another instance of the re-shuffling of already existing Communist-controlled organizations into a new organization. This will be clear from a tabulation of the speakers and officers of the organization together with their other Trojan Horse connections. It has already been noted that a characteristic tactic of the Communist Party is to re-shuffle its members, sympathizers, and Trojan Horses to form a new organization whenever the aims of the Party seem to justify it. Let us look at the composition of the Conference on Constitutional Liberties in America in order to make this point clear once more:

Speakers, officers, and sponsors:

Elizabeth Gurley Flynn, member, National Committee of the Communist Party

Merle D. Vincent, president, Washington Committee for Democratic Action
Pearl M. Hart, chairman, Civil Liberties Committee of the National Lawyers Guild
James Dombrowski, member, Southern Conference for Human Welfare
Max Yergan, president, National Negro Congress
Carey McWilliams, chairman, American Committee for the Protection of the Foreign Born
Alfred K. Stern, chairman, National Emergency Conference for Democratic Rights
Josephine Truslow Adams, vice-president, Descendants of the American Revolution
Morris Watson, vice-president, American Newspaper Guild
Joseph Curran, president, National Maritime Union
Frances Williams, administrative secretary, American Youth Congress
John P. Davis, secretary, National Negro Congress
Edwin S. Smith, executive board member, American League for Peace and Democracy
Franz Boas, chairman, American Committee for Democracy and Intellectual Freedom
Bella V. Dodd, secretary, Joint Committee for Trade Union Rights
Carol King, secretary, International Juridical Association
Colston Warne, president, Consumers Union
Vito Marcantonio, president, International Labor Defense
Gardner Jackson, chairman, Council for Pan American Democracy
Michael Quill, president, Transport Workers Union
Donald Ogden Stewart, president, League of American Writers
Robert W. Dunn, director, Labor Research Association
George Seldes, editor, *In Fact*

The foregoing list, while not complete, is sufficient to show how the Communist Party brings together its sympathizers, fellow travelers, and members into new groupings. A knowledge of this tactic is an indispensable key to the identification of the Party's Trojan Horses. So far as any given individual in such a list is concerned, his presence in the aggregation is not conclusive proof of his connection with the Communist Party, but on the other hand if he appears regularly on such lists, his presence there may well constitute a part of cumulative evidence with respect to his connection.

One of the several Trojan Horses which the Communist Party used to raise funds from sympathizers with the Loyalist cause of Spain was known as the American Relief Ship for Spain. Joseph Curran was listed as one of the trade union sponsors of this organization. Listed together with him were the following: Julius Emspak, secretary-treasurer of the United Radio, Electrical, and Machine Workers, Lewis Merrill, president of the United Office and Professional Workers of America, Morris Muster, president of the United Furniture Workers, Mervyn Rathborne, president of the American Communications Association, and Marcel Scherer, national organizer of the Federation of Architects, Engineers, Chemists and Technicians. It is noteworthy that, of the seven trade unions which had representatives on the sponsoring group of the American Relief Ship for Spain, six were found by the unanimous report of the Special Committee on Un-American Activities to have Communist leadership entrenched in them. Marcel Sherer, who was among the seven trade union sponsors of the Relief Ship, is an avowed Communist Party member.

Not long ago, the Communist Party set up an organization known as the Mexican and Spanish American Peoples

COMMUNIST CONTROLS SHIPPING 189

Congress. The plans for this new Trojan Horse were made at a very secret meetings of the top-ranking leaders of the Party in the Southwest. That meeting was held in San Antonio, Texas, on April 24, 1938. Among those present were Homer Brooks, Texas state organizer of the Communist Party, Emma Tenayuca, chairman of the Communist Party of Texas, Luz Salazar, delegate from the Communist Party of New Mexico, a man named Irwin, delegate from the Communist Party of Colorado, and Peggy Vance, a Party leader in San Antonio. In planning to set up the Mexican and Spanish American Peoples Congress, this group of Communist Party functionaries decided to prepare a "Call" for the first meeting of the organization and to obtain the signatures of "prominent individuals" who were prepared to sponsor it. A copy of that "Call" shows the following sponsors: Joseph Curran, president of the National Maritime Union, Rockwell Kent, president of the Artists Union, Mervyn Rathborne, president of the American Communications Association, Vito Marcantonio, member of Congress, George Soule, editor of the *New Republic*, Harold Pritchett, president of the International Woodworkers of America, Reid Robinson, president of the International Union of Mine, Mill and Smelter Workers, Donald Henderson, president of United Cannery, Agricultural, Packing and Allied Workers of America, Herbert Biberman of the Screen Directors Guild, and Lionel Stander of the Screen Writers Guild.

Curran's closeness to the Communist Party is further evidenced by his associates in his own union. Some of the most important officials of the National Maritime Union are avowed members of the Communist Party. If Curran were opposed to their holding such positions, there is no doubt concerning his ability to have them removed. The educational director of the National Maritime Union, for example, is one Charles L. Keith. On May 10, 1940, at a district convention of the Communist Party held in Public School 11 in New York City, Keith placed the name of Al Lannon in nomination for Congress on the Communist Party ticket. Al Lannon is an important figure in the National Maritime Union. Lannon is also a member of the national committee of the Communist Party of the United States. In the position of educational director of the National Maritime Union, Keith has an extraordinary opportunity to propagandize among seamen on behalf of the Communist Party and, in fact, does so propagandize.

The editor of the *Pilot*, official publication of the National Maritime Union, is one Corby Paxton. The Special Committee on Un-American Activities is in possession of a letter written by Paxton to Mike Quin in which Paxton discloses the fact that he was a member of unit F#9 of the Communist Party in San Francisco. Paxton's signature on the letter has been authenticated.

For several years, the Communist Party has conducted a marine training school in which Party workers were trained for organizing among seamen. The school is located at the Communist Party's camp near West Point, Camp Nitgedaiget. Frederick Myers and Ferdinand Smith, two of the leading officials of the National Maritime Union, are among the many graduates of this "Red Annapolis." The director of the school is Al Lannon. One of Lannon's latest announcements of the Marine Training School states that "the school will be held in pleasant, healthful surroundings in upstate New York beginning October 15th and ending December 15th, 1939," and that among the courses to be taught will be one on the 18th Congress of the Communist Party of the Soviet Union.

One of the important tests by which a union's political affinities may be judged is whether or not its members march in the Communist Party's May Day parades. In 1940, the National Maritime Union led the May Day parade in New York. It was followed immediately by the Marine and Shipbuilding Workers Union which was in turn followed by the American Communications Association. The Communist Party and the Young Communist League composed the 10th Division of the parade.

The very latest Trojan Horse which the Communist Party has built is known as the American Peace Mobilization. The organization was formally launched at a Labor Day meeting in Chicago. Among the permanent officers and council members of the American Peace Mobilization are most of the familiar figures which are usually found in a Communist Party Trojan Horse. Joseph Curran and Mervyn Rathborne, two of the three labor leaders in the shipping industry which we have under consideration, are members of the national council. Jack McMichael of the American Youth Congress is one of the vice-presidents. Donald Ogden Stewart of the League of American Writers, John P. Davis and Max Yergan of the National Negro Congress, Morris Watson of the American Newspaper Guild, Donald Henderson of the United Cannery, Agricultural, Packing and Allied Workers, Moses Miller of the Jewish People's Committee, Carey McWilliams of the American Committee for the Protection of the Foreign Born, Michael Quill of the Transport Workers Union, James B. Carey of the United Electrical, Radio, and Machine Workers of America, Bella V. Dodd of the American Federation of Teachers, Franz Boas of the American Committee for Democracy and Intellectual Freedom, Louis Berne of the Federation of Architects, Engineers, Chemists and Technicians, Aline Davis Hays of the League of Women Shoppers, and George Seldes of the publication *In Fact* are all on the national council. Earl Robinson, composer of the "Ballad for Americans," is also a national councilman. At the Chicago meeting over the Labor Day week-end, Joseph Curran was one of the principal speakers. Prior to the gathering, Curran pledged the support of the entire National Maritime Union to this Communist-dominated organization. In New York where Curran is head of the newly-formed C.I.O. Council, a number of the C.I.O. unions which are free from Communist domination protested Curran's activities on behalf of the American Peace Mobilization. Their protest was based upon the charge that the Communist Party is in control of this so-called peace movement. It goes without saying that the American Peace Mobilization adheres strictly to the Communist Party "line" of combating all efforts to build up the national defenses of the country.

It must be emphasized here that the major activity of the Communist, as well as of the Nazi, Fifth Column in the premilitary phase of attack on a country has been well described as "the softening process." The very essence of "the softening process" is agitation against national defense. Curran has thrown the full force of his maritime union, with from 75,000 to 100,000 members, into this Communazi movement to combat America's military preparedness for any emergencies that may arise. Harry Bridges' control of the International Longshoremen's and Warehousemen's Union has made that union's 35,000 members an ally of the Communazi attack upon American preparedness, and Mervyn Rathborne's leadership of the American Communications Association, with its 15,000 strategically-placed radio and telegraph operators, has placed that union on the side of America's enemies. We must guard against the assumption that all or even a majority of the rank-and-file members of these three unions are Communists or Communist sympathizers. The menace to national defense which these unions present is to be found in the Communist leadership which has entrenched itself in them.

Both Curran and Rathborne went through an anti-Communist phase in their labor careers. In a letter in his own handwriting, Curran wrote to Peter Innes, Jr., on August 23, 1936, as follows: "I frankly do not believe there is anything here as I believe the C. P. [Communist Party] have broken all our chances up." Again, on October 8, 1936, Curran wrote to Innes, as follows: "They think they are big shots now that the C. P.s have about got control of the outfit now with Tommy Ray director of operations here in New York." Tommy Ray is the Communist Party's commissar on the waterfront of New York. A few months after these letters were written, Curran capitulated to the Communists, according to witnesses who appeared before the Special Committee on Un-American Activities. In a letter dated February 4, 1931, over his own signature, Mervyn Rathborne wrote to Frank B. Powers warning him that the Communists were "eager" to organize the radio operators and explaining to him the danger of such an organization campaign, in the following language: "Of course their idea is to cause a tie-up of American shipping and to make trouble."

Eventually, Rathborne, having made his peace with the Communist Party and having become the head of the union of radio operators, publicly threatened the same kind of a "tie-up of American shipping" which he had previously charged the Communists with planning. In a speech before the League of Women Shoppers in New York, the New

York *Times* reported Rathborne as saying that all maritime workers "would agree not to handle war materials" in the event of the United States' becoming involved in war.

We have already noted Rathborne's connections with some of the Communist Trojan Horses with which Curran is also connected. In addition to those previously noted, Rathborne was a member of the national labor committee of the American League for Peace and Democracy and a sponsor of the Conference on Pan American Democracy of which Gardner Jackson is now chairman. Rathborne has also been a sponsor of the Consumers National Federation. When the avowed Communist Party member, Simon W. Gerson, was appointed assistant borough president of Manhattan, Rathborne was one of the numerous Communists and fellow travelers who signed a public statement in support of the appointment.

Rathborne was a member of the Coordinating Committee to Lift the Embargo. This committee was an auxiliary of the North American Committee to Aid Spanish Democracy, and both groups have been shown beyond any shadow of doubt to have been instruments of the Communist Party for raising funds around the appeal to aid the Spanish Loyalist cause. Associated with Rathborne on the Coordinating Committee were such avowed Communist Party members as the following: Ben Gold, president of the International Fur Workers Union; Donald Henderson, president of the United Cannery, Agricultural, Packing and Allied Workers; and Marcel Scherer, international organizational director of the Federation of Architects, Engineers, Chemists and Technicians.

When we turn to consider the verbal testimony of numerous witnesses who have testified under oath that Bridges, Curran, and Rathborne are Communists, we find that that testimony is strongly backed by the large amount of documentary evidence of which a part has been set forth in this discussion. An entire volume devoted exclusively to the situation in the shipping unions which are headed by these three leaders in the C.I.O. would be required to present all of the evidence which goes to prove that Bridges, Curran, and Rathborne are important figures in the Communist Party's network of organizations. Whether or not these three men now hold membership in the Communist Party is a question which only they and certain officials of the Party can answer. The question is, however, of relatively minor importance. The fact which has been established beyond any possibility of doubt is that all three of them are at work just as effectively on behalf of the Communist Party and its revolutionary objectives as they could be if they held membership cards.

The urgent issue for American national defense is whether or not the Communist Party is to be allowed to continue its domination of our vitally important shipping industry through its entrenched leadership in these three unions. The Special Committee on Un-American Activities in a unanimous report, after hearing a great volume of testimony on the subject, found that Communist leadership is entrenched in the International Longshoremen's and Warehousemen's Union, the National Maritime Union, and the American Communications Association. That is a situation with which the Government of the United States must deal promptly, before it is too late.

CHAPTER XIV

THE COMMUNIST PARTY IS RUN FROM MOSCOW

If Stalin placed himself at the head of 150 divisions of uniformed Soviet troops and marched them through the streets of our cities, the American people would have no doubts about our being invaded by a foreign foe. The people of this country would know exactly what to do about such an invasion, and they would do it with a lightning stroke that would make Hitler's blitzkrieg look like slow motion. If any American demanded in the name of "civil liberties" that Stalin and his troops should have free access to our streets and highways, it would go pretty hard with him. He would be treated as a confederate of the Soviet dictator and his invading columns. If any high government official in Washington tried to ridicule those who were defending our homes against the Red Fuehrer and his troops, such an official would be dealt with as an obvious member of Stalin's fifth column.

The differences between such an imaginary invasion, led personally by Stalin, and the real invasion led by an agent of Stalin are not very great. Perhaps the only important difference is that the real invaders just do not happen to wear uniforms. Of course they have left the uniforms off purposely, and that makes the red army of invasion a vastly greater menace to our homes and institutions. They are able to reach points of great strategic value in our defenses simply because they do not wear the uniforms of the Red

Army. If they had worn uniforms, they would not have been able to get the several thousand government positions which they now hold. If they had worn uniforms, they would not have been able to place themselves in the leadership of a dozen C.I.O. labor unions which they now dominate. If they had worn uniforms, they would not have been allowed to fill the hundreds of college professorships from which they now teach the doctrine of loyalty to the Soviet Union.

Let us make no mistake about it. The Soviet invasion of the United States has already taken place. The followers of Stalin in this country number something less than 2,000,000 individuals who, according to Earl Browder, "go with the Communist Party all the way to its full program." These two million individuals about whom Browder spoke are not, of course, dues-paying members of the Communist Party. At the highest estimate, the Party has only one hundred thousand card-holding members. The larger army who, Browder informs us, go all the way is composed for the most part of those who believe in Communism but do not for one reason or another wish to accept the rigid discipline of Party membership.

Browder himself is the completely subservient agent of Stalin, for whom Stalin's word is law. Stalin's followers who are members of the Communist Party are subject to a rigid, military discipline. Stalin's followers who are not dues-paying members of the Communist Party submit voluntarily to the rule of Moscow, or, as Browder put it, they "go with the Communist Party all the way to its full program."

Even though Stalin's invaders do not wear military uniforms in this country, they give such ample evidence in other ways of their Soviet allegiance that a military uniform would add very little to the proof of their treason. Time and time again they have grown bold in utterance. While thousands of individuals—especially among intellectuals and professional people—hold their Communist Party membership in strict secrecy, nevertheless the Party itself has withheld little that is necessary to establish its complete subservience to Stalin and its complete disloyalty to America.

The *Daily Worker*, for example, proudly published the revealing words of one of the outstanding labor heroes of the Communist Party in this country. Here are the words:

> I told the police the hell with the U.S.A. flag. I said that the flag I claimed was the one with the hammer and sickle, the Red Flag, which we will have some day. Not only the Red Flag but a Workers' and Farmers' Government here in the U.S.A.

This was not the impulsive outburst of some nameless Communist whose words on some street corner were forgotten as soon as they were uttered. These were the words of a Communist Party leader who had just returned from the Soviet Union, and whose words were considered important enough to be published in the columns of the official organ of the Party.

Within the limitations of available space, we can do little more than summarize the vast amount of evidence which the Special Committee on Un-American Activities has assembled to prove that the Communist Party of the United States is a tool of Stalin.

Leaders of the Communist Party in the United States have admitted that the Communist Party of the Soviet Union is the model after which all other Communist Parties are patterned. The American Communist Party is engaged in a systematic study of the History of the Communist Party of the Soviet Union, which has as its avowed aim the inculcation of the idea that the Communist Party of the Soviet Union is the true "model" Party for all other Communist Parties in the world. The Communist Party of the United States published 200,000 copies of this History of the Communist Party of the Soviet Union. Every member of the Party was required to purchase a copy and to study it thoroughly. Each member was also under strong pressure to see that Party sympathizers bought copies.

Present leaders of the American Communist Party have admitted that they look upon, and have spoken about the Soviet Union as the "Fatherland of the working class of the world." Otto Kuusinen in his speech at the Seventh World Congress for the Communist International discussed at length the way in which the American Youth Congress was to be used by the Communists in supporting the Soviet Fatherland. Clarence Hathaway addressed the Youth Congress in the same vein.

It was clear from the testimony of every member of the Communist Party who appeared before the Special Committee on Un-American Activities that his loyalty in the event of any conflict between the United States and the Soviet Union would force him to choose the side of the Soviet Union. When he was a witness before the Committee, Earl Browder stated frankly that he would try to precipitate a civil war in this country if we should become involved in a conflict with the Soviet Union.

The Communist Party of the United States has regularly maintained a number of official representatives in Moscow for the purpose of interlocking the American Party with the ruling Party of the Soviet Union. Scores of outstanding members of the American Communist Party have served in this capacity in Moscow. Most of them have gone there on false passports.

The Statutes of the Communist International provide for the sending of its representatives to the various Communist parties throughout the world. The basic law of the Communist International invests these representatives with complete authority over the affairs of the various sections of the Communist International. Among these plenipotentiaries from Moscow who have directed the activities of the Communist Party in the United States at one time or another have been John Pepper, Harry Pollitt, Dengel, Gussev, and F. Brown.

Walter Krivitsky, one time head of the Soviet Union's western European military intelligence, testified before the Special Committee on Un-American Activities that Soviet spies looked upon the United States as one of the places in which their work could be done with the least interference from local government agencies. From many sources, the Committee has learned that Stalin's spy system is closely interlocked with the work of the Communist Party itself. There is abundant evidence to indicate that leaders of the American Communist Party are kept under constant surveillance by Stalin's secret agents just to be sure that they carry out the Soviet dictator's will in every respect. Aside from such spying upon his own agents in the United States, counterfeiting, kidnaping, military espionage, underground organization, and other illegal activities have been assigned to the Soviet spies who are at work in the United States. The Committee has in its possession a set of instructions in which Moscow ordered the American Communist Party to set up an organization whose responsibility would be to transmit industrial secrets direct from American factories to Moscow.

Scores of the leaders of the American Communist Party received their training in Communist theory and tactics in the Lenin Institute in Moscow. This was a school which the Russian government maintained for the training of the leaders of foreign Communist parties. Clarence Hathaway, editor of the *Daily Worker*, was one of the many American Communist leaders who received instruction at the Lenin Institute.

The leaders of the American Communist Party have made so many visits to Moscow that few of them can recall either the number of visits or the dates. The Special Committee on Un-American Activities was entirely unsuccessful in eliciting exact information concerning these Moscow visits from such witnesses as William Z. Foster and Earl Browder. Among the Communists of the world, Moscow has been described as "Mecca." In one of his speeches addressed to the American delegation which he had called to Moscow in 1929, Stalin described the Communist International as "the Holy of Holies."

From the very beginning of the Communist International, it has been a part of the system of control to require the leaders of Communist parties to make periodic reports to Moscow. In some of the books which he has published in the United States, Earl Browder has included some of his formal reports delivered in person to the executive committee of the Communist International. These reports are subjected to thorough criticism by the officials of the Communist International who are at the same time officials of the Soviet government, and on the basis of this criticism Stalin's agents in the United States are expected to improve or modify their activities.

The control of Moscow over the American Communist Party has extended to such detailed matters as analyzing and criticizing each day's issue of the *Daily Worker*, official newspaper of the Communist Party of the United States. The Special Committee on Un-American Activities received in evidence a copy of one of these elaborate Moscow analyses of the *Daily Worker*.

According to several witnesses, it was necessary to obtain Moscow's permission before the headquarters of the Communist Party of the United States could be moved from Chicago to New York. The Party's own manifestoes published in the columns of the *Daily Worker* indicate that Moscow's permission has been necessary to hold a convention of the Party here.

It would require many volumes to reprint the actual instructions, usually described as "directives," which have been sent to the American Communist Party from Moscow. Hundreds of these "directives" which are in the possession of the Special Committee on Un-American Activities leave no possible doubt about the thoroughness of Stalin's control of the Communist Party of the United States.

Time and time again Stalin is hailed as the leader of the American Communist Party. In numerous articles, Stalin's advice has been gratefully acknowledged by leaders of the American Communist Party. At the 10th convention of the American Communist Party, Stalin was made a member of the honorary presiding committee of the gathering.

Whenever changes in the "line" of the Communist Party of the United States are made, those changes closely parallel the shifts of policy made by Stalin's government. When Stalin was working for an alliance between the Soviet Union and the democracies under the formula of "collective security," the Communist Party of the United States threw all of its energies into agitation for such an alliance.

There seemed to be absolutely no limits to which Communist leaders were willing to go in their professed admiration for democracy if only they could lure the United States government into an alliance with Stalin. There was no language too vehement to use in describing Hitler back in those days when Stalin's line and Browder's imitation of it called for the destruction of the Nazis. In the twinkling of an eye, however, and apparently without giving the slightest warning to his agent Browder, Stalin dropped the idea of an alliance with the democracies and signed a series of pacts with Hitler. Browder was so taken by surprise that he put himself entirely out of reach of the press for 24 hours, until he could get new instructions from Moscow and also, probably, adjust his mind to the sudden change. But Browder was obedient, precisely as he and all other members of the Communist Party in the United States must be obedient to the will of Stalin.

It is not only the Communist Party which is under the absolute control of Stalin. Numerous Communist auxiliary organizations are subject to the same type of foreign domination. The Trade Union Unity League, the American League for Peace and Democracy, the International Labor Defense, and the International Workers Order, in fact hundreds of auxiliaries, have all been a part of what the Communists call their international solar system. These and hundreds of other Trojan Horse organizations set up in the Communist Party have their ultimate control in the hands of the Great Red Fuehrer, Stalin.

CHAPTER XV

COMMUNISM PREACHES VIOLENCE

AT ITS tenth national convention in May, 1938, the Communist Party of the United States adopted a new constitution, one better suited to the Trojan Horse tactics upon which the Party had embarked three years before.

In May, 1938, the People's Front policy of the Communist Party was at full tide. Stalin and his emissaries throughout the world were professing a devoting to democracy which, on the surface at least, was so touching that many sentimental liberals everywhere were hoodwinked into joining forces with Moscow. These liberals appeared honestly to believe that the Communist Party had turned over a new leaf, and that strict adherence to democratic procedures was thenceforth to take the place of the earlier communism which so frankly stated its violent intentions with respect to all bourgeois institutions. As a matter of fact, almost everybody now knows—including the most sentimental and gullible of the liberals—that Stalin wanted only to find powerful allies among the democratic nations of the world. The whole profession of devotion to democracy was simply a part of the Trojan Horse tactic. One phase of that democratic pretense was a world wide agitation by the Communist parties against Hitlerism. Browder persuaded a lot of Americans that his Party was the one and only uncompromising foe of Nazism. History has now recorded the fact that Stalin, and after him Browder, dropped the anti-Nazi agitation the very moment that Hitler was willing to enter into an alliance with the Kremlin. When that alliance cracks up, as it is certain to do one of these days, we shall again hear from Browder an appeal to join forces with the Soviet Union for the defense of democracy against Hitlerism.

The Communist Party is so organized that a mere word from Moscow is enough to set aside one constitution in favor of another. The fact that the present constitution of the Party expresses its devotion to democracy and its opposition to violence is to be looked upon as nothing more than a tactical maneuver. The basic doctrines of Communism, resting upon the authoritative words of Marx, Engels, Lenin, and Stalin, were not abrogated by the tenth national convention of the Communist Party of the United States when it adopted its new constitution.

Article VI of that constitution declares that the Communist Party "opposes with all its power any clique, group, circle, faction or party which conspires or acts to subvert, undermine, weaken or overthrow any or all institutions of American democracy whereby the majority of the American people have obtained power to determine their own destiny in any degree." On the surface, that declaration appears so completely loyal to Americanism that it stamps the Communist Party as an ultra-patriotic organization. It was in fact, however, as we shall show, a direct contradiction of all that the un-repudiated authorities of the Communist Party have taught. That declaration, which appears to oppose any conspiracy against American institutions, was itself the result of a conspiracy to hoodwink unthinking liberals into support of the Communist Party's numerous Trojan Horses.

Again, in Article X of its new constitution, the Communist Party declares that "Party members found to be

". . . advocates of terrorism and violence as a method of Party procedure . . . shall be summarily dismissed from positions of responsibility, expelled from the Party and exposed before the general public." The Communist Party has recently used, in court, these portions of its present constitution as arguments to combat the charge of subversion. They are, in fact, evidence of subversion. They have only one purpose, like that of the Trojan Horse itself: to deceive the unwary. Let us look at the facts.

There is another constitution under which the Communist Party of the United States also operates. It is the Constitution of the Communist International. It has been published in several editions by the Communist Party of the United States under the title, *Program of the Communist International Together with Its Constitution.* When William Z. Foster, the chairman of the Communist Party of the United States, was a witness before the Special Committee on Un-American Activities on September 29, 1939, he testified under oath, as follows:

Mr. Matthews: Mr. Foster has already stated that he accepts the Program of the Communist International; that is correct, is it not?

Mr. Foster: That is right.

Mr. Matthews: And in your book you have quoted extensively from the Program of the Communist International; that is also correct, is it not?

Mr. Foster: That is right.

Among the quotations from the *Program of the Communist International* which William Z. Foster used in his book, *Toward Soviet America,* and the acceptance of which he reiterated under oath on the stand was the following:

The conquest of power by the proletariat does not mean

peacefully "capturing" the ready-made bourgeois state machinery by means of a parliamentary majority.

The *Program of the Communist International* which has the endorsement of the chairman of the Communist Party of the United States goes on to declare:

> The conquest of power by the proletariat is the violent overthrow of bourgeois power, the destruction of the capitalist state apparatus (bourgeois armies, police, bureaucratic hierarchy, the judiciary, parliaments, etc.), and substituting in its place new organs of proletarian power, to serve primarily as instruments for the suppression of the exploiters.

That puts the Communist International, the Communist Party of the United States, and William Z. Foster clearly on record in favor of the doctrine of violent revolution.

One of the chief propaganda campaigns put on by the Communist Party of the United States during its entire history has been the publication and dissemination of a volume entitled *History of the Communist Party of the Soviet Union*. This book was published only last year in an edition of two hundred thousand. All Party members were required to purchase and study the volume as well as to push its sale among Party sympathizers. The Communist Party press and the Party leaders hailed the book as one of the most authoritative statements of Communist tactics and principles ever published. On the subject of violence, the *History of the Communist Party of the Soviet Union* says:

> Marx and Engels taught that it was impossible to get rid of the power of capital and to convert capitalist property into public property by peaceful means, and that the working class could achieve this only by revolutionary violence against the bourgeoisie, by *a proletarian revolution*, by establishing its own political rule—the dictatorship of the proletariat—which must

crush the resistance of the exploiters and create a new, classless, communist society.

That, too, puts the Communist Party of the United States as well as the Communist Party of the Soviet Union on record in favor of the doctrine of violent revolution. Both Foster's declaration of allegiance to the *Program of the Communist International,* which we have cited, and the Party's publication of the *History of the Communist Party of the Soviet Union* post-date the adoption of the Trojan Horse constitution in May, 1938, which appeared to eschew violent revolution.

Attention has already been called to Earl Browder's testimony before the Special Committee on Un-American Activities when he asserted in answer to questioning that he would try to precipitate civil war in the United States in the event of a war between the United States and the Soviet Union. That testimony will bear frequent repetition. It shows conclusively where Browder's allegiance lies as well as the means he is prepared to employ in the expression of his allegiance to the Soviet Union. The questions and Browder's answers to them were as follows:

Mr. Matthews: But assuming that it should attack the Soviet Government, or become involved in a war against the Soviet Union, what then?

Mr. Browder: If it were possible for the American Government to do that, or if we assume that the American Government should make an aggressive war against the Soviet Union, I would stand as absolutely opposing such a war, as doing everything possible to stop it.

Mr. Matthews. Even to turning such a war into a civil war?

Mr. Browder: Yes, sir; in every way I could stop it.

That puts Browder on record in favor of the doctrine of violent revolution. Browder was, of course, simply repeat-

COMMUNISM PREACHES VIOLENCE

ing one of the standard slogans of the Communist International which declares in its official *Program* that the Communist parties of the world must, whenever an opportunity arises, "turn imperialist war into civil war."

Browder was likewise echoing the words of Lenin in his *Letter to American Workers* in which the Russian leader said:

> The representatives and defenders of the bourgeoisie, as well as the socialist-reformists, frightened by the bourgeoisie, cannot understand and do not want to understand the necessity and the legality of civil war.

That puts Lenin, the most authoritative teacher of present-day Communists, on record in favor of the doctrine of violent revolution.

Among the works of Lenin, the one held most valuable by Communists is the *State and Revolution*. In that treatise on basic Communist principles, Lenin declared: "The replacement of the bourgeois by the proletarian state is impossible without a violent revolution." In other words, the ballot is out, American democratic institutions are out, and violence is decidedly in. Once more Lenin is on record in favor of the doctrine of violent revolution.

In his book, *The Proletarian Revolution and Renegade Kautsky*, Lenin declared: "The proletarian revolution is impossible without the violent destruction of the bourgeois state machine and its replacement by a *new one*." That, too, puts Lenin on record.

In his booklet, *Foundations of Leninism*, published by the American Communist Party in an edition of 100,000, Joseph Stalin, held up by Communists everywhere as the foremost pupil and practitioner of Leninism, declared: "The dictatorship of the proletariat is a revolutionary power based on violence against the bourgeoisie." Again, in the same work, Stalin said: "The dictatorship of the proletariat is the domination of the proletariat over the bourgeoisie, untrammeled by law and based on violence . . ." That puts Stalin on record in favor of the doctrine of violent revolution, the Trojan Horse constitution of the American Communist Party to the contrary notwithstanding.

In an interview with H. G. Wells, published by the Communist Party of the United States, Stalin declared: "As you see, the Communists regard the substitution of one social system for another, not simply as a spontaneous and peaceful process, but as a complicated, long and violent process." This was Stalin's way of stating the case of *Marxism* vs. *Liberalism*, the title under which the interview with Wells was published. That, too, puts Stalin on record in favor of the doctrine of violent revolution.

In his book, *What Is Communism?*, Earl Browder offered to American readers the most authoritative of all interpretations of communism written by an American Communist. In dealing with the question in hand, Browder wrote: "History does not show a single example in which state power was transferred from one class to another by peaceful means, whether in the form of voting or some other method of formal democracy." That gives the lie to the Trojan Horse constitution of the Party, and puts both Browder and the Party on record in favor of the doctrine of violent revolution.

Attention has already been called to a pamphlet entitled *Negroes in a Soviet America* written by James W. Ford, now candidate for the vice-presidency of the United States on the Communist ticket, and Sol Auerbach alias James S. Allen. These leaders of the American Communist Party wrote: "We must fight for these rights . . . Anyone who tells you to depend upon the ballot and civil rights for your defense is betraying you." That is precisely the opposite of what the constitution of the Communist Party says about the Party's belief in and defense of "any or all institutions of American democracy." It also puts Ford and Auerbach on record in favor of the doctrine of violent revolution, particularly as applied to Negroes in the United States.

Both Browder and Foster testified under oath in September, 1939, before the Special Committee on Un-American Activities that the volume entitled *The United Front* by Georgi Dimitroff was one of the authoritative expositions of the current "line" of the Communist Party. In that work, published by the American Communist Party, Dimitroff called the idea of peaceful revolution an allusion. He said:

> The Right opportunists, on the other hand, tried to establish a special "democratic intermediate stage" lying between the dictatorship of the bourgeoisie and the dictatorship of the proletariat, for the purpose of instilling into the workers the illusion of a peaceful parliamentary passage from the one dictatorship to the other.

That puts Dimitroff and the American Communist Party on record in favor of the doctrine of violent revolution.

Many years before Dimitroff spoke of the illusion of a peaceful change from a bourgeois society to a proletarian dictatorship, one of the leaders of the American Communist Party, H. M. Wicks, wrote in the *Daily Worker* about the attitude of the newly-formed Communist organization in this country toward that "illusion." Wicks wrote: "The Workers Party will destroy the illusion fostered by the yellow Socialists and Reformists that the workers can achieve their emancipation from the oppression and exploitation of capitalism thru the election of a majority of members of the legislative of the capitalist government . . ." That put the Communist Party on record in its very infancy in favor of the doctrine of violent revolution.

In 1933, the Communist International officially hailed the triumph of Hitler as a means of "destroying all the Democratic illusions among the masses." The resolution of the Communist International which embodied this theory was published by the Communist Party of the United States in its official organ, the *Daily Worker*. This theory of Communist advantages issuing from Nazi dictatorship was stated as follows: "The establishment of an open Fascist dictatorship, by destroying all the Democratic illusions among the masses and liberating them from the influence of social democracy, accelerates the rate of Germany's development towards proletarian revolution." Once again we find the highest body of world communism discarding the idea of peaceful change as an illusion and placing itself on record in favor of the doctrine of violent revolution.

One of the leaders of the Communist Party in the United States, William Dunne, contributed a series of articles to the Party's newspaper, the *Daily Worker*, in which he wrote, as follows: "There never has been and there never can be an orderly revolution. 'Orderly revolution' means no revolution. The whole international experience of the working class, immeasurably enriched by the Russian Revolution, proves this beyond question." Naturally, if there can be no orderly revolution, the Communists are preparing for a disorderly one, which means a violent overthrow of the government. That puts the *Daily Worker* and William Dunne on record beyond question.

When William Z. Foster was being examined in New

York at a hearing on the Communist riot of March 6, 1930, he said in answer to a question from Aldermanic President McKee: "We explain to the workers, and we teach the workers that only by violence finally can a revolution be accomplished. All revolutions have been accomplished by force and violence." This statement was published in the *Daily Worker* and may be properly taken as an authoritative expression of the Communist Party's position. As we have previously pointed out, the Communists deliberately provoked the rioting and violence which marked the demonstrations of March 6, 1930—demonstrations which were explicitly ordered by Moscow. That puts Foster once more on record in favor of the doctrine of violent revolution.

Robert Minor, long a leading member of the Communist Party, was one of those apprehended for the rioting in New York on March 6, 1930. When Minor appeared before Mayor Walker, he declared that the class struggle "has never been solved and never can be solved without violence." That puts Robert Minor on record in favor of the doctrine of violent revolution.

In Canton, Ohio, the Communist demonstration of March 6, 1930, was described in the *Daily Worker*, as follows:

> As we looked out over the sea of hungry and angry workers, we saw 10,000 workers ready to fight, ready to unite under revolutionary leadership, cowing the police into permitting us to march and to denounce the capitalists from the steps of their own capitalist government, City Hall—hurling a dare into the faces of the classes which robs and oppresses them.

It should be pointed out that the Communist Party does not as a rule approve an individual member's verbal advocacy of violent acts. The theory of the Party is that the individual member should commit overt acts of violence but keep his mouth shut. If apprehended by the authorities, the defense then offered in court is that the Party member was provoked by the police into committing violence. The Communist Party not only does not expel a member for perpetrating acts of violence, it defends and extols him.

When we consider the present so-called anti-war movement of the Communist Party, such as that of the American Peace Mobilization and that organized around the slogan, the Yanks Are Not Coming, we must bear in mind the established teachings of the Communists with respect to their anti-war movements and their plans for civil war. The official theoretical magazine of the Communist Party in this country is known as the *Communist*. This organ declares: "In fighting *against war*, the Communists must prepare even now for the transformation of the imperialist war into civil war, concentrate their forces in each country, at the *vital parts of the war machine* of imperialism." The Communist Party is clearly on record in describing the present European war as an imperialist war. The Party's violent and revolutionary intentions, in the event of the participation of this country in that war, have been announced in advance.

Again, the *Communist* declares that "the main enemy is within one's own country. Such is the correct principle for action by a revolutionary workers' party. 'Turning the imperialist war into a civil war,' such is the correct slogan." These statements of basic Communist principle put the Communist Party on record in favor of the doctrine of violent revolution.

In connection with the foregoing statements of principle, it is alarming to consider that the Communist Party now has its own leadership entrenched in several of the trade unions which cover basic industries essential to national defense. One of these trade unions, as we have shown, has a local in almost every navy yard, shipbuilding concern, and aircraft factory in the country.

Despite the overwhelming evidence that the Communist Party preaches violence—evidence which could be expanded to fill an entire volume—Communists are accustomed to argue, whenever they are pinned down on the question, that they resort to violence only because they meet resistance from the bourgeois state. In other words, there would be no violence if the government acceded unprotestingly to the revolutionary demands of the Communist Party. The situation is exactly analagous to that of a man whose home is being plundered by a burglar. If the owner makes no protest against the burglar's demands and offers no resistance to his plunder, there is a fair chance that violence may not be committed. The speciousness of the Communist argument, that it is not responsible for violence whenever the bourgeois state resists a Communist revolution, is perfectly apparent. What the Communists ignore in their argument is that the violence begins with the Party's own revolutionary demands, even in case they do not proceed at once to overt acts of violence in anticipation of "bourgeois" resistance.

No greater deception was ever attempted than that which is embodied in the Trojan Horse constitution of the Communist Party, adopted at its tenth national convention in May, 1938. The unadulterated truth is that the Communist Party represents a foreign-controlled conspiracy which plans civil war in the United States. Any one who aids and abets that conspiracy must be looked upon as *particeps criminis*. Any other view of the Communist

Party is intolerable nonsense. Any other view of its numerous auxiliaries masquerading under progressive slogans is liable to lead its holder into crimes against our national safety.

CHAPTER XVI

STALIN'S AGENTS OF CRIME

OUT of all the mass of detailed evidence which has been presented to the Committee on Un-American Activities in two years of its existence, there has emerged one fact the importance of which probably exceeds that of all others; the Communist Party is an agency for the planning and perpetration of misdemeanors and high crimes.

We must hasten to observe that the crimes and misdemeanors of the Communist Party belong in a special class. Behind the Communist violations of our statutes, there is a special motive which requires a special kind of understanding. The Communist criminal is not an ordinary criminal even when he is committing ordinary crimes.

The extraordinary thing about a Communist crime is that it rests upon an elaborate philosophy which is summed up in the doctrine that *the end justifies the means.* The Communist Party usually recruits its members and sympathizers by painting the Communist goal or end in glowing terms of justice, security, brotherhood, peace, and democracy. The communist *end,* in other words, is a beautifully depicted Utopia. Only after the new recruit has become wedded to the communist Utopia is he initiated into the *means* by which the Communist Party proposes to attain its Utopia. Included among these *means* are all the opposites of the high ideals which are supposed to be achieved when the goal is reached.

One aspect of the Communist goal is said to be greater

democracy; but the means for attaining it is a frank and ruthless dictatorship.

The Communist says that peace will reign in his Utopia, but in order to arrive at that estate he must wage merciless war, class war and civil war. The Communist declares that in his re-arrangement of society all men will be brothers and comrades, but in order to build this new social order he must school himself in hate.

The viciousness of the doctrine that *the end* justifies *any means* lies in the fact that the means, when in conflict with the end, destroy it. Stalin's Utopia is nothing more than the complete fulfillment of all the brutal means that were employed to achieve it. The reckless disregard for truth, justice, and human life, which the Communists defend as *means*, has become the abiding characteristic of their social order, now that they have achieved it over one-sixth of the world's surface.

But when criminal methods are used for Utopia's sake, criminal methods become a habit which carries over into Utopia.

Even according to its professed tactics, the Communist Party is an agency for the planning and perpetration of misdemeanors and high crimes. Lenin himself made this perfectly clear when he said: "Revolutionaries who are unable to combine *illegal* forms of struggle with every form of legal struggle are very poor revolutionaries." Lenin launched the Communist movement on the theory that the end justifies the means and that among the means to be employed were "illegal forms of struggle" as well as legal.

What we have said explains why Earl Browder has been convicted and sentenced for obtaining a United States passport through *fraud*.

It explains why William Weiner, head of the International Workers' Order and financial secretary of the Communist Party, has been convicted and sentenced for fraudulently representing himself as an American citizen.

It explains why Nicholas Dozenberg, agent of Stalin's secret military intelligence service, has been convicted and sentenced for perjury in obtaining an American passport.

It explains why Dr. Valentine Burtan, Communist agent for Stalin's counterfeiting ring, is now serving a sentence in the Federal prison in Lewisburg, Pennsylvania.

It explains why the Communist Party practices fraud on a large scale in obtaining signatures for its election petitions.

It explains why Communists defied our laws to recruit four thousand American boys to send them to fight for Stalin in Spain. All of these men and thousands of others who have not yet been apprehended and convicted committed their crimes in the service of the Communist Party.

The criminal character of the Communist Party must be brought home at once to all government officials who have been lax in the exercise of their appointive powers, and have thereby permitted Communists and sympathizing "partyliners" to land in government jobs, where they may add to the seriousness of their crimes by perpetrating them under the cover of official acts. The least we can do is to make an end of tax-supported crime. The Special Committee on Un-American Activities has found unanimously that the Communist Party is a "foreign conspiracy masked as a political party." This means that Communist Party members, who are subject to a strict Party discipline in all their activities, are foreign conspirators who cannot honorably or honestly serve the American government.

Recently, the Special Committee on Un-American Activities had before it a witness who for eight years served as an agent of the Moscow International Red Aid in various parts of the world, a man who was a charter member of the Communist Party in the United States. The man was one James H. Dolsen. Through his own testimony, it was developed that he obtained a position as an instructor on a WPA project. His lecture notes, which he identified as having been used by him in his tax-supported position on WPA, revealed that he had been teaching the Communist doctrine of the destruction of our form of government.

Dolsen admitted that he had given false information with respect to his previous employment when he filled out his application for a position on WPA. He stated falsely that he had been employed by a number of highly respected firms while in fact he was lecturing in one of Stalin's schools in Moscow. He admitted possession of a Communist Party membership book made out in the name of the President of the United States—a fraudulent, even if silly, act of contempt for the United States Government and its highest office. This man defied the Special Committee on Un-American Activities by refusing to answer questions put to him, and has been cited for contempt by the House of Representatives. The Communist Party is doing its utmost to make a martyr out of this man. It pretends that he is being attacked because he belongs to the labor and progressive movement, and it asks gullible citizens to contribute money for a "defense fund." While striking at the very foundations of our democracy, the Communist Party yells lustily about its rights under our democracy.

The criminal nature and aims of the Communist Party must be brought home to all leaders and members of labor unions who have been guilty of laxity in allowing Communists and sympathizing "party-liners" to land in positions of leadership in the unions. The coddling of

Communists in such positions is a betrayal of the millions of patriotic American citizens who carry trade union cards.

The Special Committee on Un-American Activities had before it another witness who held an organizer's position in the Steel Workers' Organizing Committee. This man now goes under the name of George Powers although his real name is Morris Pobersky. Both before and after he held that position of trust in one of the C.I.O. unions, he was an official of the Communist Party. This man arrogantly declared that he was born in the Soviet Union and that he came to the United States when he was 19 years of age, but that he could not remember what his or his father's name was when he landed in this country. He was forced to admit that he had used more than one name since his arrival in America.

The Special Committee on Un-American Activities has listened to undisputed testimony that hundreds of Communist Party members—loyal agents of Stalin whose names are in the records of public hearings—have held positions of leadership in labor unions, particularly in the unions of the C.I.O.

Some of the highest leaders in the Communist Party have testified that at least fifty thousand Communist Party members are working in the various labor unions of this country. The Special Committee on Un-American Activities found unanimously that Communists are entrenched in the leadership of at least ten of the C.I.O. unions. Many of these unions cover our basic industries. The Communist leadership of these unions exposes these industries to the grave risks of sabotage and espionage in a time of national emergency. Stalin is in a position to strike at the very foundations of our security through his command of these Moscovite agents who masquerade as labor leaders. They are, in fact, agents of crime. Is Democracy so weak and defenseless that it must remain exposed to such a menace without even the power to investigate and expose it? A great many pseudo liberals appear to think so. The Communist Party has set up the cry that we are attacking the labor movement and has demanded the protection of the Bill of Rights for the purpose of shielding its conspirators who have penetrated the ranks of organized labor. The Communist Party is no more a legitimate part of the labor movement than it is a Sunday School class.

The criminal nature and aims of the Communist Party must be brought home to the millions of Americans who have allowed themselves to be recruited into the huge Trojan Horse stable which the Party runs. The American League for Peace and Democracy, which served the interests of Stalin's foreign policy during the late period of the People's Front, is now dead, and gullible Americans can no longer be hoodwinked by its professed aims; but, in the place of the American League, as we have shown, the Communist Party is now setting up Yanks Are Not Coming committees. College students of America have been asked to rally in a so-called peace demonstration under this slogan. This student demonstration was under the leadership of Stalin's Trojan Horse organization, the American Student Union and several other organizations which together call themselves the United Student Peace Committee. The program of all these groups calls eventually for treason against the United States.

New organizations designed to carry out the purpose of the new Communist Party "line" are being set up all over the United States. Many of the old organizations are still functioning, such as the Workers' Alliance, the American Youth Congress, the International Workers' Order, the International Labor Defense, and the League of American Writers, but all of these older organizations have obediently flopped over to the newer Communist Party "line" dictated from the offices of the Kremlin in Moscow.

The main strategy of the Communist Party in building its numerous organizations is to bring millions of non-Communists under the influence and control of the Party, but these "fronts" also serve as feeders into the regular Party membership and as organizations for the recruiting of outright espionage agents for the Soviet military intelligence. Patriotic and intelligent Americans will refrain from joining or sponsoring these "front" organizations lest they become unwittingly the dupes of a criminal foreign conspiracy.

The influence and the strength of the Communist Party must not be measured in terms of its card-holding membership alone. For every actual, dues-paying member, there are ten to twenty sympathizers; and for every sympathizer there are a half dozen "innocents" who through ignorance are drawn into the work of furthering the Party's revolutionary and illegal purposes. Together, these dues-paying members, fellow travelers, and "innocents" number several millions. Acting under the leadership of a criminal organization which in turn is obedient to a foreign power, this group constitutes a national menace which Americans dare not ignore. For the sake of all that we hold dear, we must devise methods of bringing about the dissolution of this foreign-controlled conspiracy.

If some Dillinger or Al Capone had a hundred thousand loyal henchmen, organized into a criminal racket in this country, the whole nation would be aroused to the menace. But Capone's racket, compared to Stalin's was small and easy to handle. It was not predicated upon the promise of any Utopia. On the whole it was devoid of pretense and masquerade. It had no respectable sponsors who were willing publicly to lend it the prestige of their names. Capone dealt in illegality for the sake of some millions of dollars. There the matter ended. Stalin's racket is organized in the most clever and elaborate fashion ever conceived by the human brain. It is deliberately calculated to defy understanding or detection. It confuses ideals with crime. Capone wanted only our loose pocket change. Stalin wants our entire national income. Capone was satisfied to leave to us our thoughts, our liberties, our free institutions, our religion. Stalin plots to rob us of everything, to enslave us body, mind, and soul.

The criminal character of the Communist Party should be fully understood by every law-enforcement agency in the land. Failure to prosecute Communists for their Lenin-inspired and Stalin-directed illegalities, or leniency in the meting out of punishment for their political-motivated crimes will be interpreted in Moscow as evidence of the spinelessness of democracy and its inability to defend itself. Dismissals of indictments against Communists on the ground that their crimes have worked no public injury will raise doubts in the minds of many of our own people about the ability or willingness of public officials to defend our democracy with the vigor that is required for its survival in these times when more than one democratic people has become the prey of totalitarian aggressors.

As a matter of fact, the modern totalitarians of all schools —Stalin's, Hitler's, and Mussolini's alike—look with contempt upon any democracy that is worth having. They believe us to be such fools as well as weaklings that they can catch us on their totalitarian hooks with the bait of more and better democracy than we now have.

When we have questioned Communist witnesses, such as

the state secretary of the Communist Party of Maryland, on whether or not they believed in our American democracy, they have replied that they believe in an extension of democracy and all of them have maintained that Stalin's regime in Russia represents such an extension of democracy. That reminds one of the traveler who, journeying by night down a road which ended at the edge of a precipice, "extended" his journey beyond the point where the road had come to its end. The law of gravity took over the situation and left his body a mangled heap at the foot of the cliff. Any "extension of democracy" according to the formula of the Communists and the Nazis is a step over a precipice and a fatal plunge into the abyss of totalitarianism.

No man in this country can be a member of the Communist Party or a member of the German-American Bund and at the same time be a loyal American. These two organizations are loud in their clamor for their constitutional rights and at the same time brazen in their defiance of their constitutional loyalty and duties. They have regard for the Constitution of this country only when they think that this charter of our freedom may be used as a cover under which they may plot and carry out its destruction. The *Daily Worker*, official newspaper of the Communist Party, has baldly declared: "Our flag is the red flag of the international working class."

Time and again when the leaders of the Communist Party have been witnesses before the Special Committee on Un-American Activities, they have been challenged to declare their allegiance to the government of this country in the event of a conflict between the United States and the Soviet Union. Not one of these Communist leaders has been willing to make any such declaration of loyalty to America. Browder, Foster, Bedacht, Trachtenberg, Weiner, and

Blumberg, have tried to hedge and evade when confronted with the question of their loyalty under the Constitution. Their stock reply to any request for a declaration of their loyalty to America has been to say that the question is a purely hypothetical one, which they refuse to answer.

No one should be fooled by this evasion. The real fact is that the question is not at all hypothetical for members of the Communist Party. They are all committed already to the defense of the Soviet Union as their first obligation. The Seventh World Congress of the Communist International with those resolutions Browder and Foster admitted they agreed and with whose resolutions all members of the American Communist Party must agree, declared unanimously that "the defense of the Soviet Union must be considered paramount." Browder, Foster, James W. Ford, Gil Green, and other leaders of the American Communist Party were voting delegates to the Seventh World Congress which adopted unanimously that pledge of paramount loyalty to the Soviet Union.

The plain fact of the matter is, therefore, that these American Communists have already answered what they now choose to call a hypothetical question, and in their answer they have taken their stand on blind and implicit loyalty to the regime of Stalin. If any one of them had *refused* to declare by his vote at the Seventh World Congress that "the defense of the Soviet Union must be considered paramount," and had then tried to explain his refusal by telling Stalin that the issue was hypothetical, he would have been in a tougher spot than any Congressional Committee in the United States will ever put him.

"No man can serve two masters," said Jesus; and Stalin is the master of the American Communist Party.

When by their statement of silence or evasion these

American Communists place themselves on record to the effect that they will not support this country in any emergency or eventuality, they disclose the treasonable and conspiratorial character of the Communist Party. The least we are entitled to know is who the members of such a party are. No man can claim a constitutional right to conceal the identity of those who conspire to destroy our institutions. Those who are not engaged in such activities will not hesitate to make their identity known. Legitimate organizations and legitimate political parties have nothing to hide.

For a little more than a year, the Special Committee on Un-American Activities heard numerous witnesses who testified at length and in great detail on the nature and aims of the Communist Party. Incidentally, let us note that that testimony has stood up under all manner of ridicule, distortion, and abusive criticism. However, during the year that we were hearing these witnesses against Communism, there was a persistent chorus of demand from the Communists and their fellow travelers that they themselves be permitted to take the stand and tell the "whole truth" about the Communist Party and its activities. We have accorded numerous Communist leaders this opportunity for which they clamored so loudly, but when they have had the opportunity to speak, they have decided to follow the "line" of defiant and contemptuous silence. The truth of the matter is that they have never wanted to come forward and tell the whole truth about the Communist Party. In the first instance, they wanted to use the Committee's hearings as a sounding board for their propaganda. When the Committee declined to be used for any such purpose, they adopted the present party "line"—which is to be found in contempt of Congress and to seek martyrdom or the appearance of martyrdom. The defiance and contempt of these Communist witnesses is for the double purpose of concealing the truth and of making themselves martyrs. One of the basic principles of Communism is to make martyrdom pay good dividends.

One of the crucial questions facing democracy today is whether it can develop a method of defending itself without doing violence to its own essential nature, whether it can hold its undemocratic minorities in check without resorting to the repressive measures of totalitarianism. The answer to this question must lie on the one hand in permitting the greatest freedom to all individuals to think and express their own thoughts, however fantastic or Utopian, and on the other hand in acting promptly and decisively in punishing crime, that is, overt acts of illegality. The courts must deal with the Communist Party, not because it professes certain Utopian ideals or beliefs, but because it is a self-proclaimed violator of our laws owing a self-proclaimed allegiance to a foreign power. It is one thing to think and express thoughts that are revolutionary; it is an entirely different thing to engage in violence, racketeering, conspiracy, counterfeiting, perjury, fraud, sabotage, espionage, illegal recruiting, and allegiance to foreign principals. Democracy must protect with all its powers the former, and refuse just as emphatically to condone or leave unpunished any of the latter.

CHAPTER XVII

TREASON IS A COMMUNIST VIRTUE

EVERY report which has reached us from war-stricken Europe during recent months serves to pile up evidence showing that Stalin and Hitler rely upon treason as a powerful ally in their conquests of other peoples. Making every allowance for their mighty war machines, especially Hitler's, we are still forced to the conclusion that without their deliberate cultivation of treason the dictators would never have been able to sweep through twelve countries in exactly that many months.

Every advance in our industrial and mechanized civilization has served to magnify the menace of treason, to a country that is under attack. A single hand to throw a switch in a great power plant, a lone telegraph operator to send out a false order or to withhold a bona fide command, a radio announcer to create panic among the populace, a mechanic to loosen a bolt in an airplane, a lone hand (like that of Sinon's in Troy) to open a door which bars the way of the attacker, or a seaman to put the vast and intricate mechanism of a modern ship out of commission—any one of these acts, if treasonably performed at a critical place and time, may be enough to cost a people its liberties. These are a few of the thousands of ways in which traitors, single-handed, may seal the doom of their countries.

Whether the Communist Party has a million dues-paying members or only ten thousand is relatively unimportant when we consider what havoc a single act of treason committed by a single individual may work under the conditions of modern civilization.

And yet, the Communist Party has put itself on record again and again with respect to its intentions of disloyalty to the American government and with respect to its actual loyalty to a foreign state, the Soviet Union. Of course, if the Soviet Union really represents the interests of the great majority of Americans better than the government of the United States does, as the Communist Party has openly declared on many occasions, then history will commend its treason to the latter and its loyalty to the former. Reasoning from the premises of Communism, treason is a virtue. But to all those Americans who believe that their own form of government is the best and wisest that human minds have yet conceived, there can be only one judgment passed upon the Communist Party of the United States: guilty of treason.

The great difficulty which confronts us today is that so few Americans have ever taken the time and trouble to examine the basic program of the Communist Party, or, if they have informed themselves of its treasonable plans for the violent overthrow of the United States government, that they have discounted its seriousness. Even though we have dealt with that basic program of the Communist Party in an incidental fashion in other connections throughout this discussion, we do well to consider it in all of its aspects. At this point, let us examine it as an elaborate and carefully conceived plan for treason. The Communists themselves may be allowed to do most of the speaking.

The *Program of the Communist International*, printed in English by the Communist Party of the United States, contains the following statement:

Expressing the historical need for an international organization of revolutionary proletariat—the gravediggers of the capitalist order—the Communist International is the only international force that has for its program the dictatorship of the proletariat and communism, and that openly comes out as the organizer of the international proletarian revolution. The ultimate aim of the Communist International is to replace world capitalist economy by a world system of communism.

The *Program of the Communist International* then goes on to indicate how large numbers of people are to be prepared for the acceptance of the "ultimate aim" of communism, namely, by convincing them first that the Communist Party is an everyday friend in helping them to achieve their immediate needs, a purely tactical pretension of concern for their day-to-day welfare.

The dictatorship of the proletariat, it continues, is a stubborn fight—bloody and bloodless, violent and peaceful, military and economic, pedagogical and administrative. . . .

The party advances certain transitional slogans and partial demands corresponding to the concrete situation; but these demands and slogans must be bent to the revolutionary aim of capturing power and of overthrowing bourgeois capitalist society. The party must neither stand aloof from the daily needs and struggle of the working class, nor confine its activities exclusively to them. The task of the party is to utilize these minor everyday needs as a starting point from which to lead the working class to the revolutionary struggle for power. . . .

The mass action includes a combination of strikes and armed demonstrations, and finally the general strike conjointly with armed insurrection against the State power. . . .

The Communists disdain to conceal their views and aims. They openly declare that their aims can be attained only by the forcible overthrow of all the existing social conditions . . .

Let the ruling class tremble at a communist revolution . . . Workers of all countries, unite!

The *Constitution of the Communist International*, also published in English by the Communist Party of the United States, contains the following statements:

Membership in the Communist Party and in the Communist International is open to all those who accept the program and the rules of the respective Communist Parties and of the Communist International, who . . . abide by all decisions of the Party and of the Communist International . . .

After a decision has been taken by the Communist International . . . the decision must be unreservedly carried out even if a part of the party membership or the local party organizations are in disagreement with it.

The decisions of the executive committee of the Communist International are obligatory for all the sections of the Communist International and must be carrier out . . .

This control by the Communist International over its sections, such as the Communist Party of the United States and its auxiliary organizations, is shown by many rules written into the *Constitution of the Communist International*, even to the necessity for permission to hold congresses. "Congresses of the various sections, ordinary and special, can be convened only with the consent of the executive committee of the Communist International."

The Special Committee on Un-American Activities has indisputable evidence to prove that the Communist Party of the United States is a section of the Communist International at Moscow, and that the International does issue special directives to its Section in this country, and that the Section here has carried out those directives.

The Communist Party adopted what it called a "new

constitution" for the American section at its May, 1938, Congress, held in New York City. The following statement is to be found in this constitution:

> The new constitution is profoundly connected with the political life of America and is realizing in practice the instructions of Comrade Dimitroff who called on us at the Seventh World Congress of the Communist International to learn as quickly as possible how to sail on the turbulent waters of class struggle . . .
> The emblem of the party shall be the crossed hammer and sickle . . . with a circular inscription, having at the top "Communist Party of the U.S.A.," and in the lower part "affiliated to the Communist International . . ."
> The Communist Party of the United States is affiliated with its fraternal Communist Parties of other lands through the Communist International and participates in international congresses, through its national committee . . .

At the Party congress where this new Trojan Horse constitution was adopted, resolutions were also adopted, one of which, in the form of a cable to Moscow, stated:

> The tenth national convention laid down as the most important task for the party the further struggle for united action of all forces of the working class, for the purpose of securing joint action of all democratic elements of the country. The convention indicated the concrete forms of the struggle for unity of the working class; in the first place to overcome the split in the trade-union movement in the United States of America, by creating a uniform confederation of labor. The convention formulated the program of the democratic front, the program of uniting the American people.

A few days later, the Trojan Horse made its appearance again when the Communists began explaining why they had suddenly begun to sing the Star Spangled Banner and to use

American flags, along with the Internationale (the Communist song) and red flags. In the *Daily Worker*, July 4, 1938, is their explanation:

> When we sing the Star Spangled Banner and the Internationale together, when we decorate our platform today with the American flag and the red flag of the socialist revolution . . . this is the way we express the fusion of our Communist program for socialism and the American tradition.

Instructions of the Communist International are "to learn as quickly as possible how to sail on the turbulent waters of class struggle." There was no actual remolding of the Communist Party into an American organization. It remained as un-American as ever, even while trying to beguile Americans with its newly acquired doctrine of the People's Front. Communists were merely carrying out the instructions of the Communist International to adopt the Trojan Horse methods suggested by Dimitroff.

The Communist Party honored Dimitroff for his inspiration when it sent the following message to Moscow:

> The tenth national convention of the Communist Party of the United States of America sends its warmest revolutionary greetings to the Communist International and its helmsman, George Dimitroff, true comrade-in-arms of Stalin, leader of the struggle against fascism and war, hero of all anti-Fascists, hero and leader of the working class.
>
> We have learned from you how to rekindle that fire. We have learned from you how to fuse the internationalism of our socialist heritage with the best traditions of the revolutionary patriots of past history.
>
> The international working class under your leadership is building unity . . . and at the head of the forces of peace stands the Soviet Union, the socialist country . . . Our convention pledges to you and to the Communist International

our steadfast determination to be worthy of the model you have set for us . . . the goal of the leadership of Marx, Engels, Lenin, and Stalin—the winning of a socialist world . . .

It would be financially prohibitive for Stalin to employ 100,000 spies to carry out his program and to do his bidding in the United States. However, through the Communist appeals to class hatred and the promise of Utopia, Stalin has been able, without substantial cost to Russia, to build up within the United States a legalized organization of agents who can be depended upon to follow his instructions at little or no hazard to themselves.

The hold which Stalin has upon his agents here is fantastically binding. It is almost inconceivable that people who had been denouncing Fascism and Nazism in all their speeches and publications could perform overnight an ideological somersault simply because Stalin aligned himself with Hitler. It is almost unbelievable that any man could change the "convictions" of his followers by the mere announcement of a change of foreign policy. Communists are permitted, even authorized, by the Party to lie about most things, but, with reference to the question of allegiance, Stalin does not permit any equivocation or deception. Consistently, when Communists are asked whether they would support the United States in the event of war with Russia they dare not declare their loyalty to the United States in such eventuality.

People whose "convictions" come and go at the whim of a foreign dictator will not hesitate to obey any orders issued by their master. We need not indulge in speculation with respect to the willingness of Communists to obey the orders of Moscow. We have indisputable proof of the fact.

In view of its known character and proven record, it is

almost unbelievable that government officials, labor leaders, and so-called liberal organizations have continued to treat the Communist Party with tolerance or sympathy. But notwithstanding the revelations before the Special Committee on Un-American Activities, many Communists remain unmolested in government service, labor unions, and in vital industries such as transportation, communications, shipping, and even in airplane factories and naval yards.

Organized society has always regarded treason as one of the most heinous offenses that can be committed. Every country has the most stringent laws for dealing with treason. We have been taught that a traitor is a most despicable character. We have had traitors held up to us as horrible examples, and yet in the United States today we not only tolerate, but we actually legalize an organization made up of thousands of traitorous-minded people. Communism is nothing more nor less than organized treason, and those who abet or encourage it run grave risks of being *particeps criminis*.

CHAPTER XVIII

COMMUNISM IS THE OPIATE OF THE PEOPLE

THE drug which deadens the minds of men to the highest realities of life is Communism. Stalin knows no higher law than his own capricious will, no higher code of ethics than the changing necessities of class hatred. No other ruler of the Russians was ever drugged with such an autocratic sense of power. Under him, a nation of slaves has eaten the opiate of Communism and fallen under the grotesque illusion that they are masters of their political destiny and owners of their national economy. No Chinese coolie, under the influence of the enslaving poppy, ever entertained a more fantastic illusion. In such a regime of brutal power and hate, there is no place for religion. In the philosophy which supports that regime, there is no room for God. The missionaries of Stalin's philosophy throughout the world are likewise at war against religion and God.

In a published interview which he held with an American trade union delegation, Stalin discussed the attitude of the Communist Party toward religion. "The Party cannot be neutral toward religion," he said, "because all religion is something opposite to science." The interview which contained this unequivocal judgment by the Russian dictator was reported and published by the American Communist Party.

In accordance with Stalin's program, the Communist

Party seeks not only to change our form of government by substituting a Soviet dictatorship for democracy. It seeks also to revolutionize our basic conception and manner of life as interpreted by the fundamentals of religion.

Religion is predicated upon not less than four propositions which are essential to the highest order of living. These propositions are:

(1) Faith in Almighty God as our Father from whom we derive the blessings of freedom and sustenance;

(2) Respect for individual man as a living soul bearing in his own nature the imprint of divine creation;

(3) Love of God and man as the only possible basis for a brotherly society;

(4) Confidence that spiritual forces, not material, must rule supreme in the affairs of man.

On each of these four propositions, Communism takes the position of anti-religion. Communism denies the divine creation of man and holds that the individual is a mere cog in a collectivistic machine. Communism preaches hate and strives to mobilize the forces of hate to achieve its ends. Communism is based on materialism, holding that moral and spiritual forces are a fable and a delusion.

During the period of the People's Front which was abruptly ended or greatly modified when Stalin entered into alliances with Hitler, the Communist Party tried to carry on a one-sided flirtation with the Church. Earl Browder declared that the Communist Party was prepared "to extend the hand of fellowship to the Church." That offer was on a par with the Communist Party's pretense of espousing democracy.

From the time of Karl Marx down to the present, the true position of Communists has been that religion is the opiate of the people. In his book, *What Is Communism?*,

COMMUNISM IS OPIATE OF THE PEOPLE   239

written before the "extended hand of fellowship," Earl Browder declared: "We Communists do not distinguish between good and bad religions, because we think they are all bad for the masses." Karl Marx declared that "the social principles of Christianity are lickspittle."

Some years ago the Communist Party of the United States brought out a pamphlet entitled *The Church and the Workers*. This pamphlet bore the name of Bennett Stevens as author. Bennett Stevens is an alias for Bernhard J. Stern, a Columbia University professor. Professor Stern's alias was admitted by Alexander Trachtenberg, head of International Publishers, a Communist Party publishing house. According to Professor Stern, Communists hold that "it is necessary to link the fight against the church and religion with the fight against capitalism and imperialism." In this same pamphlet, Professor Stern stated that "the Soviet Union under a workers' and peasants' government is the only country in the world where religion and the churches are being combated with active cooperation of the government."

In another of the Communist Party's pamphlets, Corliss Lamont wrote of "the unaltering determination of the Communists to do away with religion and the inclusion of this aim as one of the chief features of the educational system from one end of the country to the other." Mr. Lamont, who was the head of the Communist Party's Trojan Horse organization known as the Friends of the Soviet Union, declared further: "The Red Army is one of the most active centers for the dissemination of atheism. Its recruits are given systematic instruction in anti-religious theory just as they are in other Communist doctrines." It is noteworthy here to point out that Mr. Lamont definitely classifies anti-religious theory as one of the Communist doctrines. Mr. Lamont, scion of great wealth, has also been a member of the faculty of Columbia University.

The whole history of the Soviet Union, from the first days of Lenin's assumption of power down to Stalin's present-day assault upon and conquest of neighboring states, constitutes a first-rate object lesson in what happens to a nation when it is systematically instructed in atheism, hate, and materialism. Since Stalin's alliance with Hitler and his attack upon Finland, many of the erstwhile gullible Americans who had been drawn for one reason or another into the Communist Party and its Trojan Horse organizations have come to doubt the excellence of life in Stalin's godless Utopia. Twenty-two years of systematic destruction of the faith and soul of the Russian people have left this vast population of 170,000,000 a prey to self-deception and cruelty. In less than a single generation, the Communist leaders of Russia have apparently drained the last drop of the milk of human kindness from the soul of a great people. This is a tragedy which it is impossible to exaggerate, and it is the tragedy which is certain to befall any people which throws the common decencies of morality and religion into the ashcan of history.

Communists aim not only to destroy the Church and to train a whole generation in atheism; they aim also to put aside all that the human race has developed in the way of high ethical or moral standards since man emerged from the jungle. Communism is the restoration of the jungle code—a code of ethics whose terrible quality is multiplied over and over again by the possession of modern instruments of propaganda and physical destruction.

It is impossible to understand the tactics and the statements of Communists and their fellow travelers unless their very special code of ethics be kept constantly in mind.

COMMUNISM IS OPIATE OF THE PEOPLE 241

Lenin summarized this moral code when he said: "Our morality is entirely subordinated to the interests of the class struggle of the proletariat . . . For the Communist, morality consists entirely of compact united discipline and conscious mass struggle against the exploiters. We do not believe in eternal morality, and we expose all fables about morality." In practical terms, this means that the individual Communist's moral judgment is rigidly subordinated to the will of the Communist Party, and the will of the Communist Party is, in turn, whatever its most politically powerful member, Stalin, decides it shall be. The Communist code of ethics says that truth must give way to class advantage. It is a hard and cynical code. By it, Communists have put the world on notice that their word, whether under oath or not, has only so much value as their momentary conception of the interests of the class struggle may dictate. When William Weiner, financial secretary of the American Communist Party, was under oath before the Special Committee on Un-American Activities, he stated that he was an American-born citizen. Weiner has since been convicted as an impostor whose real name is Warzower and whose real birthplace was Russia. It is the Communist view that perjury committed in the interests of the Communist Party is not only defensible but a virtue. There are other concrete instances where Communists have held counterfeiting, bank robbery, theft, destruction of property, beatings, shootings, stabbings, and kidnaping to be virtues under their ethical code, if only these violations of the simplest ethics, as well as statutes, furthered or seemed to further the cause of Communism. Lenin advised "manoeuvers, illegal methods, evasion, and subterfuge" as ways to penetrate trade unions, and to carry on Communist work in those unions. All this is no more than is to be expected in a movement which is based upon atheism, hate, and materialism, and which holds that morality is a fable.

Recent international events show clearly how Communists alter their moral and ethical judgments to fit the alleged necessities of the class struggle. In the brief space of a few days, the Communists in the United States performed an ethical somersault which shocked those who had not come to understand Lenin's moral code and Communism's godlessness. When Hitler—unallied with Stalin—was invading Austria and Czechoslovakia, our American Communists under Browder's leadership staged mass meetings and demonstrations, organized committees headed by highly respectable citizens, and denounced unsparingly the conquests of the Nazi dictator. However, when Stalin—allied with Hitler—embarked upon the identical course of invading neighboring countries, our American Communists stamped his conduct with their vociferous approval. Some of the Communist Trojan Horse organizations were not permitted to make such bold ethical reversals. They simply refrained from denouncing Stalin's acts. The American League for Peace and Democracy, the American Youth Congress, and the American Student Union, for example, refused to go on record in opposition to international aggression when committed by Stalin. Their silence, however, marked them none the less plainly as Trojan Horse organizations of the Stalin machine and as adherents to the Communist code of morality. By the definitions of Communism, Stalin is not a conqueror but a "liberator" when his army marches in and takes possession of another country.

Despite the clearly atheistic, materialistic, and hate philosophy of the Communist Party, numerous clergymen and religious leaders in this country have permitted themselves to be used by Browder and his various Trojan Horse organizations. One example of this unfortunate state of things came in the form of a public manifesto signed by some 98 clergymen and religious leaders at the request of the American League for Peace and Democracy. This manifesto urged the Congress to refuse continuation and a new appropriation to the Special Committee on Un-American Activities. There can be no doubt whatever about the right of these reverend gentlemen to oppose the continuation of this Committee and to petition the Congress to that effect. That is a right which they enjoy as free American citizens and which they certainly would not enjoy in a corresponding situation in the Soviet Union where all must agree with Stalin or take the bitter consequences of disagreement. When, however, these clergymen and religious leaders exercise their rights as American citizens under the auspices of a Trojan Horse organization of the Communist Party, it is the right of other American citizens to call attention to their association with the Browder-Stalin machine, whether that association be witting or unwitting. In its Report to the Congress, the Special Committee on Un-American Activities unanimously found, on the basis of the fullest evidence, that the American League for Peace and Democracy was a "front" organization set up and controlled by the Communist Party. It was not "American" and its objectives were not those of "Peace and Democracy," notwithstanding the fact that a clergyman, Dr. Harry F. Ward, was the national chairman of the organization. As a tool of the Communist Party, the American League was designed to contribute directly and indirectly to the strength and influence of the Party, and in the long run to advance the philosophy of godlessness, hate, and materialism which is the basis of Communism. These 98 clergymen and religious leaders serve as an example of how the Communist Party reaches out to enlist non-Communists for achieving its immediate objectives. It is a deplorable example. Surely, these 98 religious leaders could have found some auspices other than those of a Trojan Horse organization of the Communist Party under which to express their opposition to the work of this Congressional Committee, even if they were compelled to create their own auspices for that purpose. It is a safe assumption that they would not put their signatures to any manifesto presented to them by the German-American Bund, no matter how heartily they subscribed to the objectives of the manifesto. It will be difficult to bring about the rout of the Communist forces in this country as long as respected citizens lend their names to the various Trojan Horse organizations of the Communist Party. This is particularly true of citizens who are prominent in government, the church, and trade unions. It is heartening to observe that the overwhelming majority of our religious leaders, besides which these 98 clergymen are a negligible minority, have given their full support to efforts to expose the *isms* that threaten the existence of our institutions, including a free church.

Communists have been specifically instructed to plant themselves in religious organizations in order to carry on Trojan Horse activities. At the Seventh World Congress of the Communist International, in 1935, a resolution was adopted which declared it to be "the duty of Young Communist League members to join . . . religious organizations; to wage a systematic struggle in these organizations to gain influence over the broad masses of youth." Most Americans will find it an almost incredible thing to be told that Communists have carried their Trojan Horse operations into every conceivable type of organization, but the resolution from which we have just quoted was unanimously adopted by the highest Communist body in the world and should leave no doubt about the tactics and ethics of the Communist Party. A more cynical conspiracy has never before existed in the history of the world. Once it is thoroughly understood, however, we have provided ourselves with the greatest possible safeguard against its operations.

It would be a grave mistake for us to assume that the atheistic and materialistic philosophy of Communism or Marxism has been thoroughly and finally discredited by Stalin's alliance with Hitler. The philosophy of Marxism has corrupted our thinking in circles that are far wider than those of the Communist Party. Even in colleges and schools where there is no branch of the American Student Union and on campuses where Earl Browder has never spoken, the philosophy of Marxism has made serious inroads upon the minds of the young.

It is a tragic thing when thousands of American youth, under the guidance of the American Student Union and the American Youth Congress or under the instruction of Marxist professors, are led to the theory that the government owes them a living. This is done, of course, in the name of social justice and economic security, but it reflects a philosophy which is destructive of both personal initiative and individual development. It reflects a doctrine of the State which is wholly un-American. It is a dangerous fallacy of Marxist materialism to hold that economic insecurity is the greatest misfortune which can befall men. A far greater calamity is to be found in the loss of those liberties which are set forth in the Declaration of Independence and the Bill of Rights. This country was settled in its infancy by men who were seeking the unrestricted liberty to worship God according to the dictates of their own consciences, and not by men who were in quest of economic security or a government which would support them. In most cases, the early settlers of America turned their backs upon greater economic security than they could ever hope to achieve in the new country during their own lifetime. They were men stirred with a passion to worship God without the interference of the State and to develop their own God-given personalities free from the tyrannies of Europe. Today we are faced with the fact that many of our people would establish those very tyrannies in American government and reduce us to the conditions of slavery in which the peoples of Germany and Russia find themselves under the dictatorship of men who promised them economic security as the greatest good. The price of their acceptance of those promises has been a veritable enslavement of Russians and Germans. They have eaten the opiate of Marxism.

Another fallacy to which many of our people have fallen victims is the Marxist illusion that a "planned economy" is either workable or desirable. This fallacy has spread in circles that are far wider than those touched immediately by the Communist Party and its front organizations. Its exponents have for a period of years, recently, wielded tremendous influence and power in our federal government. Planned economy means the substitution of an enormous state bureaucracy for personal initiative. In any form which it may assume it is plain economic quackery. No body of bureaucrats anywhere on earth is wise enough to order all the economic affairs of a modern nation, but what is infinitely worse than their limitations of wisdom is the inevitable consequence that any group of bureaucrats which makes the attempt to administer the economic life of a nation must end by setting up a tyranny over the minds and souls of men. In the first place, they must possess vast powers not contemplated in the American form of government before they could ever undertake to plan our economy; and, in the second place, their inevitable failure to plan successfully would lead them to the attempt to stifle all hostile criticism and to govern our thoughts as well as our tastes. In the end we should find ourselves with one big boss bureaucrat who, like Stalin and Hitler, would try to become a Marxist god to the American people.

Ironically enough it has been Marxism which has turned out to be the opiate of the people. On the other hand, the very religion which the Marxists scorned has been shown more clearly than ever before in human history to be essential for individual and national accomplishment.

Communism and Nazism are possessed by the demon of hate which sets class against class or race against race. Religion cannot survive the triumph of Communism or the ascendancy of Nazism. The values which Americans hold most dear and which were incorporated in our institutions of government are values which are derived from a religious outlook—faith in Almighty God as Father and as the source of spiritual and physical strength, respect for human personality as a divine creation, love as the basis of the highest human relationships, and confidence in the priority and supremacy of spiritual forces.

In exposing the anti-religion of Communism and Nazism, we are getting down to the very roots of the ills which these *isms* have brought to other countries and which they will, if allowed, introduce into American life.

CHAPTER XIX

BROWDER RUNS A BIG BUSINESS

To PICTURE the Communists as a small group of idealistic and impecunious citizens trying to run a revolution on a shoestring would be to err seriously in any attempt to understand the menace of Stalin's Trojan Horse.

The fact is that Earl Browder presides over a far-flung business empire which deals in millions of dollars. The corporate set-up of Browder's big business is difficult—if not impossible—to trace in all of its ramifications. Nevertheless, it represents a grand aggregate of business operations over which this man Browder wields autocratic powers entrusted to him by his superior in Moscow—the world's foremost business, industrial, and financial czar.

Browder's big business includes far more than an income-producing "political party." It comprises several publishing houses, a printing press, and a large stationery supply concern. It maintains a national chain of retail book stores, as well as a wholesale book-handling organization. It publishes several daily newspapers, scores of magazines, and literally hundreds of local but irregular papers. It has its own insurance company. It owns and conducts schools, camps, and pleasure resorts in every section of the United States. It has its own moving picture houses, has complete control over several film-producing concerns, and runs a large film-importing agency. It operates a number of cooperative houses and restaurants. Its vast network of relief and defense committees does a business which aggregates millions of dollars annually and which provides jobs and revenues for strictly Party purposes. It exercises a controlling influence over the treasuries of a half dozen so-called labor unions, and draws upon their funds for many of its shrewdly concealed operations. For several years, it has maintained a Communist Party-U. S. Government liaison agency (Workers Alliance) which has been able to draw many millions of dollars of tax-raised funds to the support of Party members and activities. (It is not likely that Moscow's subsidies to the American Communists ever approached in magnitude the amount of the "Washington Gold" which has poured into Communist coffers here.)

It would be impossible to do more than make a rough estimate of the financial proportions of Browder's big business. Certainly John D. M. Hamilton and James A. Farley, in their conduct of the affairs of the Republican and Democratic parties, have not had anything remotely comparable to Browder's business set-up.

The Communist Party and its allied groups have received and spent millions of dollars every year in recent years. This is the sworn testimony of William Weiner, financial secretary of the Communist Party; Earl Browder, general secretary of the Communist Party; William E. Browder, financial secretary of the New York Communist Party; and Carl Marwig, accountant for the Special Committee on Un-American Activities.

The Communist witnesses before the Special Committee on Un-American Activities denied that the Party had received any subsidies from Russia, but the testimony of Gitlow, Zack, and other past Communist officials established the fact that Russia once sent large subsidies to the United States in the form of the crown jewels, which were confiscated by the Bolsheviks when they seized the reins of power in Russia. There is, of course, no definite way to determine how much money has been spent in the United States by the agents of Russia. That it is a large amount no one can deny if he will take the pains to read the testimony of the witnesses who have appeared before the Special Committee on Un-American Activities.

According to Browder and Weiner, the chief income of the Party in the United States is from membership dues, organizational activities, and contributions. The annual budget of the national office of the Communist Party in the United States is slightly in excess of $200,000, according to Mr. Weiner; but this represents only a very small amount of the actual expenditure of the Communist Party. From 1933 to 1938, the Party did not have any bank account, and did not make any record of its receipts and expenditures. During that period all its receipts and disbursements were in cash, and the funds of the Party were kept in safety deposit vaults. Since the beginning of 1938, the Party has deposited some of its money in several banks in New York City, under the names of William Weiner, David Leeds, and William E. Browder.

An accountant audited these bank accounts and found that from April, 1937, through March, 1939, William E. Browder had deposited $1,308,177.13 to his accounts in three banks. Disbursements by William E. Browder during that same period amounted to $1,296,997.80. All of this amount was deposited to the personal account of William E. Browder, and there was nothing to indicate that the funds belonged to the Communist Party of New York. Mr. Browder admitted that he had never filed any income tax returns or paid any taxes on all this money. The records also show that the Communist Party had never paid any income tax on these funds.

For a period of twelve months, ending December 31, 1938, there was deposited to the account of William Weiner, financial secretary of the Communist Party, the sum of $250,935.56. The total withdrawals from the Weiner account for the year 1938 were $224,073.43; and for two months during 1939, the sum of $58,454.22, or a total of $282,527.65. For the first six months of 1939, Weiner testified that the income of the national office of the Communist Party, from all sources, was $113,146.08. He testified that the total income from 1937 was $258,316.62.

According to Weiner and Browder, a large part of the income of the various divisions of the Communist Party is derived from the contributions of sympathizers. Browder and Weiner stated that these contributions ranged from $10 to $1,500; and that they had thousands of contributors who were not members of the Party. They testified that some of these people were wealthy people who were in sympathy with the work of the Party. Weiner would not submit the names of these contributors. The national office only gets about thirty per cent of membership dues, funds from organizational activities, and contributions, according to Weiner.

William E. Browder said that in New York State the income of the Party runs about $20 per member a year from all sources. If this average holds true for the other cities, the total income of the Communist Party in the United States is about $2,000,000 annually. This does not take into consideration any of the subsidiary and controlled organizations of the Party. Mr. Marwig, the accountant of the Special Committee on Un-American Activities examined forty-three accounts of the Communist Party and affiliated or subsidiary groups. He testified that the total deposits in those forty-three accounts, for the period covered, aggregated $10,164,730.91.

It must be borne in mind that this audit did not include all of the accounts of the Communist Party and subsidiary organizations in New York; neither did it include any of the accounts in other cities outside of New York. But based upon the testimony of Communist officials and the audit made by the Committee accountant, it is a reasonable estimate that the total income of the Communist Party and subsidiary or affiliated organizations in the United States exceeds $10,000,000 a year.

The Party does not keep any accurate records, and what records are kept are destroyed within a short time. A large part of the disbursements is in cash. For instance, there was one check of $15,000 payable in cash and drawn out by Larry Taylor, who had some minor job in the Party headquarters in New York. Weiner and Browder testified that the disbursements include expenditures for propaganda, aid to strikers, and salaries to organizers of the Party. The national office subsidizes a few of the State organizations that are not self-sustaining.

Although the financial statement of the Communist Party for the two years ending December 31, 1937, does not, to any extent, indicate the total amount spent by even the political section of the Communist movement in the United States, in that it does not include the income and expenditures of its enormous list of publishing houses, publications, and allied movements, the report does show that the expenditures of the national office of the Party amounted to $751,183.47 for the past two years, and that the assets (including only $1,403.86 cash balance) totaled $78,827.81. It shows, also that the Party collected only $146,563.42 of the

$751,183.47 in dues and $116,133 for an International Solidarity fund.

The report shows that the Party subsidized organizations in the United States to the extent of $65,816.81 and that it lent $42,000 in addition. It shows that the Party spent $68,728.88 for Communist activities in Brazil, Bulgaria, Canada, Cuba, Chile, Costa Rica, China, Ethiopia, Germany, Ireland, India, Italy, Mexico, Nicaragua, Philippines, Puerto Rico, and Portugal. It accounts for the expenditure of $32,419.77 in steel, auto, textile, railroad, marine, metal, rubber, oil, and mining strike activities, in addition to the amount other Communist organizations expended along those lines.

It costs $120,000 more to operate the *Daily Worker* than the newspaper takes in each year. In other words, it costs about $250,000 a year to operate the paper. None of this amount is included in the central committee's financial report.

The Scottsboro Committee alone spent $64,351.75 in one year, and about a half million dollars in three years. The International Labor Defense, in its financial report, shows liabilities amounting to $240,134.13 for one year. At times its reports have shown upward of $180,000 expenditures in the United States for a period of one year. The International Workers' Order report showed $487,300 annual receipts and assets totaling $598,841.08, with a surplus on hand of approximately a million and half dollars.

Aid movements in the United States for the Spanish "Red" front, according to reports made to the Department of State, raised over $1,000,000 during 1938, approximately $300,000 of which was spent for so-called advertising and office expenses of the American group.

As proof of the fact that the Soviet Government has helped finance Communism in the United States, we have the following official order issued by the Soviet Government in December, 1917, as signed by Lenin and his Commissar of Foreign Affairs, Leon Trotsky, and published in the reports of a New York State investigating committee:

> Financing the international movement. Inasmuch as the Soviet power firmly adheres to the principles of international solidarity of the proletariat and of fraternity of the toilers of all lands; and inasmuch as the struggle against war and imperialism can be brought to victory on an international scale: Therefore, the Soviet of Peoples Commissars deems it necessary to bring all possible means, including money, to the aid of the left international wing of the workers movement of all lands, quite regardless of whether the countries are at war or in alliance with Russia; or whether they are neutral.
>
> To that end the Soviet of Peoples Commissars orders to appropriate for the needs of the revolutionary international movement 2,000,000 rubles, to be taken charge of by the foreign representative of the Commissariat of Foreign Affairs.
>
> V. ULIANOFF (Lenin),
President, Soviet Peoples Commissars,
L. TROTSKY,
Peoples Commissariat of Foreign Affairs.

We have estimated that approximately $10,000,000 is spent annually in the United States for the various activities of the Communists. Where does all this money come from? Certainly not from the workers.

When Earl Browder was a witness before the Special Committee on Un-American Activities, he acknowledged his Party's indebtedness for generous financial support to men and women of large means. From the beginning of the movement to destroy American democracy and set up a proletarian dictatorship, the Communist movement has had its financial "angels" in such persons as Anita Whitney,

Rose Pastor Stokes, Bishop William Montgomery Brown, Corliss Lamont, Gardner Jackson, Robert Marshall, and Charles Garland. The case of Garland is of special importance.

Young Charles Garland, of Boston, once fell heir to a very considerable fortune, and when he refused to accept it, most of it went to financing various radical causes. He was the son of James A. Garland, a wealthy and highly respected old American, who, when he died, left his son $900,000 in very conservative securities. Charles, through his associations at Harvard, had acquired theories opposed to the private ownership of property. He refused his inheritance.

Roger Baldwin talked young Garland into the idea of contributing his fortune to the various uses of the radicals. When the securities were dug up, it was found that, in those abundant twenties, they had more than doubled in value. The $900,000 had grown to be $2,000,000.

A board of directors was set up for handling this easy money. The heads of the principal radical organization in the United States found places in it. Roger Baldwin, as originator of the idea, occupied first place. A second director was William Z. Foster, chairman of the Communist Party. Another was Sidney Hillman, author of *Reconstruction in Russia*, and recently appointed a members of the President's new National Advisory Defense Commission. Yet another was Clinton S. Golden, prominent through his association with various radical publications and schools and a C.I.O. leader in the "Little Steel" strike of 1937. Hillman has named Golden as one of his assistants on the Defense Commission.

The Garland Fund has been particularly accessible to agencies which publicize radical views. The *Daily Worker*, official voice of the Communists, received $57,000, while the *Masses* got $68,000. The Federated Press, a Communist-controlled news service with Earl Browder on its board, received $76,000.

Naturally the fund was available for the defense of William Z. Foster, one of its directors, when he was arrested at Bridgman, Michigan, and charged with plotting to overthrow the government.

Most of the men who were publicized by this Garland Fund have gained national prominence. Roger Baldwin, as head of the American Civil Liberties Union, has been thought by many to be a battler for human rights. William Z. Foster has been three times candidate for the presidency of the United States on the Communist ticket. Sidney Hillman became Labor Advisor for the National Recovery Administration, and had much to do with the selection of the personnel of the first National Labor Relations Board, and is now one of the President's intimate defense advisors. It was given to Clinton S. Golden to become an intimate friend of Professor J. Warren Madden, of the University of Pittsburgh, and to tutor him in radicalism. Madden became head of the National Labor Relations Board when it was created and made Golden his regional director in Pittsburgh. And Golden is now assistant to Hillman on the President's Defense Commission.

CHAPTER XX

A TROJAN HORSE ON THE BALLOT

IN A unanimous report submitted to the House of Representatives on January 3, 1940, the Special Committee on Un-American Activities said:

The committee feels that a careful examination of the facts justifies the assertion that the Communist Party of the United States is a foreign conspiracy masked as a political party.
The committee is forced to conclude that, in practice, the Communist Party is actually functioning as a "border patrol" on American shores for a foreign power—the Soviet Union.

It is true that the Communist Party has appeared on the ballot in most of the States of the Union. The Party, however, enters election campaigns for purely agitational purposes and not for bona fide electoral reasons. Its solicitation of votes is a way of winning sympathizers for Communism. Unlike real political parties, it is not concerned with having its candidates elected to office in order to have them exercise the normal functions of government. It is a political party in name only; it is a foreign conspiracy in fact.

Even when Communists have received a majority of the votes in a regular election, they have been required to subordinate their public offices to the conspiratorial purposes of the Communist Party. In this connection, there is an illuminating passage in the Trojan Horse speech which Georgi Dimitroff delivered at the Seventh World Congress of the Communist International in 1935. In Saxony and Thuringia in Germany, in 1923, Communists were elected to public office. Twelve years later, Dimitroff bitterly denounced these Communists as "right opportunists." In their public offices, according to Dimitroff, "the Communists should have used their positions primarily *for the purpose of arming the proletariat.*" Because these Communist office-holders failed to use their positions "primarily for the purpose of arming the proletariat," Dimitroff excoriated them with the observations that "they behaved in general like *ordinary* parliamentary ministers 'within the framework of bourgeois democracy.'" It was nothing to Dimitroff that the Communists in Saxony and Thuringia were elected as "ordinary parliamentary ministers within the framework of bourgeois democracy." In his view—a view which Browder has described as the official "line" of the Communists throughout the world today—they should have ignored the purposes for which they were chosen by the electorate under the German Constitution and should have used public office simply and primarily to carry on the conspiratorial work to which Communist allegiance had committed them.

Dimitroff's words of denunciation of the Communists of Saxony and Thuringia are worth remembering when the question of the Communist Party's place on the American ballot is under consideration. If, by some strange behavior of the electorate, a Communist candidate should be elected to public office in the United States, he will be required by the Communist Party to engage in its conspiratorial work while in the pay of American citizens. The Party will expect such a Communist *not to* behave like an ordinary office-holder within the framework of American bourgeois democracy, but like a conspirator within the framework of Communist Party discipline. The American people in each of the forty-eight States must shortly come to grips with the question of whether or not such an organization as the Communist Party is to be permitted to place candidates on the ballot. The "line" laid down by Dimitroff as the authoritative spokesman for the Communist Party of the United States is ample justification for denying the Party a place on our bourgeois ballot.

From the very beginning, the Communist Party has been a conspiratorial organization. Lenin made this clear when he described the Communist Party as "a small kernel consisting of reliable, experienced and steeled workers with responsible agents in the chief districts and connected by all the rules of strict conspiracy."

Some years ago, when the Communist Party was much younger in this country, it published a volume entitled *Lenin on Organization*. The book bears the imprint of the Daily Worker Publishing Company and the date 1926. It appeared as volume 1 of the Lenin Library. It is not necessary to dwell upon the absolutely authoritative character of Lenin's writings for all Communists. They are the first to assert their unquestioning acceptance of his teachings. In this book, Lenin used the words "conspiracy" and "conspiratorial" in connection with Communist organization more than a score of times.

Let us look at what Lenin had to say about the nature of an "organization of revolutionaries," or a Communist party as it was set forth in his book published by the American Communists.

"Such an organization," wrote Lenin, "must of necessity be not too extensive and as conspiratorial as possible." Naturally, a conspiracy must restrict its membership drastically. That is why Lenin remarked that a Communist

Party "must of necessity be not too extensive." On this important point, a conspiracy and a political party are opposite in nature. A political party aims to enlist in its membership a majority of the voting population. A conspiracy aims to enlist a small, highly disciplined, and trained minority of malcontents. In the parlance of the Communists, this small minority has commonly been described as "the vanguard of the proletariat."

Something of the amazing breadth and complexity of the Communist conspiracy is indicated in Lenin's volume which we have under consideration. He wrote: "All the other groups serving the movement should be organized—the university students and high school students groups, the groups, let us say, for assisting government officials, transport groups, printing groups, passport groups, groups for arranging conspiratorial meeting places, groups for tracking spies, military groups, groups for procuring arms, organization groups, such as for running income producing enterprises, etc. The whole art of conspiratorial organization consists in making use of everything and everybody and finding work for everybody."

For conspiratorial work, the alien is as good as the citizen. By the admission of its own leader, Earl Browder, the Communist Party admits aliens to membership. Obviously, the alien is not eligible to vote and cannot, therefore, belong to a political party as we ordinarily understand the words. The only country to which the members of the Communist Party owe any real allegiance is the Soviet Union, and for the purposes of that allegiance it does not matter whether a person is a citizen of the United States or not.

Furthermore, from the very beginning of its existence, the Communist Party of the United States has placed aliens on its highest governing body, the central committee. These

A TROJAN HORSE ON THE BALLOT 261

aliens on the central committee of the Communist Party have usually been representatives of the Communist International who have been vested with powers of veto over any and all acts of the American Party.

One such alien, a representative of the Communist International on the Central Committee of the American Communist Party, was John Pepper, alias Pogany, alias Schwartz. Eventually, Stalin became displeased with Pepper and his work in the United States, and the Communist International demanded the return of its representative. When Max Bedacht was editor of the Party's publication, the *Communist*, he published an article in which it was stated that the American Communist Party had received its "ideologic education" at the hands of Pepper.

We find, therefore, that the Communist Party admits aliens to membership, places aliens on its highest governing body, and once at least received its ideologic education at the hands of an alien. To maintain, in the face of these facts, that the Communist organization is a bona fide political party is impossible.

The Communist Party is further marked as a conspiracy by its members' use of aliases. It is the rule rather than the exception that a member takes a Party name which is different from his real name. On numerous membership books which are in the possession of the Special Committee on Un-American Activities, the letters "p. n." appear after the name of the owner of the book. The letters are initials for "party name." On transfer cards which are also in the possession of the Committee, two names often appear, one followed by the letters "p. n." and the other followed by the letters "r. n." (meaning "real name"). It is a conspiratorial organization and not a political party which practices that type of secrecy.

While the outstanding leaders and even lesser functionaries of the Party usually hold their membership openly, the great majority of the members deny their connection with the Party, whenever they consider it expedient to do so. Such secret membership is the rule rather than the exception. If the Party were a bona fide political party, there would be no point in such secrecy.

For many years, the *Party Organizer* was the official magazine of the Communist Party dealing with tactical questions. In the *Party Organizer* for May, 1937, there was an article which read, in part, as follows: "The district and section should pay attention to the wish of many professionals to stay under cover. That has been done here, and the result is that a lot of good work has been done in places we should not otherwise have reached." These professionals who "stay under cover"—doctors, lawyers, professors, and government officials—are the mainstay of the Communist Party in its conspiratorial penetration of so-called middle class organizations. The article from which we have just quoted observed that "it is easy and important to win key positions in the middle class organizations. We can find many individuals there to follow us, and even win the whole group for the People's Front, for Spain, against war and Fascism." In other words, the Communist Party admitted precisely what has so often been charged against it: that secret members carry out its "line" in numerous organizations. Each such secret member is a Trojan Horse all by himself.

The complete story of one such secret member has now been told in the official Communist Party newspaper, the *Daily Worker*. It is the story of Norman Bethune, now deceased. When he was alive, Dr. Bethune vigorously denied his membership in the Communist Party, but all the while he had an agreement with Earl Browder personally that Browder was to make public his membership in the Party in the event of Dr. Bethune's death. Dr. Bethune was a member of the editorial board of the Communist Party's magazine, *Health & Hygiene*. He went to Spain under the auspices of the Medical Bureau of the North American Committee to Aid Spanish Democracy. When he returned from Spain, Browder sent him to China. In the *Daily Worker* for June 11, 1940, Browder told the story of Bethune's mission to China, as follows: "When Dr. Bethune, at my proposal, immediately and unhesitatingly agreed to go to China . . . he knew that the chances of his coming back were very small, and he said: 'I accept on one condition, that if I don't come back, you will let the world know that Norman Bethune died a Communist Party member.'"

Even though Browder now says that he sent Dr. Bethune to China, we read in the *Daily Worker* for March 21, 1938, that Dr. Bethune was "sent to China by the American League for Peace and Democracy." The China Aid Council was a subsidiary of the American League for Peace and Democracy, according to the letterhead of the two organizations. The true situation set forth in these admissions by Browder was that the general secretary of the Communist Party (Browder himself) was running things behind the scene, commissioning a Party member to go to China, while the American League was simply the public front for Browder's activities. Many innocent persons were hoodwinked into supporting these Communist Party activities by the lie that they were maintained by independent, progressive organizations. In the very same issue of the *Daily Worker* from which we have quoted, it was announced that Mrs. Franklin D. Roosevelt had made a financial contribution to the China Aid Council of the American League for Peace and Democracy, for the support of Dr. Bethune in China, and that her donation had been forwarded through the Motion Picture Artists Committee. Here we have a graphic illustration of the interworkings of the Communist Party, the China Aid Council, and the Motion Picture Artists Committee. The systematic falsehood which pervades the whole aggregation of Communist Trojan Horses is the mark of a conspiratorial organization and not of a political party.

In a multitude of instances which could be cited, professionals who do the work of the Communist Party employ aliases to cover up their Party activities. A few examples will illustrate this secretive technique. Arthur Kallet, head of Consumers Union, was editor of the Party's magazine, *Health & Hygiene*, under the name of "Edward Adams." Sol Auerbach, one-time college professor, has written numerous volumes for the Party, under the name of "James S. Allen." Dale Zysman, teacher in the public schools of New York, has written books for the Party under the name of "Jack Hardy." Bernhard J. Stern, Columbia University professor, has written and taught for the Party under the name of "Bennett Stevens." Herbert Rosen, member of the staff of the newspaper PM, was editor of the *Communist* under the name of "David Ramsey." This list could be extended to the proportions of an entire chapter. These examples are sufficient, however, to make clear the point that the Communist Party does not operate out in the open.

Elsewhere in this volume, we have discussed the Party's use of the secret "fraction" for the control of organizations, the fact that it is careful to destroy records, the fact that it relies ultimately on violence and not on the ballot, the fact of its treasonable aims with respect to the United States, and the fact of its complete subservience to a foreign government. All of this evidence, with much more that could be adduced, goes to show that a Trojan Horse, whose outstanding characteristic is fraud, is permitted a place on one of the sacred institutions of American democracy, the ballot.

CHAPTER XXI

A RAILROAD MECHANIC BECOMES AN INTERNATIONAL SPY

How many members of the Communist Party in the United States have been recruited for the spy work of the Soviet Military Intelligence, there is no way of our knowing. All of the former Communist leaders who have testified before the Special Committee on Un-American Activities have declared that there is a close working relationship between the Communist Party and Stalin's vast international spy ring.

The former head of the Soviet Military Intelligence for Western Europe, General Walter G. Krivitsky, stated that he personally had known immediate members of Earl Browder's family who were engaged in Communist espionage.

Former Communist friends of Juliet Stuart Poyntz have testified that she was recruited from her leading position as one of the outstanding Communist Party women into the service of the Soviet Military Intelligence. Under circumstances that were highly mysterious, Miss Poyntz disappeared not long ago without leaving a trace of what happened to her. Communist Party leaders created a justifiable suspicion that they knew more about what happened to Juliet Stuart Poyntz than they were willing to tell. From our established knowledge of what Stalin does to his spies when he is through with them, we may safely assume that the lips of this American woman have been sealed forever. Witnesses have testified that she knew too much, and that she was on the point of breaking with her Russian master.

A RAILROAD MECHANIC BECOMES A SPY 267

We know and have already observed that the Communist Party has always been a reservoir from which Stalin has drawn his Soviet Military Intelligence agents whenever he has required them for his system of espionage. But it is also true that the Communist auxiliary organizations have been utilized as reservoirs for Stalin's espionage work. We have from his own lips the story of at least one of the former agents of the Soviet Military Intelligence who started his journey downward into Stalin's espionage by working in consumers' co-operatives and among the unemployed. But that is a story of the direst tragedy which will have to be told elsewhere. Suffice it to say, the young man, who for the present must remain nameless, was a graduate of one of our best American universities, and before he left the international ring of Stalin's spies, he had served three full years in solitary confinement in a dungeon far removed from his American homeland.

We know a great deal, however, with respect to at least one of Stalin's Military Intelligence agents who was recruited in this country. His name is Nicholas Dozenberg.

Nicholas Dozenberg might have lived and died a successful railroad machinist. Migrating from his native Russia to the United States as a young man, he found his adopted land one of opportunity. He never knew what it was to be unemployed. He worked his way steadily to a position as mechanic on the New York, New Haven & Hartford railway. He had no complaint concerning his hours, wages, or working conditions. For fourteen years he lived the machinist's life, and but for one thing, his life story would have been a story told a million times over of men who left the restrictions of Europe behind them and found opportunity in the New World.

But Nicholas Dozenberg fell in with the Communists.

Just why he chose to cast his lot with the Stalin-controlled conspiratorial group of revolutionists, is not altogether clear. At least it was not because he was the victim of prolonged unemployment, depression, or any other dire state of underprivilege. At any rate, he joined the Communists, and became an important functionary in the elaborate organization which Browder heads in the United States. He was, indeed, a charter member of the Communist Party. He was successively the business manager of the *Voice of Labor* and of the *Daily Worker*. During his residence as a Communist functionary in Chicago, he was accused of major responsibility for the Herrin massacre in which two score men lost their lives during the early twenties when the Illinois mine fields were ablaze with class conflict. An official account of the labor troubles of that period, published by the United Mine Workers of America under the leadership of John L. Lewis, names Nicholas Dozenberg as the Communist leader who incited the massacre.

Dozenberg's life as a Communist functionary was not different from that of thousands of others until he met one Alfred Tiltin in 1928. Tiltin and his wife, Marie, came to the United States as spies for the Fourth Division of the Red Army, sometimes known as the Soviet Military Intelligence. The couple recruited Dozenberg for espionage work.

Among the first instructions which Dozenberg received from Tiltin was an order to apply for an American passport under a false name. This Dozenberg did, and, for using the fraudulent passport issued in the name of Nicholas Dallant, Dozenberg is today serving a sentence in one of our federal penitentiaries.

During the eleven years of his operations as a Soviet spy, Dozenberg was assigned to work in many parts of the world, beginning and ending with assignments in the United States. His final apprehension and conviction were due largely to the attention focused upon him by two of the witnesses who appeared before the Special Committee on Un-American Activities. Both of these witnesses testified concerning Dozenberg's connection with Stalin's counterfeiting of American currency. These witnesses were Krivitsky and Benjamin Gitlow, the latter having been a former secretary of the Communist Party. Both men had knowledge of the counterfeiting in Moscow of millions of dollars worth of American bills.

Benjamin Gitlow related to the Special Committee on Un-American Activities the story of Stalin's counterfeit ring. He told of the part which Dr. Valentine Burtan had played in the business. Dr. Burtan is now serving a long prison term in the same institution where Dozenberg is incarcerated.

Dozenberg and Burtan were close personal friends. It was during one of their meetings that Dr. Burtan introduced Dozenberg to the woman who became his wife. Later, when Dr. Burtan was arrested in connection with the counterfeiting case, one of the first persons he met, on being released in bail, was Nicholas Dozenberg. They met in a New York restaurant, and immediately thereafter Dozenberg decided to get out of the United States. Dozenberg has stated that it was only after the arrest of Dr. Burtan that he was apprised of the fact that his own espionage operations were to have been financed with the proceeds from the counterfeited American bills.

Whatever the facts may be concerning Dozenberg's connection with Stalin's counterfeiting ring, there is no question about other activities in which he engaged during his eleven-year service in the Fourth Division of the Red Army. It has been only a few weeks since Stalin's Red Army marched into and took possession of a large part of Rumania. The plans for Stalin's extension of his imperialist rule westward into Carol's kingdom were associated with one of the first duties assigned to Nicholas Dozenberg as far back as 1932. He was instructed to set up for himself a respectable business front as an American agent for moving picture camera equipment in Rumania. To this end, he obtained an agent's contracts with one of the largest and most respectable firms producing moving picture camera equipment in the United States. In obtaining these business credentials, Dozenberg was able to use the names of highly placed American officials, including at least one United States senator.

Dozenberg's assignment in Rumania included the photographing of the country's fortifications. His success in carrying out this task bordered on the phenomenal. If we did not possess the complete documentary evidence showing the nature and extent of his Rumanian operations, it would be impossible to believe that a mere railroad mechanic could have hoodwinked so many leading government officials.

As a cover-up for his espionage work in Rumania, Dozenberg organized the American-Rumanian Export Corporation which was to be engaged, ostensibly, in the film and camera equipment business. He actually succeeded in persuading one of the highest government officials in Rumania —the head of the country's secret police, indeed—to make an investment of $15,000 in this espionage-shielding concern. He obtained a contract with the Rumanian government which gave him an absolutely free hand to operate without any serious danger of detection. Before he had completed his task of photographing Rumania's fortifications, Dozenberg had made King Carol himself the prize dupe of his espionage work. Dozenberg obtained the royal airplane from the King and then used it to make aerial photographs of the country's defenses. These photographs were then transmitted to Moscow.

After his work in Rumania was completed, Dozenberg was assigned to work in China, the Philippine Islands, and the United States. The details of his activities in these countries would fill volumes. No fictional stories of international spies ever surpassed the true story of Dozenberg who spent more than a decade as one of Stalin's most successful agents in many parts of the world.

The one fact about Dozenberg which stands out as the most significant aspect of his entire career is the proof which it provides of the complete integration between Stalin's political Trojan Horse, the Communist Party of the United States, and Stalin's espionage Trojan Horse, the Fourth Division of the Red Army. Every member of the Communist Party of the United States is a *potential* member of the Military Intelligence Service of Moscow. The Party, we must reiterate, is a reservoir from which hundreds of Russia's espionage agents have actually been drawn. Dozenberg entered Stalin's spy work with the full knowledge of the leaders of the Communist Party of the United States. It was even necessary for Dozenberg to obtain the full approval of these Party leaders before he could be transferred from one branch of Stalin's service (the political branch) to another branch of that service (the military intelligence branch).

It is almost incredible that our country has gone along for these twenty years tolerating the presence and activity of an organized group which aims at the complete destruction of our American government and economic system. Surely the time has passed when intelligent people will be moved by the argument that democracy and the Bill of Rights compel us to give an espionage agency a free hand to work for the wiping out of our democracy and the Bill of Rights.

It is even more incredible that, after the full exposure of the true nature of the Communist Party, the Special Committee on Un-American Activities should be under the unpleasant necessity of calling attention to the fact that Communists and their fellow travelers are continuing to hold important positions in the federal government. Some have recently been appointed to positions with the President's National Defense Commission. We cannot make it too clear that men or women who have for any reason whatsoever lent their names and prestige to Stalin's subversive work in this country are not men whose good judgment may be trusted to plan the defense of the United States in a time when national defense means first of all an adequate defense against the Trojan Horse tactics of Stalin, Hitler, and Mussolini.

The time has come to make an end of all pussyfooting with treason, and to assert a bold Americanism which has a brain as well as a generous heart.

CHAPTER XXII

A LITTLE MAN AND A BIG BATTLESHIP

In the attainment of his objective of a world-embracing totalitarian empire, Joseph Stalin has displayed great versatility of tactics. We have seen how he employs a far-flung organization of espionage as well as agencies that operate openly—even if with camouflaged purposes. He directs an international spy ring with one hand and a local legislative lobby for cheaper milk with the other hand, thus indicating a range of activity that has omitted little. He bores from within Christian churches through agents who profess devotion to the teachings of Jesus and at the same time maintains an organization which promulgates atheism, showing that it is the end only and not the integrity of the means which determines the character of Stalin's enterprises. He operates within the strict limits of legality when that aids his cause and at the same time pursues almost every known type of illegality when that seems to promise desired results, proving that he has a program which is subtle, elaborate, and, above all, thoroughly unscrupulous in reaching its end. When Stalin wants a large following of gullible sympathizers, his agents will picture babies crying for milk; when he wants munitions or battleships, they will resort to old-fashioned nepotism, political wire-pulling, and just plain scratching of itching palms.

Let us consider how Stalin's campaign is conducted when his agents are instructed to build up his armaments, remembering that it is the same fixed and unalterable goal which is being pursued even though the methods differ strikingly from those which we have examined up to this point. We present the story, fantastic as some of its aspects may appear, just as it was unfolded in testimony before the Special Committee on Un-American Activities.

Sam Carp was a little business man who had worked himself up to the first rung of the success ladder when he was operating a gasoline filling station in Bridgeport, Connecticut. His business capital was small but his family connections were big.

When Carp came to the United States thirty years ago, he left behind him in his native Russia a sister. Fortune or fate (a thin line divides the two in Stalin's realm) made his sister the wife of the Prime Minister of the Soviet Union. So Sam Carp became the brother-in-law of Vyacheslaff Molotov, right-hand man of Joseph Stalin.

We may assume that Carp, who had climbed from the position of a day laborer to that of filling station operator, wanted, after the lapse of a quarter of a century, to return to Russia to see his sister who had scaled such impressive heights in the workers' paradise. At any rate, Carp went back to Russia in 1934, "trying," as he said, "to get business to make a dollar."

Carp was unsuccessful in trying "to make a dollar" by his visit to the Soviet Union in 1934, but in 1936 a second visit was crowned with overwhelming success. What happened then and subsequently shows what it means to know the "right people" in a socialist society. The little business man from Bridgeport came back to the United States, his pockets bulging with money—cash—and an authorization to spend the fabulous sum of $200,000,000. He had orders to purchase armaments for Russia. In addition to several hundred thousand dollars which were given Carp in American currency in Moscow, a similar sum was drawn by him from Amtorg, the Russian Trading agency in the United States.

Rosengoltz, who later faced one of Stalin's firing squads, was the Soviet official who commissioned Carp to purchase war materials in the United States and also gave him the American currency with which to operate his purchasing enterprise. Carp had not been acquainted previously with Rosengoltz whom he described as "the purchasing agent of the whole Russian government." But he did know Molotov, and Molotov knew Rosengoltz, of course. The delightful simplicity of the transaction—as Carp understood it or as he told the Special Committee on Un-American Activities he understood it—was, to use Carp's words:

> Just simply called on him (Rosengoltz) and told him that I wanted to do some purchasing. I wanted to do some purchasing for Russia.

The principal item which Carp was instructed to purchase was a battleship—"the biggest battleship in the world." It appears from the record that Carp's sole qualification for this impressive commission was the fact that he had a sister —a sister who was the wife of Vyacheslaff Molotov who was, in turn, the right-hand man of Joseph Stalin. Outside of fiction and the world's first socialist state, it is not probable that such a story could be written. Again and again when Carp was on the stand as a witness before the Special Committee on Un-American Activities, he explained with modesty: "I didn't know anything." Nevertheless, along with his complete ignorance of battleships, Carp had his assignment to aid in the arming of the Soviet Union, and to carry out this assignment he had the authorization to dispose of $200,000,000 of Stalin's gold. Marxist theoreticians and Soviet propagandists have written volumes on the inefficiency, nepotism, and graft of the bourgeois state. They have argued learnedly to the effect that the Marxist state would change all that and put their socialist Utopia on a strict efficiency basis with a pure and profitless devotion to the working class. The case of Sam Carp, armaments agent of Stalin, may help to explain how little Finland stood off the Red Army so long.

Obviously Sam Carp did not know anything about battleships, but he had some knowledge of human nature. He knew how to "grease" a political machine as well as he knew how to grease a filling station pump.

In addition to knowing something about human nature, Carp also knew some of the "right people" here in the United States. He made it his business—with the help of Stalin's money—to get acquainted with the "right people" whom he did not yet know when he set out to buy the biggest battleship in the world. To begin with, Carp knew Aaron Benenson, assistant district attorney under Thomas E. Dewey in New York. Benenson, in turn, knew Joseph Zionson Dalinda, and proceeded to introduce him to Carp. (Benenson was later rewarded with the sum of $600 by Dalinda for his favor in introducing him to Carp. A sizable portion of Stalin's money, as it will appear later, was spent for such introductions.)

Joseph Zionson Dalinda was only one of the parade of colorful figures who entered the life of Sam Carp after he had his good luck while visiting his sister in Moscow. Dalinda was a suave cosmopolitan salesman who had been many places and learned to know many people since he quit his native Russia. He had known Rasputin, the "mad Monk" of Russia. He had had at least a passing personal acquaintance with President Harding, and back in 1916, Dalinda had been in Venezuela where he had met the United States Minister, Preston McGoodwin.

Eleven years later McGoodwin was working for the Democratic National Committee as assistant to Charles Michelson. Dalinda told Carp that he should meet McGoodwin if he wanted help "in getting the necessary permits" to buy his battleship for Stalin. The introduction was arranged in due time, and without Carp's knowing about it Dalinda arranged with McGoodwin to get a cut of McGoodwin's fee for introducing him to Carp. McGoodwin's fee was $25,000, of which $12,500 went eventually to Dalinda.

It is not clear from the record what services Preston McGoodwin performed in return for the $25,000 of this Stalin-Carp bounty, other than to extend the string of introductions. At least, McGoodwin suggested that Scott Ferris, National Democratic Committeeman and former member of Congress, should meet Sam Carp. Accordingly, Carp, Dalinda, McGoodwin, and Ferris met in a Washington hotel. As a result of their conference, Ferris was employed. When asked for what purpose Ferris was employed, Dalinda testified before the Special Committee on Un-American Activities, as follows: "If you want to know what you have to have, it was pull by anybody with influence here, a man who knows the people and knows somebody personally and calls him by his first name." Dalinda had been much more explicit about the employment of Mr. Ferris in a memorandum which he wrote to Carp at the time. "Scott Ferris is the national committeeman from Oklahoma," Dalinda explained in his memorandum, and he was qualified for the job in hand "because he was in Congress together with Hull for 14 years, and is a close friend of his for 30 years, also because he is exceptionally close to the President, all of which Carp and Wolf were well aware." (Wolf was a New York business associate of Carp.)

Carp gave Ferris $5,000 on the spot, as a retainer. Subsequently, Carp paid Ferris at least $25,000 more. What happened to that sum of money is described in the following questions and answer during Dalinda's testimony before the Special Committee on Un-American Activities:

Mr. Whitley: And the agreement which you had—you and Mr. Ferris and Mr. McGoodwin—was that any fees aside from that initial $5,000, any further fees received by Mr. Ferris from Carp would be divided three ways?
Mr. Dalinda: Yes.
Mr. Whitley: That was a definite agreement?
Mr. Dalinda: Yes.
Mr. Whitley: Did Mr. Carp know anything about this arrangement that you and Mr. Ferris and Mr. McGoodwin had among yourselves to split the fee?
Mr. Dalinda: No. He was not supposed to know.

In order to send munitions and other implements of war to the Soviet Union, it was necessary for Carp to obtain "export permits" from the munitions control board of the Department of State. Hence all the business of getting introductions to the right people. Hence all the fanfare of "pull" and fee-splitting. In the end Carp, however, did not get his "battleship." What happened to it is a long story.

There was much reluctance among the large shipbuilding concerns to undertake the construction of so large a warship. The shipbuilders wanted assurances that the State Department was prepared to issue the necessary permits. They needed prodding before they would consider seriously the construction of the biggest battleship in the world. In this situation, pressures, introductions, influence, and fee-splitting were called into play.

A LITTLE MAN AND A BIG BATTLESHIP

Dalinda wrote to Chase Mellen, Jr., as follows:

> Mr. Sam Carp is a brother-in-law of Mr. Molotov, the Prime Minister of Russia, and due to this relation and personal friendship with Stalin, Mr. Carp was charged by the Soviet Government to place certain orders in the United States, primarily of a military nature.

In the remainder of the letter, it appears that Dalinda wanted Chase Mellen, Jr., to use his good offices with one of the large shipbuilding concerns. Mr. Mellen had both political and banking connections that were important.

When it appeared that Carp's big battleship was not materializing, Scott Ferris became impatient and wrote the following note to Dalinda:

> I submit 11 months have passed with $200,000,000 on deposit to pay for the necessities that Russia requires—with a company fully authorized to apply for, pay for, contract for, and export such supplies. I submit with shipbuilders and ways on every hand anxious for the business, that surely two great countries like the United States and Russia, at peace with each other—with harmonious relations existing between them—with each country anxious to do its full duty—this commercial undertaking deserves to be solved.

Eventually naval architects in the United States provided Sam Carp with plans for his proposed battleship. These plans were the subject of much correspondence between the members of Carp's business circle. On November 19, 1937, Dalinda wrote to McGoodwin as follows:

> My own personal thought is that the President and Secretary Hull will be entirely within their rights in standing very erect in helping Russia to secure the arms and munitions they desire. My own personal notion is, frail as it may be, that they can well afford to stand out and take an important part in seeing

this is done. With Russia one of the greatest countries in the world, and surely one of the largest ones, and right over in the very crotch of our enemies, Italy, Japan, and Germany, surely we should do what we could—first, to maintain their friendship—second, to make them able to sustain themselves and ward off the blows of these three enemy nations.

It is apparent from the foregoing letter that international politics as well as business entered into this whole battleship matter.

On March 16, 1938, Scott Ferris wrote to Dalinda as follows:

I repeat, I am so anxious to be helpful to you, Mr. Carp, and Mr. Wolf, in every way I know. I am perfectly sure that, from the President down, they will all be glad to cooperate and help any way they can within the laws and rules and regulations. I have no way on earth of making these shipbuilders bid—no way of making these architects prepare plans and submit them. I am perfectly sure our good Government headed by President Roosevelt—Secretary Hull—Admiral Leahy and the Board, have no way and do not have the right under the law to do more than give their approval and cooperation and their helping hand insofar as they can do it within the law.

It would seem, from the correspondence in the case, that Carp was able to bring his enterprise to the attention of the highest personages in Washington. One aspect of this whole Carp story can be understood only in the light of the Russian sympathy which prevailed for several years in high administrative circles in Washington, a period during which the Russian embassy gave government and labor officials—notably Edwin S. Smith of the National Labor Relations Board and John L. Lewis of the C.I.O.—the best champagne dinners in town.

According to one of Dalinda's memoranda, Carp's battleship was discussed at Cabinet meetings. Under date of March 21, 1939, Dalinda wrote:

> However, all that has nothing to do with the business itself, and here is only one thing to be stated—all that was contracted to be performed, was actually performed when his matter was discussed at a few Cabinet meetings, and decision taken to accommodate the Russians. At this very moment, all that was humanly possible to do in this connection under a democratic form of government, was done, as Secretary Hull told you. When the President saw Gibbs with the plans and sent word "down the line"—as Wolf claimed it was necessary, that was, as a matter of fact, unnecessary, because a decision at the Cabinet meeting, was after all, all that is required.

Whether or not the President saw Carp's battleship plans and discussed them at meetings of the Cabinet, we have only the various memoranda to indicate. A matter of greater moment was the fact that the plans for the battleship were sent to Moscow for approval or rejection. The naval architects considered the matter of such importance that they consented to the transmission of the plans to Moscow only on condition that a naval captain accompany them. Despite this precaution, it is clear that the Soviet Government had ample opportunity, during the ten days that the plans were in Moscow, to make photostatic reproductions of them.

In the light of events of the past year, during which time Stalin has shattered the illusions of the more naive of his former sympathizers in Washington, it is necessary to account for the cordiality which existed between Soviet officials and members of the administration in Washington. One of the outstanding facts of our national life during the years 1936 to 1939 was the degree to which members of the Communist Party and their fellow travelers wielded their influence in Washington. The situation in Washington was a close approximation to the People's Front of France. Communists and their sympathizers operated openly, and brought about a situation in which Carp and his battleship found an extraordinary welcome in official circles.

So little did some Washington officials understand the dictatorship of Stalin, and so sympathetic were others to the Soviet regime, that there was a disposition to put Russia's armaments program ahead of the armaments defense needs of the United States. Scott Ferris, national Democratic committeeman, wrote to Dalinda, under date of January 10, 1939, as follows:

If Carp loses his battleship, which I hope he does not, it will be by reason of the blunders of Mr. Gibbs, although I suppose it would be lese majesty to suggest that in the presence of Mr. Carp or Mr. Wolf who are so thoroughly and completely sold on Mr. Gibbs. From what I gather in the papers and through other sources, I am afraid our much talked of battleship is going to be crowded out for want of facilities to build it. In other words, I think our own country is going to utilize all the shipbuilding facilities that are available and make it very difficult to get a company to build our ship. That has been more or less the trouble all the time. Of course, however, Russia's willingness to pay a large sum for the construction of a battleship might induce some of the shipbuilders to squeeze this ship in notwithstanding the demands of the United States to the contrary.

The case of Carp and his battleship was one of the most revealing things which the Special Committee on Un-American Activities exposed. Its ramifications were wide. It involved small men and great. Dictators, presidents, prime ministers, admirals, ambassadors, cabinet members, and lesser figures contributed their part to writing the story of the little man and the big battleship. One of the leading figures in Sam Carp's battleship transaction was convinced that the whole affair of Molotov and his American brother-in-law was a piece of sinister Soviet intrigue whose sequel is yet to be written. His opinion, incorporated in a memorandum, includes a prognostication so startling that it belongs in this story, as illustrative of the Russian Communist mind, even if it is not destined to become historical fact. The memorandum speaks for itself:

March 20th, 1939

MEMORANDUM

If the State Department has agreed, after such a prolonged examination and consideration, to grant the permit for a 55,000 ton ship, it was a foregone conclusion that it automatically agreed to grant the same kind of permission for anything below 45,000. That is as clear as can be. You can be sure that the Russians realize this, and from this very moment, Rodriguez' "usefulness and imperative necessity" ceased. That does not mean that he was "fired," but it is a normal reaction of Soviet people,—"The Moor finished his business, the Moor can go."

It is imperative to explain a point which may not be understood unless one is familiar with the "ways and means" in which Stalin keeps himself on top. Out of the 123 members of the Central Committee under Lenin,—only two are alive in Russia, *i.e.*, Stalin and Kalinin, the latter being the figurehead President. Others, with the exception of 17 men—who died natural deaths—were shot, and Trotsky—alive in Mexico. You have seen the clipping about the number of Army and Navy people, the very heads of both of these services, who were shot. Stalin always keeps "something" in reserve to spring at the next victim, and to "liquidate" one or the other, as he has done up to now with everyone, including his classmates or such faithful dogs like Bluecher, until recently the head of the Far East Army. At present his right-hand man is Molotov, officially the Prime Minister of Russia. Rodriguez is the brother-in-law of

Molotov. Rodriguez received a commission from Molotov to help build the Russian Navy. Rodriguez does it in consideration for substantial remuneration of 5 per cent of cost. You, no doubt, appreciate that this figure is most exorbitant for such a service. But it is not expensive for Stalin, because at one time or the other, when it will suit him, he will "find out" that Molotov and his wife, (the sister of Rodriguez) got part of this commission. How could Molotov and Rodriguez' sister prove that they didn't get it? They never will be able to.

Those versed in the Russian "art" are as sure on this point as it is possible to be.

CHAPTER XXIII

THE TROJAN HORSE IN GOVERNMENT

STALIN baited his hook with a "progressive" worm, and New Deal suckers swallowed bait, hook, line, and sinker.

Probably, never again in the annals of American government will such a story be recorded. Faithfulness to the facts, to say nothing of loyalty to Americanism, compels the telling of that story of subversive influences entering our federal government, or at least such parts of the story as space permits.

Seven years ago, in a letter dated November 16, 1933, Maxim Litvinoff, Soviet Commissar for Foreign Affairs, addressed the President of the United States with a solemn assurance "to respect scrupulously the indisputable right of the United States to order its own life within its own jurisdiction in its own way and to refrain from interfering in any manner in the internal affairs of the United States, its territories or possessions," and further, on behalf of the government of the Soviet Union "to refrain, and to restrain all persons in government service and all organizations of the Government or under its direct or indirect control, including organizations in receipt of any financial assistance from it, from any act overt or covert liable in any way whatsoever to injure the tranquillity, prosperity, order or security of the whole or any part of the United States, its territories or possessions," and further "not to permit the formation or residence on its territory of any organization or group—and to prevent the activity on its territory of any organization or group, of representatives or officials of any organization or group—which has as an aim the overthrow or the preparation for the overthrow of, or the bringing about by force of a change in, the political or social order of the whole or any part of the United States, its territories or possessions."

The duplicity with which Litvinoff entered into this agreement may be judged from his gleeful account of the negotiations as he gave it to his associates, D. H. Dubrowsky, former head of the Russian Red Cross, Boris Skvirsky, attaché of the Soviet Embassy, and Peter A. Bogdanov, chairman of the board of directors of the Amtorg Trading Corporation. When Litvinoff met these men only a few minutes after the conclusion of negotiations for the recognition of the Soviet Government by the Government of the United States, he entered, all smiles, with the remark, "Well, it's all in the bag." He rubbed his hands with satisfaction, as he added: "They wanted us to recognize the debts we owed them and I promised we were going to negotiate. But they did not know we were going to negotiate until doomsday." Litvinoff continued, sarcastically: "The next one was a corker; they wanted us to give them freedom of religion in Russia. And I gave it to them. I was very much prompted to offer that I would collect all the Bibles and ship them out to them."

When Dubrowsky testified before the Special Committee on Un-American Activities, he explained: "You see, the general motive is that any promise given to a bourgeois state is not worth the paper it is written on."

Subsequent developments have confirmed Dubrowsky's observation and demonstrated the naïveté of the New Deal suckers who dealt with Stalin's emissary. They had yet to

THE TROJAN HORSE IN GOVERNMENT 287

learn that broken pledges litter the path of Europe's totalitarian dictators.

Since 1933, when Litvinoff gave his assurances, the Communist Party of the United States, an affiliate of the Communist International operating with headquarters in Moscow as a subsidiary of the Soviet Government, has spread its tentacles throughout the length and breadth of the land, penetrating the labor unions in key industries vital to national defense, building Trojan Horses of every description, and even reaching into the federal government itself.

The strangest aspect of Litvinoff's broken pledge is the total absence of resentment on the part of those New Dealers who were hoodwinked by it. Not only has there been no visible resentment, there has actually been a disposition to offer encouragement to the agents of Stalin who scoff at promises given to bourgeois governments.

The very organizations which Litvinoff promised to restrain from operating on American soil have been supported by the prestige of government officials high in Administration circles. The leaders and representatives of these organizations have found the White House doors thrown open to them. Let us look at the facts.

On June 16, 1938, there was a scene at the White House which should have a humiliating effect on all Americans, and particularly on those who were responsible for it. The scene was photographed, and then reproduced in the *New Order*, official organ of the International Workers Order. The photograph shows Secretary Marvin H. McIntyre surrounded by five Communists, most of them admittedly members of the Party. On McIntyre's left stands Welwel Warzower, alias William Weiner, president of the International Workers Order. At the very time the picture was taken, Warzower was financial secretary of the Communist Party of the United States—a fact about which there was no secret. He was, in addition to his treasurership of the Party, a member of its highest governing body, the central committee. Warzower has since been convicted for fraudulently representing himself as an American citizen, and faces a penitentiary sentence. On McIntyre's right stands Max Bedacht, general secretary of the International Workers Order. At the time the picture was taken, Bedacht was also a member of the central committee of the Communist Party—a fact about which there was no secret. Formerly, Bedacht was secretary of the Communist Party of the United States and editor of its theoretical magazine, the *Communist*. On left and right of McIntyre, stand three other officers of the International Workers Order, Peter Shipka, John Middleton, and Joseph Brodsky—all prominent in the affairs of the Communist Party for many years. The occasion of the presence of these Communists in the White House was a presentation from the International Workers Order of a portrait of the President. In an earlier chapter, we have seen how completely Communist controlled is the organization headed by Warzower and Bedacht.

Some months later, in December, 1938, there was another scene at the White House in which Secretary Marvin H. McIntyre also presided over a group of smiling visitors. On that occasion, there was a delegation from the Federation of Architects, Engineers, Chemists and Technicians. The scene was photographed and reproduced in the *C.I.O. News* for December 26, 1938. The delegation went to the White House to present the President of the United States with "a drafting board, T-square and honorary membership in the union as a 'great social architect.'" In the

THE TROJAN HORSE IN GOVERNMENT 289

center of the picture, stands Marcel Scherer who had just been elected vice-president of the Federation of Architects, Engineers, Chemists and Technicians. Scherer has a long record of service in the Communist Party. There is no secret about his Party membership. In 1931, he ran as a candidate for alderman on the Communist Party ticket in New York. In 1930, he was the representative of the Workers International Relief in Southern Illinois, an organization with its main headquarters in Moscow. In the same year, he was active with the National Miners Union in Kentucky, one of the affiliates of the Trade Union Unity League which was headed by William Z. Foster. In 1932, he was national secretary of the Friends of the Soviet Union, a Communist Trojan Horse if there ever was one. In 1935, he was listed as one of the owners of the magazine, *Soviet Russia Today*, one of the Party's chief propaganda organs. In 1938, he was a sponsor of the American Relief Ship for Spain, and in 1940 he was connected with the United American Spanish Aid Committee, both Communist Party Trojan Horses. While he was national secretary of the Friends of the Soviet Union, Scherer wrote an introduction to one of the organization's pamphlets in which he said: "This organization aims to bring home to the American workers a true picture of conditions in the Soviet Union, to establish a closer contact between the American and Russian workers, to promote the recognition of Soviet Russia and the extension of trade between the two countries; to point out to the American workers the necessity of defending the Soviet Union, the Workers' Fatherland; to enforce a 'Hands Off Russia' policy upon the grabbing imperialist powers; and, finally, to counteract the lying statements against the new Russia in the capitalist press, radio and pulpit." It is hardly likely that Scherer ever thought, in his wildest imagination, that he would one day be cordially received at the White House by the Secretary of the President of the United States. From its very beginning, Scherer has been the dominant figure in the Federation of Architects, Engineers, Chemists and Technicians. Another officer of the Federation shown in the picture taken at the White House is Jules Korchien, one-time consulting architect for the Soviet Government in Moscow. Korchien has recently been an employee of the federal government in the Department of the Interior, and even more recently the housing expert for the newspaper *PM*. He was among the 563 government employees who belonged to the American League for Peace and Democracy in Washington, D. C. When that organization folded up as a result of a decision of the Communist Party, Korchien became a member of its sucecssor organization, the Provisional Committee for a Washington Committee for Democratic Rights. He was a member of the executive committee of the Inter-Professional Association for Social Insurance and a sponsor for the National Congress for Unemployment and Social Insurance, both of whose Communist connections have been described in an earlier chapter. Also present in the picture taken at the White House is Lewis Alan Berne, president of the Federation of Architects, Engineers, Chemists and Technicians. Berne has been a sponsor of the American Committee for Democracy and Intellectual Freedom, a sponsor of the American Committee for the Protection of the Foreign Born, a sponsor of the Refugee Scholarship and Peace Campaign, a member of the national labor committee of the American League for Peace and Democracy, and is now on the national council of the American Peace Mobilization, the Communist Party's latest Trojan Horse for fighting conscription and other preparations for national defense. In its unanimous report to Congress, the Special Committee on Un-American Activities found that Communist leadership was entrenched in the Federation of Architects, Engineers, Chemists and Technicians. The organization was not only received at the White House in order to present the President of the United States with an honorary membership, but, what is even more serious, it has units in the navy yards at Boston, Brooklyn, Philadelphia, Portsmouth, Norfolk, Washington, and Pearl Harbor. It also has units in the following plants: Westinghouse Electric, Pittsburgh and Philadelphia; General Electric, Lynn, Massachusetts, and Philadelphia; the Radio Corporation of America; Sperry Gyroscope; Douglas Aircraft; Glenn Martin Aircraft; New York Shipbuilding Corporation; Bethlehem Shipyard, Los Angeles; Bethlehem Steel, Los Angeles; Brill Car Company, Philadelphia; Baldwin Locomotive Works, Philadelphia; American Bridge Company, Pittsburgh; New York City Water Supply; Jones and Laughlin, Pittsburgh; and others too numerous to list, but most of which are equally vital to national defense. With the prestige of a cordial reception at the White House, it is easy to see how these Communists and Communist fellow travelers go out successfully to draw technical men into their organization.

Another picture taken at the White House shows the president of the Workers Alliance leaving a conference with the President of the United States. This picture was made after the Special Committee on Un-American Activities had found unanimously that the Workers Alliance is a Communist Trojan Horse. The erstwhile head of the Alliance has since concurred in that finding, having belatedly broken with the comrades.

The prestige of the White House is immense. If Fritz

Kuhn, William Dudley Pelley, George Deatherage, Joseph E. McWilliams, Robert E. Edmondson, and Edward James Smythe had even been cordially received there, the Nazi-Fascist movement in the United States would have acquired a popular influence in the United States which it will, happily, never possess. On the occasion when the Special Committee on Un-American Activities was examining the leaders of two Communist Trojan Horses, the American Youth Congress and the American Student Union, those same leaders were entertained at the White House.

Both the American Youth Congress and the American Student Union have proudly displayed in their publications letters of greeting which they have received from the President of the United States. Three other Communist Trojan Horses have been the recipients of similar White House greetings, namely, the National Negro Congress, the Workers Alliance, and the American Committee for the Protection of the Foreign Born.

The First Lady of the Land has been one of the most valuable assets which the Trojan Horse organizations of the Communist Party have possessed, due to the immense prestige which her sponsorship has conferred upon them. She has been a speaker for the following organizations: the American Youth Congress, the World Youth Congress, the League of Women Shoppers, the Daughters of the American Depression, the Southern Conference for Human Welfare, the American Communications Association, the Workers Alliance, the National Negro Congress, and the Southern Negro Youth Congress. She has otherwise lent her prestige to the Motion Picture Artists Committee, the China Aid Council of the American League for Peace and Democracy, the United Student Peace Committee, and the American Federation of Teachers, Local No. 5.

Following the lead of the White House, cabinet officers have done their part to add to the influence of some of the Communist Trojan Horses.

The Secretary of the Interior, Harold L. Ickes, has spoken for the National Negro Congress. He endorsed the meeting of the American Committee for the Protection of the Foreign Born, held in Washington in March, 1940. He permitted himself to be made the honorary chairman of the Spanish Refugee Relief Campaign which the Communist Party abandoned when it lost control of the organization by the narrow margin of one vote. He signed the "Call" of the American Youth Congress for its annual gathering in 1939. He contributed to the publication of the International Labor Defense. He wrote for the League of American Writers, and he sponsored the Descendants of the American Revolution.

The Secretary of Agriculture, Henry A. Wallace, endorsed the American Committee for the Protection of the Foreign Born. He was a speaker for the American Committee for Democracy and Intellectual Freedom and for the Consumers Emergency Council; and he has contributed writings to the magazine *Equality* and to the League of American Writers.

The Attorney-General, Robert H. Jackson, sent a telegram of endorsement of a parade of the American League for Peace and Democracy which was led by two hundred Veterans of the Abraham Lincoln Brigade. He has spoken for the Consumers National Federation, and has written for the League of American Writers.

When Frank Murphy was Attorney-General, he endorsed the American Committee for the Protection of the Foreign Born, and sent a letter of greetings to the International Labor Defense.

Right down the line, lesser Washington officials have given their endorsement to the Trojan Horses.

Merle Vincent, Department of Labor, was a speaker, along with Harry Bridges, at the May Day demonstration under the control of the Communist Party in Washington in 1939. He served as chairman of the National Conference on Constitutional Liberties in America, a gathering which was completely controlled by Party members and fellow travelers. He sent his greetings to the International Labor Defense. He sponsored the meeting of the Descendants of the American Revolution, held in Washington this year. He is president of the Washington Committee for Democratic Action, and also president of the Washington chapter of the National Lawyers Guild.

A. A. Berle, Assistant Secretary of State, withdrew from the National Lawyers Guild on the ground that it would not in any way take a position contrary to the Communist Party "line." If Berle was right—and the evidence is conclusive that he was right—what is to be said of the hundred or more New Deal office-holders who have remained in the National Lawyers Guild up to the present time?

Henry T. Hunt, Department of the Interior, was chairman of the meeting of the Descendants of the American Revolution, held in Washington in March of this year. He was honorary chairman of the Lawyers Committee on American Relations with Spain. He is a member of the national committee of the International Juridical Association. He is a sponsor of the Washington Committee for Democratic Action, and for the National Emergency Conference. He is a member of the National Lawyers Guild. In March of this year, he signed a letter protesting the ban on Communists in the American Civil Liberties Union.

Archibald MacLeish, Librarian of Congress, has had one

THE TROJAN HORSE IN GOVERNMENT 295

of the longest records of association with Communist-controlled groups to be found among New Deal appointees. His connections have included the following organizations: the American Friends of Spanish Democracy, the North American Committee to Aid Spanish Democracy, the Spanish Refugee Relief Campaign, the Friends of the Abraham Lincoln Brigade, Frontier Films, Writers and Artists Committee, Motion Picture Artists Committee, the *New Theatre*, the New Theatre League, the Workers Dance League, the American Youth Congress, the League of American Writers, the Connecticut Writers' Conference, the *New Masses*, the Julius Rosenthal Memorial Committee, the National Writers' Congress, and the American Committee for the Protection of the Foreign Born.

Robert Morss Lovett, appointed by the President to the Virgin Islands, comes close to holding the all-time record for fellow-traveling with Communist organizations in this country. His connections have included the following: the American Friends of Spanish Democracy, the *New Masses*, the Committee to Save Spain and China, the Boycott Japanese Goods Conference, the American Committee for Struggle Against War, the American League Against War and Fascism, the American League for Peace and Democracy, the American Committee for the Protection of the Foreign Born, the Non-Partisan Committee for the Re-election of Congressman Vito Marcantonio, the American Youth Congress, the Friends of the Soviet Union, the National Writers' Congress, Film Audiences for Democracy, Films for Democracy, the National People's Committee Against Hearst, the Refugee Scholarship and Peace Campaign, the National Mooney Council of Action, the magazine *Champion*, the United States Congress Against War, the Golden Book of American Friendship with the

Soviet Union, the National Committee for the Defense of Political Prisoners, the Open Letter for Closer Cooperation with the Soviet Union, the National Committee for People's Rights, the Student Congress Against War, the Open Letter to American Liberals on Trotskyism, the Letter Protesting the Ban on Communists in the American Civil Liberties Union, and the National Conference on Constitutional Liberties in America.

Mary McLeod Bethune, director of Negro affairs in the National Youth Administration, was one of the vice-chairmen of the American League for Peace and Democracy. She has sponsored the Washington Committee for Democratic Action, the American Youth Congress, the National Emergency Conference, the Spanish Refugee Relief Campaign, the American Committee for the Protection of the Foreign Born, the National Negro Congress, and the Daughters of the American Depression.

Edwin S. Smith, member of the National Labor Relations Board, was elected a member of the presidium of the World Congress Against War and Fascism when it held its gathering in Mexico City two years ago. Smith also addressed the meeting. The World Congress was the parent body of the American League for Peace and Democracy. At the Mexico City gathering, Leon Jouhaux of France lauded the well-known Communist Henri Barbusse as the founder of the organization. Smith's connections with that affair have been recounted previously, but they must be retold here for the purpose of showing the extent to which government officials, as such, have sponsored Moscow's Trojan Horses. Smith has also sponsored the National Emergency Conference and the National Conference on Constitutional Liberties in America. He was a member of the executive committee of the Washington branch of the American League for Peace and Democracy.

Paul Sifton, formerly deputy administrator of the Wages and Hours Administration and now in another federal job, has been connected with the Congress of American Revolutionary Writers, the American League Against War and Fascism, the National Committee for People's Rights, the Consumers National Federation, the New Theatre League, the Workers Dance League, the National Film and Photo League, the National Committee Against Censorship of the Theatre Arts, Frontier Films, and the National Committee for the Defense of Political Prisoners. In the magazine *Fight*, Sifton wrote a revolutionary piece in which he said: "Tell them they and their fancy pieces of paper and the whole capitalist shell game can sink and be damned. Tell them that we've got another war on, closer home, a war to establish a workers' peace, a workers' government."

Tabulations such as the foregoing could be extended to fill an entire volume. Several thousand federal government officials and employees have been involved in the support of Communist Trojan Horses in recent years. While a few of them have broken away from their former Muscovite sympathies since the signing of the Soviet-Nazi Pact, most of them have continued to support Stalin's Trojan Horses —without in any way jeopardizing the jobs which they hold at the expense of American taxpayers. When the Communists staged their anti-national-defense rally in Chicago at the beginning of September, 1940, a delegation which chartered two special cars went from Washington, D. C., to attend the meeting. It was at that rally that the American Peace Mobilization was formed. It is through that latest of the Muscovite Trojan Horses that the same Communists and fellow travelers, who hail every measure of military preparedness in Russia with great rejoicing, have organized their attack upon the military preparedness of the United States. A check-up of the delegation which went from Washington to Chicago has revealed that its leaders are the same people who a year ago were carrying on agitation for Stalin's foreign policy under the guise of the American League for Peace and Democracy. They are not only the same people, but they continue to hold the same government jobs. One of the leaders of that delegation was fired from the finger-printing bureau of the F.B.I. a few years ago only to become employed immediately thereafter in the Social Security Board.

W.P.A. was the greatest financial boon which ever came to the Communists in the United States. Stalin could not have done better by his American friends and agents. Relief projects swarmed with Communists—Communists who were not only the recipients of needed relief but who were entrusted by New Deal officials with high administrative positions in the projects. In one Federal Writers' Project in New York, one third of the writers were members of the Communist Party. This was proven by their own signatures. Many witnesses have testified that it was necessary for W.P.A. workers to join the Workers Alliance—high-pressure lobby run by the Communist Party—in order to get or retain their jobs. One witness in California testified that she was compelled to resign from the D.A.R. in order to get a relief job, and, furthermore, that she was coerced into joining the Communist Party.

Several hundred Communists held advisory or administrative positions in the W.P.A. projects. Only two illustrations are cited here: Alfred Kreymborg, director of the Federal Poetic Theatre, and H. W. L. Dana, advisor of the Federal Theatre Project. Kreymborg signed the call for the support of the Communist candidates in the very election in which his future New Deal employers were victorious. He was a member of the League of Professional Groups for Foster and Ford when those two Communists were running for president and vice-president respectively. He has been a contributor to the *New Masses* and the *Sunday Worker*, as well as a contributing editor of the *New Theatre* magazine. He has been a member of the John Reed Clubs, the League of American Writers, and the National Committee for the Defense of Political Prisoners. His sponsoring has included the League of Workers Theatres, the Workers Dance League, the National Film and Photo League, the National Committee for People's Rights, and the American Committee for Democracy and Intellectual Freedom. He signed the Open Letter for Closer Cooperation with the Soviet Union, and was a member of the National Committee Against Censorship of the Theatre Arts. H. W. L. Dana has been just as clearly identified as a Communist. Dana was a member of the Committee of Professional Groups for Browder and Ford, as well as a member of the League of Professional Groups for Foster and Ford. He has been a contributor to the *New Masses*, *Soviet Russia Today*, and the *New Theatre* magazine. He was a member of the National Committee to Aid the Victims of German Fascism, the Friends of the Soviet Union, the National Committee for People's Rights, the National Committee for the Defense of Political Prisoners, the American Committee for Struggle Against War, the United States Congress Against War, and the Student Congress Against War. He was one of the American delegates to the World Congress Against War. He signed the Statement by American Progressives on the Moscow

Trials, and is now a sponsor of the United American Spanish Aid Committee.

All over the United States, the Federal Theatre Project produced plays which were nothing but straight Communist propaganda. This is not at all surprising in view of the personnel chosen by the New Deal to supervise the Project. Let us take a look at one of these Communist plays.

At the Adelphia Theatre in New York in May, 1936, a capacity audience of theater goers saw W. H. Auden's poetic play, the Dance of Death. As the play opened, an announcer stepped in front of the curtain and recited the following lines:

We present to you this evening a picture of the decline of a class. Of how its members dream of a new life, but secretly desire the old; for there is death inside them. We show you that death as a dancer.

Near the beginning of the Auden play, an imaginary audience, one McLaughlin, and a chorus spoke the following lines:

AUDIENCE: One, two, three, four—the last war was a bosses' war. Five, six, seven, eight—rise and make a workers' state. Nine, ten, eleven, twelve—seize the factories and run them yourselves.
McLAUGHLIN: We will liquidate—
CHORUS: The capitalist state!
AUDIENCE: Overthrow!
CHORUS: Overthrow!
AUDIENCE: Attaboys!

The revolutionary seizure of our factories; the overthrow of the capitalist state: such was the theme of the play which an audience just off Broadway was witnessing on that opening night in May, 1936. How the play ended may best be told in the words of the *Daily Worker* a few days later. That official newspaper of the Communist Party hailed the production as a great achievement in the theater. It described the ending, as follows:

> With Death the Dancer dead, we witness the appearance of a huge shadow on the backdrop. It is Karl Marx, who announces: 'The instruments of production have been too much for him. He is liquidated.' Exeunt, to a Dead March, as capitalism is borne out on the shoulders of four pallbearers.

That and scores of other plays equally freighted with Moscow's propaganda were what the American people spent millions of dollars to have produced all over the country. A great deal of time would be required to find a parallel for such a betrayal of the American people by their own federal officials. Of course, it was all done in the name of humanitarianism and in the name of relief for the needy. The situation became so intolerable that the Congress of the United States stepped into the picture and made an end of the whole shameful use of the taxpayers' money to spread Communist propaganda. The Communists and their fellow travelers are, of course, clamoring for the restoration of the Federal Theatre Project. Naturally, they want the feed-bag put back to the mouth of their Trojan Horse, but they also want the Government of the United States to pay for Stalin's propaganda.

The facts which have been set forth in this chapter could be added to indefinitely. They constitute one of the most astonishing stories in the annals of American history, no matter from what standpoint they are viewed.

Even if we should concede for the sake of argument that the Communist Party is a bona fide political party, it would still be an amazing thing that a political group with almost negligible strength in dues-paying membership has been able to command such tremendous patronage and influence in our federal government. But when we reflect that the Communist Party is nothing more nor less than a foreign-controlled conspiracy aimed at the destruction of our form of government, the story of Stalin's infiltration into official Washington must be viewed in its true light as one of the major political scandals of American history.

Not all of the members and employees of the Administration have been *suckers* for Stalin's progressive bait in their support of the Communist Trojan Horses. Many of them have known very well what they were doing. There are not less than two thousand outright Communists and Party-liners still holding jobs in the government in Washington.

So far as the suckers in the New Deal are concerned, the most generous interpretation which can possible be put upon their pro-Communist activities is that their intentions have been good but that they have been thoroughly duped. Even such an interpretation does not acquit them of allowing the Red Fuehrer of Moscow to penetrate our federal government, to channel off our tax funds to the support of his American agents, to dominate a dozen labor unions with the assistance of the National Labor Relations Board (fifty-five of whose attorneys are members of the Communist-controlled National Lawyers Guild), to sabotage American industry, to fight against our military preparedness for any international emergency, or to corrupt our political life and thought with the fallacies of his planned economy. This is an age when totalitarian conquerors work as effectively through dupes as they do through conscious allies. A half dozen dupes high in the federal government are more useful to Stalin and Browder than are ten thousand ordinary dues-paying members of the Communist Party.

Parachutes are not always made of fine-spun silk. They may be woven of soft words and a glistening web of Utopian promises. Fifth columnists are not always garbed in the uniform of foreign troops nor do they always speak with a foreign accent. They may be native-born American citizens. Such figurative parachutists have already landed in the federal government. They await the "zero hour" when Stalin will give the command to attack. Before that "zero hour," their work does not consist of any overt acts of violence against our form of government. It is their present duty to work at the "softening process" on our national spirit and determination to preserve American institutions from their planned assault.

The Communist Party's highly synchronized and highly disciplined organization has been permitted to entrench itself deep in our body politic. It will not be rooted out until the powerful voice of the American people makes itself heard and demands effective action.

CHAPTER XXIV

KUHN RIDES A TROJAN HORSE FOR HITLER

Soon after the success of Mussolini's Black Shirt movement in Italy and the rise of Hitler to power in Germany, these dictators put into effect plans to win the support and sympathy of Germans and Italians in the United States. Agents of Hitler and Mussolini were sent to the United States to organize Nazi and Fascist movements in this country. This was in line with their philosophy that Nazism and Fascism are world theories.

The dictators wanted to encourage Nazi and Fascist movements in America for many reasons. First of all, they wanted to build up sympathy for the Nazi and Fascist regimes in this country among people of German and Italian descent. This would enable them to neutralize the pro-British and pro-French sentiment in America. The Nazi and Fascist organizations to be set up would also serve as vehicles for the dissemination of propaganda and as window dressing for espionage work. Through ideological followers and sympathetic organizations, Hitler and Mussolini hoped to build up in America an effective and valuable espionage service to supply them with industrial and military secrets.

These organizations were to take the same lines as the Nazi and Fascist parties in Germany and Italy. They were to profess bitter opposition to Communism; and in the case of the Nazi organizations, to the Jews.

These organizations began violent attacks upon the Communists, which continued with unabated fury until the Soviet-Nazi pact was signed. After this alliance was entered into by Hitler and Stalin, the Nazi publications in the United States ceased to attack the Communists and began to attack British imperialism. The Communist Party, which had held itself out as the chief opponent of Nazism and Fascism, adopted the same line after the pact was concluded. "Down with British imperialism!" became the battle cry of the Communists and Nazis in America and throughout the world.

Almost all of the Nazi and Fascist organizations are outspoken and vociferous in their praise of Adolf Hitler and Mussolini. A few others are more cautious and clever; but all of them disclose a strong sympathy for the axis partners which they cannot conceal.

The spearhead of the Nazi movement in this country has been the German-American Bund. This organization was an outgrowth of the Friends of New Germany. It was set up in March, 1936, in Buffalo, New York. Its predecessor, the Friends of New Germany, was organized in May, 1933, but was dissolved in 1936 because orders came from Germany instructing German citizens in America to withdraw from affiliation with any political groups in this country. The German-American Bund was formed with the declared purpose of permitting only United States citizens to become members.

When the Bund was formed, Fritz Kuhn was elected president and continued to serve in this capacity until recently. He had been a member of the Friends of New Germany, and was its local unit leader in Detroit. George Frobesse was made the district leader of the Middle West; Herman Schwinn, district leader of the West; and Rudolph Markmann, district leader of the East.

The Bund is divided into three districts: East, Middle West, and West. Each division is divided into districts, which correspond to the states. There are 47 districts, divided into 100 units. The unit is the smallest administrative group of the organization. The only state which has no district or unit organization is Louisiana. Each district organization has a department leader; and each unit has a leader. Representatives of the local units meet in national conventions where the president is elected. The president, in turn, appoints all the other officers of the national organization. The local unit heads are appointed by the department leaders, subject to the approval of the president.

The constitution provides that to be eligible for membership, an applicant must be an American citizen and an Aryan.

Kuhn testified that when he was a member of the Friends of New Germany he heard that the German Government, through its consular service, had ordered German citizens to get out of every political organization. He said: "I was in Detroit at that time and I cooperated with a representative of the German Government in helping get the addresses of those in the former organization, the Friends of New Germany; I gave them the addresses so far as I knew them, of those who were German citizens."

The Bund has approximately 100,000 members in the United States, composed of regular members who have voting privileges in the organization, and members of the sympathizer sections, who do not have voting privileges. The sympathizers pay the same dues as regular members. There is an initiation fee of $1 and a dues payment of 75¢ a month, which would yield the Bund a total income of $900,000 a year.

In his statement on March 25, 1939, Kuhn said: "We

have hundreds of thousands of people who cannot afford to be seen with us, but still wholeheartedly or partly sympathizing with us. It is hard to make an estimation, but I have feelings—the way the reaction comes from the groups —I have a feeling that our sympathizing groups is very much more. You can say it is from 1 to 10."

On the application blank for membership in the Bund, there is a provision for voluntary propaganda contributions; and the requirement that two references be furnished. One reference must reside in Germany and one in America. On the application blank are the words: "Only United States citizens are eligible for office."

The national offices of the Bund do not keep any record of the names of the members of the organization; and shortly before the Special Committee on Un-American Activities began its work, orders were issued by Fritz Kuhn to the various district and unit leaders to destroy all their records. Kuhn testified that the Bund received many contributions from outsiders who are in sympathy with the purposes and aims of the organization.

The attitude of the organization toward Nazi Germany is indicated in the following questions and answers in the examination of Fritz Kuhn:

The Chairman: Over and above that, you will admit that you have published articles praising the new Germany?
Mr. Kuhn: Yes, sir.
The Chairman: You do not deny that?
Mr. Kuhn: No, sir.
The Chairman: Praising what Hitler had done for Germany?
Mr. Kuhn: Yes, sir.
The Chairman: That was the objective of your articles?
Mr. Kuhn: Yes, sir.
The Chairman: And they reflect your honest views?

Mr. Kuhn: Yes, sir.

The Chairman: So that, as a matter of fact, you are a great admirer of Hitler and the new Germany?

Mr. Kuhn: I am an admirer of Hitler.

The Chairman: You feel that he has done a great job?

Mr. Kuhn: Yes, sir.

The Chairman: You have said that many times in the past?

Mr. Kuhn: Yes, sir.

The Chairman: And one purpose of the organization is to bring that viewpoint to the United States?

Mr. Kuhn: No, sir, I did not say that. I said to enlighten the public. What you read in the paper is wrong. You read only one side of the story.

The Chairman: That is, that our people may have the same viewpoint with reference to the German Government and Hitler that you have?

Mr. Kuhn: Yes, sir.

The *Weckruf*, published in New York City, is the official organ of the German-American Bund. In an issue of the *Weckruf* dated March 5, 1939, there is a statement captioned, "We Accuse—Press statement made at Chicago by Oscar C. Pfaus." This article was a reprint of the mimeographed article of the same caption which was sent out from Hamburg, Germany.

In the *Weckruf* dated August 31, 1939, there is an article which is a reprint from a Swiss paper. The caption of that article, which is in German, is "Fritz Kuhn, America's Henlein. German-American Bund, the organization of which he is the leader, 8 to 10 thousand uniformed storm troops. The duel, Kuhn versus Dewey."

In another issue of the paper, there appears the following statement: "We may have lying in the closet different citizenship papers and yet we are all German men and links of a big German community of hundreds of millions."

In an article which appeared in the *Weckruf* dated December 10, 1936, and which quotes from a speech which Fritz Kuhn made in San Francisco describing his trip to Germany on the occasion of the Olympic Games, there is a statement that Hitler told Kuhn: "Go back and continue your fight." In another issue of the same paper, August 13, 1936, there is a front page story attributing this same statement to Hitler.

Another issue of the paper speaks of "Our eternal loyalty to Germany and our eternal loyalty to Der Fuehrer."

In the issue of the *Weckruf* for October, 1936, there appeared an editorial which reads, in part, as follows:

If you prefer the term "American-Germans" to the term the "German-Americans" you do so for the same reason for which the former German-Russians called themselves Russo-Germans and the German-Brazilians, Brazilian-Germans, namely, for the reason that we are first of all Germans in race and blood and language. We belong to the great humanity of German people.

By obtaining your citizenship you have not lost your German character. You remain what you were, Germans in America. American-Germans because we do not become Americans by taking out second papers.

In 1936, a delegation of the members of the German-American Bund went to Berlin to attend the Olympic Games. This delegation, which was headed by Fritz Kuhn, carried $3,000 in cash with them which they donated to Hitler for the winter relief fund. They marched under the swastika; and at Hanover, Germany, Kuhn made a speech which, according to the *Weckruf*, contained the following statement: "We feel bound with Germany and are fortunate to belong to such an organization. To be in Berlin and see the Fuehrer eye to eye was for us an experience. We will bear everything and will continue to fight further for the cause."

Testimony before the Special Committee on Un-American Activities, both from hostile and friendly witnesses, shows that the German-American Bund receives its inspiration, program, and direction from the Nazi government of Germany through the various propaganda organizations which have been set up by that government and which function under the control and supervision of the Nazi Ministry for Propaganda and Enlightenment.

The program and the activities of the German-American Bund, according to the evidence received by the Committee, are similar to Nazi organizations in Germany and in other countries.

The Bund newspaper makes constant use of material emanating from Nazi propaganda sources, such as *World Service*.

The emblem of the National Socialist Party, the swastika, is (if it has not been recently changed) the emblem of the German-American Bund.

It was established through the testimony of Fritz Kuhn that the Bund had worked sympathetically with other organizations throughout the United States and had cooperated with them. Kuhn testified that these groups included the Christian Front, the Christian Mobilizers, the Christian Crusaders, the Social Justice Society, the Silver Shirt Legion of America, the Knights of the White Camellia, and various Italian Fascist, White Russian, and Ukrainian organizations. Kuhn testified that the leaders of some of these groups had addressed meetings sponsored by the Bund, and that representatives of the Bund in turn have appeared frequently as speakers at meetings sponsored by the above-named organizations. It was also established that the Bund has cooperated with some of these organizations and their leaders by publishing material, emanating from them, in the official organ of the Bund. Numerous articles have appeared in the Bund newspapers expressing its approval of the activities of the organizations mentioned. Furthermore, the literature put out by the various groups and individuals named has been distributed or sold at the Bund camps, meetings, and other gatherings.

With reference to the exchange of literature and propaganda material between the Bund and various Nazi or Fascist groups, the Special Committee on Un-American Activities received testimony that the following are standard reading in Bund camps: Hitler's *Mein Kampf*, Pelley's booklets and his publication, *Liberation*, the books of Julius Streicher (German propagandist), and the Reverend Charles E. Coughlin's publication, *Social Justice*.

The German-American Bund, like the National Socialist Party in Germany, pays particular attention to the training of its youth. Testimony was heard that members of the youth movement are taught nothing concerning American institutions or ideals, and that they are encouraged to be extremely critical of the United States and its government. It was also found that the uniforms worn by the members of the youth groups, their camps, and their program of activities are similar in every respect to those of the Hitler youth movement, and, further, that the Nazi salute is the accepted gesture of greeting.

It was established that groups of leaders of the German-American Bund youth movement are frequently sent to Germany for special training. Testimony was received from a witness who was a member of a group of fifteen boys and fifteen girls from various parts of the United States who were selected by the Bund to be sent to Germany for special training. According to the witness, all instructions concerning arrangements and the trip came from V.D.A. (League of Germans Living Abroad), one of the Nazi propaganda agencies, and all plans for the trip were carried out with the utmost secrecy.

It was established through two witnesses, both former Bund members, that there is a political agent on all German ships and that these political agents maintain contact with the Nazi representatives in foreign countries. They are intermediaries for transmission of instructions to the Bund leaders in the United States, and they receive reports from these leaders concerning the Bund's activities.

A former Bund member on the West Coast testified that German agents are engaged in espionage activities, and have sought and received the cooperation of Bund leaders in that work. This witness also testified that he had heard discussions among Bund leaders with reference to the manner in which the Bund, through its members in various industrial plants, intends to carry out a program of sabotage in case such action becomes necessary in the interest of Hitler.

Evidence was heard by the Special Committee on Un-American Activities that members of the Bund had assisted German agents, whose arrests were sought by officials in the United States, in avoiding apprehension, and had helped get them out of the United States with the cooperation of German ships.

Evidence was taken indicating that Nazi propaganda agencies, through officials of the German Government in the United States, have attempted to propagandize educational institutions in this country. It was testified that a German consul general had offered, on behalf of the German Government, to subsidize German departments in American universities provided the professors were "acceptable" to the Nazis.

Doctor Otto Albert Willumeit, who is the leader of the Chicago unit of the German-American Bund, appeared before the Special Committee on Un-American Activities under subpoena and testified at length. He said that the Chicago unit was actually organized in 1933 under another name. "First it was under the 'Teutonic Sons of Germany' and then later on became the 'Friends of New Germany' and then later on in 1933 became the 'German-American Bund.' " said Dr. Willumeit.

Doctor Willumeit succeeded Peter Gissibl as the leader of the Chicago Unit Post. He said that he could not say how many members the Chicago unit of the Bund has because all the records of membership were destroyed several years ago in obedience to orders issued by Fritz Kuhn. Since that time the Chicago Bund post has kept no records, and when new members join the application blanks are filled out and forwarded to New York. He estimated that the total membership of the local unit was about 500.

After Fritz Kuhn issued an order that German citizens would have to sever their connections with the Bund, a separate organization in Chicago, known as the German Bund, was established. No one is eligible to belong to this organization except German citizens and Doctor Willumeit estimated the membership at a few thousand people. Later he said: "I have once or twice attended an official celebration at the Germanic Club, which was given by the German Consulate and arranged by this German Bund here, and according to the crowd that I have seen there I think it probably must be 800 or 1,000."

The head of the German Bund according to Doctor Willumeit, is Fritz Heberling who is connected with the German consulate in Chicago. At one of the meetings of the German Bund, Eric Von Schroeder was ejected because of the manner in which he asked a question concerning Nazism.

Doctor Willumeit said that only a few of the thousand members of the German Bund have applied for citizenship. He admitted that members of the German Bund and the German-American Bund had made trips to Germany. He said that the Bund had purchased the publications of William Dudley Pelley, R. E. Edmundson, James True, and Father Coughlin.

He said that the purpose of the Bund "is to teach people in the United States to appreciate the new Germany, or rather to understand the new Germany"; that he felt that Hitler had accomplished a great deal in Germany for the Germans, and that Nazism was a splendid thing for the Germans and was the only answer to their problem.

In explaining his attitude toward Jews, he said: "I feel this way—that you cannot make any distinction, there are good and bad among all nationalities; but the Jew as a race has been unassimilable, especially the Talmudian Jews." He expressed his views as follows: "I mean, let them stay in their own group, just as we do with the Negro and with the Asiatics; and have them partake in the government and so on according to their racial number . . . I would allow them government positions, professional jobs, etc., according to their numerical strength." He said that he would do the same thing with reference to the Negroes, the Chinese, and the Japanese.

When he was asked how many sympathizers the German-American Bund has in Chicago, he answered: "To judge by the attendance at our meetings, approximately 6,000 or 7,000." He said that the majority of the Bund members are laboring people, skilled laborers, artisans, professional men, and that they work in practically all of the industries in and about Chicago, and that most of them are naturalized citizens.

When he asked, "Didn't most of them serve in the World War, are any of them veterans of the German Army?" he replied: "Yes, quite a number of them, I would say, because they are of that age when they were drafted for military service."

Doctor Willumeit testified that while the Bund was not affiliated with the German-American National Alliance, the Alliance is sympathetic with the new Germany and that the societies which are affiliated with the Alliance are also sympathetic to the new Germany. He testified that all singing societies, societies of World War veterans, the German-American Technical Association, and some of the beneficial societies are affiliated with the Alliance.

CHAPTER XXV

A TROJAN HORSE OF GERMAN WAR VETERANS

WE HAVE in the United States a German organization which pretends publicly to have a strictly cultural interest but which, by its own written principles, judges its members on the basis of their ability to do "confidential" work. Its public pretense is punctured by its private membership instructions which lay stress on the importance of pistol practice as well as "confidential" work.

Adolf Hitler is the arch-enemy of German culture. Hitler and Goethe do not mix any better than oil and water. Yet, the agents of Hitler have set up this Nazi Trojan Horse under the guise of preserving German culture among Americans of German descent. The organization is known as the Kyffhauserbund, or, in English, as the League of German War Veterans.

The Special Committee on Un-American Activities has listened for many hours to the testimony of members of this organization as they stoutly maintained that their sole purpose was to keep German culture alive in America. Their claim, made with wearisome repetition and in the face of overwhelming evidence to the contrary, was that they were interested only in the German language, its literature and songs.

Let it be clearly understood that no one can justly charge the overwhelming majority of Americans of German descent with any lack of loyalty to this country, and further, that this loyalty is consistent with a genuine desire to preserve their cultural heritage. Their patriotism is not clouded by any doubt in their own minds or in the minds of their fellow citizens whose ancestors migrated to America from lands other than Germany. These German Americans also know that the vulgarity and ruthlessness of Nazism are the very opposites of true German culture. They know, as do all the rest of us, that when the spirit of Goethe, Wagner, Ehrlich, and Kant lives again in Germany, then Hitler, Goering, Gobbels, and Hess will be dead or removed from power. Beyond any doubt, our great German American population resents the use of legitimate German cultural interest as a camouflage for Nazi propaganda and espionage.

Compared with the millions of our citizens whose forbears came from Germany or who are themselves of German birth, the number of those who are involved in the Trojan Horse activities of the German-American Bund or of the Kyffhauserbund is very small. At the same time, we must never forget that the dangers of espionage are not to be measured only by the number of persons engaged in it.

Most of the members of the Kyffhauserbund have come to this country since the World War of 1914-1918, and a very large proportion of these have not become American citizens. Their own testimony has revealed their deep sympathies with Nazism.

The Kyffhauserbund was organized in the summer of 1937. It was first incorporated in the State of Pennsylvania. It has spread from Philadelphia to New York, New Jersey, Massachusetts, Connecticut, Michigan, Illinois, and Texas.

In New York City, the Kyffhauserbund has its headquarters in the offices of the German American Vocational League, an organization which sponsored lectures in this country by the Nazi agent, Dr. Colin Ross.

The Kyffhauserbund was a continuation of an organization known as the Stahlhelm or the Steel Helmets. In the State of Texas, the Kyffhauserbund still operates under a charter issued in the name of the Stahlhelm.

The Kyffhauserbund is affiliated with the Kriegesbund, the War Front, which has its international headquarters in Germany. The larger organization has all the earmarks of a Nazi international.

The Special Committee on Un-American Activities came into possession of one of the membership books of the Kyffhauserbund. The description of the organization set forth in its membership book is as follows:

The Kyffhauserbund in North America is a consolidation of former German soldiers that have served in the German armies or those of their allies. The organization is spread over the whole Continent of North America.

In our fatherland the Kyffhauserbund has become the standard bearer of all inactive German veterans and veterans' organizations, and it is hoped that this bund here in America will accomplish the same results. There are no official connecting ties with the fatherland organization outside of a strong social nature.

Despite the assertion in the foregoing statement that there are no "official connecting ties" between the Kyffhauserbund and Germany, one of the leaders of the organization testified before the Special Committee on Un-American Activities that it is a part of the Kriegesbund which has headquarters in Berlin, and it goes without saying that any organization in the Third Reich can exist only with the approval of Adolf Hitler.

Not everything in the Kyffhauserbund is open and above board. This is clear from the organization's membership book itself. There we find a space to be filled in which is headed as follows:

> Recommendation of organization leader as to members ability of being trusted with confidential work.

The membership book also admonishes those who belong to the Kyffhauserbund to "promote rifle and pistol practice." There is the further admonition to "induce your organization to participate in the yearly national rifle matches of the Kyffhauserbund."

Surely, every patriotic American will agree that there is no place in this country for any foreign-controlled group which asks its members to do "confidential work" or to "promote rifle and pistol practice." Our objections to such a group are reinforced by any evidence that it is controlled by one of the totalitarian regimes which specializes in the Trojan Horse penetration of other countries for subversive purposes.

One of the State Commanders of the Kyffhauserbund wrote a memorandum which is in the possession of the Special Committee on Un-American Activities and which contains the following declaration of political allegiance:

> We did not need to un-learn anything when Hitler came to power in Germany. We were already Nazis when he took up the reins of government in the Reich.

In an article which appeared a few weeks ago in the Philadelphia *Herold*, a German Language newspaper, under the caption "What Are the Aims of the Kyffhauserbund Outside of Germany," we read the following:

> At present we are doing everything in our power to band together all Germans in this country to help our old homeland, Germany, in its present strife and struggles. These efforts have

been repaid, but not in such proportions as we have Germans in the United States . . . It is not only a point of honor for the entire German population, but a holy duty to the fatherland to help along so that we can say proudly, "I, as a German, have done everything in my power to help and I am not ashamed of being a German."

Statements such as the foregoing, which are plentiful in the evidence which has been collected on the Kyffhauserbund, indicate far more than a non-political interest in the German language, its literature, and songs. They establish the fact of a close political tie with the Nazi regime in Germany. The uses to which Hitler has put such organizations in Poland, Norway, Holland, Austria, Belgium, and France are now matters of historical record. The caption of the statement itself implies that the Kyffhauserbund exists "inside" as well as "outside" of Germany.

Not long ago the Kyffhauserbund held a meeting in Philadelphia which was attended by four United States Army and Navy officers. One of these officers had been warned in advance that the meeting was of a subversive character, but he attended in spite of the warning. These American officers stood up with the rest of the gathering during the singing of the Horst Wessel song—the official song of the Nazi movement. At all meetings of the Kyffhauserbund, according to the information gathered by investigators, the Nazi salute is given, the "Heil Hitler" is used, and the swastika and pictures of Hitler are displayed. This was true of the Philadelphia meeting attended by the United States Army and Navy officers.

Early this year, the Kyffhauserbund held another meeting in Philadelphia which was addressed by the Reverend Sigmund von Bosse. The national leader of the organization, Karl Schumacher, presided at the gathering. Reports to the Special Committee on Un-American Activities indicate that this meeting was a typical gathering of the organization for the spread of Nazi propaganda. A large banner draped across the stage had on it the slogan, "Gold gab Ich fuer Eisen" ("I give gold for iron"). The slogan referred to a campaign for the raising of war funds for Hitler's rape of Europe.

At still another meeting which was held in Philadelphia, the German consul in that city, Mr. Erich Windels, greeted the audience with the Nazi salute and the audience responded in like manner. Hitler was hailed as a great saviour and conqueror. The Horst Wessel song was sung by the audience with arms raised in the Nazi salute at the end of Windels' speech. Most of the five hundred present at the meeting were American citizens.

The Special Committee on Un-American Activities is in possession of evidence that German consular agents throughout the United States have made it a practice to interfere in the political affairs of German Americans who are citizens of the United States. Such conduct on the part of American consular agents in Germany would lead to their immediate expulsion from the country.

The Nazi Consul-General in New Orleans, Baron Edgar Von Spiegel, wrote a threatening letter to the editor of a German-language newspaper in Texas. That letter, together with scores of other such communications from German consuls, is in the possession of the Special Committee on Un-American Activities. It reads, in part, as follows:

> I intended to discuss with you the manner and the spirit in which you sometimes report activities in Germany in your paper . . . I cannot imagine what causes you to make such statements, nor can I imagine their sources. Your articles could

just as well appear in a paper hostile to Germany ... The Fuehrer has declared that Germany, in the future, will take *drastic steps* against any untruthful international newspaper propaganda.

The editor who received this threat from Baron Von Spiegel is an American citizen. The evidence shows that the Kyffhauserbund is one of the Fuehrer's instruments used to bring such matters, as the allegedly unfriendly articles in the Texas newspaper, to the attention of German consular agents.

Members of the Kyffhauserbund have used the German language press in this country to carry on propaganda for the Third Reich and the principles of Nazism. In some instances, the editors and publishers of these German language papers are members of the Kyffhauserbund. The case of the Texas *Herold* and its editor, Hans Ackerman, is typical.

In one issue of the Texas *Herold*, there appeared the following evaluation of Hitler's work:

It is the greatest achievement of Adolf Hitler that he has created the German Volksgemeinschaft ... It is our desire that many more German societies join the great movement of the German-American Union for the salvation of German Volkstum and for the creation of true Volksgemeinschaft.

The foregoing statement is merely a repetition of the idea which has been propagated from Hitler's Germany since the beginning of Nazi rule, namely, that persons of German origin or descent, no matter what their present citizenship status may be, are first of all subjects of Hitler's domain—a German Volkstum which extends to any part of the world where those of German blood may reside.

The Texas *Herold* has made it clear that the German

Weltanschauung (World View) is an essential part of German culture. "Whoever," said the *Herold*, "stresses the preservation of German cultural values and refuses to acknowledge the German 'Weltanschauung' does not know what he is talking about." The Weltanschauung of Hitler is something entirely different from the Weltanschauung of Goethe and the other creators of the true German culture. It is the "World View" of Nazism which the Texas *Herold* insists is an indispensable part of German culture.

With a flourish of complete contempt for our American intelligence, the Texas *Herold* announces: "We see exactly that Reichsfuehrer Hitler is no dictator." Communists also, with equal disregard for our American common sense, insist that Stalin is no dictator. There is hardly any limit to the affronts which both Nazis and Communists offer to our American intelligence.

The editor of the Texas *Herold* went to Germany last year. His travel expenses were paid under circumstances which made it perfectly clear that the costs of the trip were met from Hitler's propaganda budget. The editor returned to America to sing Hitler's praises. The Special Committee on Un-American Activities has assembled evidence which proves conclusively that Stalin's government over a period of twenty years and Hitler's government during the past seven years have financed the journeys of thousands of American citizens to their respective realms. In all but a few cases, these dictator-subsidized Americans have returned to their own country to engage in the subversive activities of their subsidizers.

CHAPTER XXVI

PELLEY TRIES TO SELL SILVER SHIRTS

WE COME now to the story of a would-be American Fuehrer who has not been able to make the grade. The inspiration to ape Hitler, if such an ambition may be called an inspiration, has undoubtedly moved many maladjusted personalities during the past decade. It moved one William Dudley Pelley in our own country. How it moved him is the theme of the present chapter.

William Dudley Pelley was born at Lynn, Massachusetts, on March 12, 1885, and, so far as is known, passed a not unusual childhood in New England. In his early manhood he became editor and publisher of *Philosopher Magazine*, at Fulton, N. Y. During the period 1909-12, he was treasurer and manager of the Pelley Tissue Corporation at Springfield, Massachusetts. Later he was editor and publisher of the Chicopee (Massachusetts) *Journal*, the Wilmington (Vermont) *Times*, and the St. Johnsbury *Caledonian*. He was with the International Y.M.C.A. in Siberia from 1917 to 1918. He is now editor of *Liberation Magazine*, a weekly publication. He is also chairman of the Foundation for Christian Economics. He founded the Silver Legion of America in 1933 and the Christian Party, in 1935.

Pelley is the author of many books, among them being *The Greater Glory*, 1919; *The Fog*, 1921; *Drag*, 1924; *Golden Rubbis*, 1929; *Seven Minutes in Eternity*, 1929. According to his own statement, he is the author of 220 published narratives—fiction enough to fill thirty volumes of ordinary novel length. He is one of the most prolific writers in the United States, and his various publications have been read by thousands of people in every section of the country.

A sample of Pelley's esoteric writings may be found in his book, *The Door to Revelation:*

Weird as it may sound to those hearing this sort of thing for the first time, I have the same adamant conviction that we actually choose our parents of our own free will, before entering life as infants. We know in advance, before we are physically born, I say, what the factors and trends in a given life will be by selecting certain parents.

Again, in the same book, he wrote:

Searching my memory honestly as I write these lines, it seems that in those far-off years I was quite as old a person as I feel myself to be at present. There were two souls of me inside—that was how it was! One knew all things. The other asked questions.

Pelley sold some of his fiction to the First National Pictures in Hollywood; and he was engaged in the real-estate business in California from 1927 to 1929. He was president of the Pelley Company and of the Brief Meal Corporation, a restaurant chain. He came to New York in 1930 and began to write and teach along psychic and spiritualistic lines.

On February 7, 1931, he incorporated the Galahad Press in the state of New York, with himself and two women, M. J. Benner and Olive E. Robbins, as incorporators. The two women were clerks in Pelley's office.

The office of the Galahad Press was located on 42nd Street in sub-rented office space. The Galahad Press was in evidence from Febuary 7, 1931, until May 1, 1934, when it was adjudged bankrupt in the District Court for the United

States for the Western District of North Carolina, at Asheville.

In 1934, Pelley incorporated the Silver Legion of America in Delaware. The Foundation for Christian Economics paid the incorporation fees of the Silver Legion, although the two organizations were entirely separate. Shortly before the Silver Legion was incorporated, Pelley sent a telegram to Harry F. Sieber, which contained the instruction: "Immediately clean records clean." The evidence before the Special Committee on Un-American Activities showed that Pelley was ordering the destruction of the records of the Galahad Press preparatory to the establishment of the Silver Legion.

In his book, *The Door to Revelation*, Pelley described the origin of his Silver Legion in the following language:

> It so happened that I was working late one night in my office at the east end of the main college building when Marion Henderson, my secretary, came in with the Asheville evening paper. I saw 8-column headlines. Curiously I picked it up. The date was January 30, 1933. And screaming from the page were the significant words "Adolf Hitler becomes German Chancellor." I looked at the lines. I read them again. I sought to comprehend them. Something clicked in my brain. . . .
>
> I laid the paper down. The prophecy heard that night in the Fifty-third Street flat before going up to Mrs. Leslie's was working.
>
> "Tomorrow," I announced, "we have the Silver Shirts."
>
> Anderson scowled. Marion was puzzled. One of them demanded, "What do you mean, Silver Shirts?"
>
> "Let me alone tonight," I begged. "Tomorrow you'll know everything."

In September, 1937, Pelley incorporated the Skyland Press. The incorporators were M. Helen Pelley, Alfred H.

Talpey and W. D. Pelley. One hundred shares of capital stock were authorized for $100,000, and the corporation was to start business when $1,000 had been subscribed. The Skyland Press is the publishing company which publishes the *Liberation*, weekly organ of the Silver Legion.

Pelley is president of the Silver Legion of America and of the Skyland Press. The Skyland Press owns the equipment of the publishing plant, but the building in which it is located belongs to Pelley personally. Pelley's express packages are sent out under the name of the Foundation Fellowship, which is not incorporated. The Special Committee on Un-American Activities heard testimony that the use of the name Foundation Fellowship for express shipments was a cover-up so that the literature or shipments could not be identified with Pelley.

The Pelley set-up appears to be as follows: the membership organization is the Silver Shirt Legion of America, Inc.; the building and the literature are Pelley Publishers; the bank account is carried under the name of Skyland Press; the express shipments go out under the name of Foundation Fellowship; the mail goes out under the name of Little Visits; the magazine is *Liberation.*

Liberation lists for sale a large number of Pelley's publications, among them the following: "Jews Say So!—Braggings of 82 Jewish leaders that Jews intend to dominate all Gentiles"; "Dupes of Judah—The inside story behind the World War"; "Forty-Five Questions—Particulars of Most Popular Interest Concerning Jews in Relation to Gentiles"; "What Fifty Famous Men Have Said About Jews"; "What the Chinaman Thinks of the Jew"; and "Protocols of the Learned Elders of Zion."

Many of Pelley's publications are sent by express to sympathizers, agents, and members of the Silver Shirt Legion.

The Special Committee on Un-American Activities obtained a record of express shipments. For example, during the first seven months of 1938, he expressed 1,154 shipments to the West Coast, and 14 to the East Coast.

Pelley has received some large contributions. For instance, one woman in Massachusetts sent him money orders totaling $3,800. George B. Fisher, who is connected with the Crowell Publishing Company, sent the Pelley Publishers a check for $2,000 on January 3, 1938, a check for $600 on March 17, 1938; and a check for $2,000 on February 6, 1939. John R. Brinkley, M.D., of Little Rock, Arkansas sent him a check for $629.64, dated November 28, 1938.

From September, 1937, until July, 1939, Pelley received approximately $66,000 so far as it was possible to ascertain the amount of donations from available records.

In Pelley's publication, *Liberation*, under date of July 28, 1938, there appears the following statement:

> It is a fact which posterity will attest that Chief Pelley of the Silver Shirts was the first man in the United States to step out openly and support Adolf Hitler and his German-Nazi program. Hitler became German chancellor on the 31st day of January 1933. This publication appeared on the 18th of the ensuing February openly and unashamedly endorsing Hitler and his program against the German Jewish "reds."

The foregoing statement clearly expressed Pelley's sympathy for Nazi ideology. Undoubtedly he has sought to build through the Silver Shirts an organization modeled after the Nazi Party of Germany. The basic propaganda of his organization has been anti-semitism. It has made considerable progress in many sections of the country and has recruited thousands of members. At one time it was a political factor in some sections of the country.

In his *Door to Revelation*, Pelley boasted:

Who in this stricken Nation has not heard of the Silver Shirts? Step up to the average man on the streets today and ask him, "Have you ever heard of the Silver Shirts?" What will he answer in these early months of 1939? "Sure, I've heard of 'em. There was a crazy fool down somewhere in the South who tried to revive the Ku Klux Klan and go after the Jews. But the Government authorities fixed him. I think he got in jail."

The average man says that, because such is the perversive intelligence that has been published. But the battle is still raging, that I started that midnight back in 1933. And I did not land in jail, though its doors opened for me.

Far and wide across this Nation in the opening months of that epochal year went the high tocsin to America's Christian patriots to form the Silver Legion.

From Maine, from Oregon, from Michigan, from Texas came back the pledges of Christian freemen to band themselves together and clean the great homestead that was the stricken United States.

The tiny lad that had stood on the knoll in summer morning behind the East Templeton parsonage and marveled at the mystery of an ant running up a grass stalk, the lad who had stood with Mabel beneath that wild-cherry tree while she broke off a sprig of cherry blossoms and put them in her hair, the youth who had lain in that Wilmington tenement and grieved for a little white casket to the drone of midnight saxophones, the fellow who had stood with Admiral Kolchak in far away Siberia, who had watched the moth wobble on his table in a Greenwich Village twilight, the man who had beheld Svende Garde's green carpet, then approached the Doors of Revelation and gone through them . . . what does the world know of the innermost thoughts of a mortal's heart when he sounds a bugle to a nation and beholds the miracle of great hordes responding. . . .

Further on in his book, Mr. Pelley said:

From Massachusetts, from Montana, from Florida, from Idaho, from Ohio, Pennsylvania, Texas, Washington, Illinois, and California the Silver Legionnaires were responding to my tocsin. It was an awe-inspiring thing.

I had known that the Nation was disgruntled with the encroaching caste of Jewry. I had never appreciated that it hungered for leadership like this. Yet had the prophecy back there in New York not stated: "When the young painter comes to power in Germany, take that as your time signal to launch your organization." There was substance to such prophecy. It was idle vaporing of subconscious mind. And always and forever in the back of my thinking was the radiant culmination. . . . I must "sit upon an iceberg in the center of a sea of hostile humanity" . . . and then something was to happen. . . .

Pelley described his purpose in forming the Silver Shirts in the following language:

My purpose in forming the Silver Shirts—in my own heart at least—was to prepare a great horde of men nationally to meet the crisis intelligently and constructively. Every Silver Shirt must know the full extent of the conspiracy, see it in its most detailed workings, get his thinking up onto a level where the size of the plot could be accredited and, if Red Communism in all its frightfulness were finally projected upon the country, be in a position to join with tens of thousands of similarly enlightened Christians, and preserve the form of constitutional government set up by the forefathers. If this last meant using force to hurl a great regime of scoundrels from the country, very well then, it meant force.

Speaking of military discipline, he wrote:

The whole Silver Shirt horde required military discipline from top to bottom. But military discipline is military discipline. It rests on severe penalties for infractions of rules. It depends on uniforms to designate rank and therefore authentic responsibilities.

After the Special Committee on Un-American Activities began its work, one Fraser Gardner applied for a position as investigator. He appeared along with many other applicants before the Committee and, under questioning, started that he was not connected with any subversive group. Gardner was not employed by the Committee, but when it was continued, he again applied for a position. He appeared before an executive session of the Committee, and, under oath, denied that he was connected with Pelley, the Silver Shirts, or the Skyland Press.

Records subsequently obtained, however, disclosed that Gardner was on the pay roll of Pelley and the Skyland Press, and that many telephone calls and telegrams had passed between him and Pelley. Gardner was indicted for perjury and pleaded guilty. It seemed clear that Pelley was seeking to place Fraser Gardner on the investigative staff of the Committee for the purpose of sabotaging the investigation.

CHAPTER XXVII

MUSSOLINI'S TROJAN HORSE IN AMERICA

The ascendancy of Mussolini as the dictator of Italy was followed almost immediately by Fascist propaganda and activities in the United States. This fact has not been generally understood because it has received little publicity outside of the Italian press which is largely pro-Fascist in sympathy. Most of the Italian newspapers are printed in the Italian language.

According to the United States census for 1930, there were almost two million Italians residing in America who were born in Italy. In that year, they constituted the largest single group of foreign-born residents in our country. Only the residents of the United States who were born in Germany ranked close to them in number. Several million other residents of our country are of Italian-born parentage or of Italian descent.

Among Italians of the first and second generations, there is a strong sympathy for Italy. They follow developments in Italy with the greatest interest. Few, if any, non-Italians attend meetings and functions of Italian societies in the United States. Many of the speeches to these organizations are delivered in the Italian language. Hence, the progress of Fascist ideology among people of Italian descent in America has not become widely known.

The revenue received from Italian citizens and sympathizers residing in the United States has been an important item to Mussolini and his government. Hundreds of thousands of dollars have been sent to Italy by Italians residing in the United States; and during the Ethiopian campaign, there was an organized effort in the United States to raise funds for the conquest of Ethiopia. The support of this group alone has been an important factor in the Italian economy. The facts show that many Italian-Americans have assisted the Fascist regime. It is difficult for the average American to appreciate the importance of this financial aid to the near-bankrupt Italian government. It must be remembered that the Italians in the United States have earned far more in wages than their racial brothers in Italy.

When we came to investigate Fascist activities and propaganda in America, we were immediately confronted with the difficulty of finding out what goes on at the meetings of Italian societies. It is known, however, that Italian consuls addressed many meetings of the Sons of Italy where Mussolini and Fascism were praised in the highest terms. It is known that the audience signified by enthusiastic applause their approval of these speeches.

Italian consular officials and secret Fascist agents are spreading Fascist propaganda throughout the ranks of many Italian-American organizations in the United States. In addition, they are expending every effort to penetrate bona fide Italian-American fraternal societies with a view to gaining control of these organizations for the purpose of increasing the influence of the Fascist dictatorship.

There is a very close tie-up between many Italian societies in this country and the Italian consular service. It has been the practice of these societies for years to invite members of the Italian consular service to deliver addresses and to participate in their meetings.

As a matter of fact, the Italian consular service in this country may be said to constitute the very spearhead of

Fascist activity and propaganda. These consuls maintain contact with Italians and their societies. They have omitted no opportunity to glorify Fascist Italy and Mussolini. This is in keeping with the foreign policy of Mussolini to build up supporters and adherents among the Italian people in every country.

Italian consular officials have addressed scores of semi-public gatherings and closed meetings in which they delivered speeches of Fascist propaganda, speeches in which they scoffed at the democratic form of government.

The participation of Italian consuls in such meetings is a matter of common knowledge among the American-Italians. Testimony before the Special Committee on Un-American Activities showed that among those who have repeatedly taken part in Fascist affairs in their respective areas are the following: Consul General Vecchiotti, New York City; Consul General Segre, Boston; Consul General P. Pervan, Philadelphia; Consul P. Decicco, New Haven, Connecticut; Consul Jannelli, Johnstown, Pennsylvania. Consular officials have participated in meetings where American money is raised for the Fascist cause in Italy.

The Committee heard testimony that consular officials have spied on American citizens and threatened those who will not subscribe to Fascism; that they have gone so far as to warn Italian-Americans that their American citizenship would be revoked, and they would be returned to Italy. It was also testified that these officials had threatened to punish the relatives of Italian-Americans still residing in Italy. For instance, we have in evidence a letter from Consul Angelo V. Jannelli of Johnstown, Pennsylvania, to Mr. Gavino Pellani of Nettleton, Pennsylvania, dated March 16, 1937. The letter gives the year of the Fascist era, XV, and it says: "Dear Sir: You are invited to come to this office for communications which regard you personally."

In a sworn affidavit, Mr. Pellani's wife said that her husband could not visit the consular office, in accordance with its invitation, because he was working; and that she went in his stead, on March 20th, with her son-in-law, Paul Cubeta. Mrs. Pellani said in the affidavit that the consul threatened to have her husband's citizenship papers revoked and have him deported to Italy.

Another letter was received in evidence written by the Consul General in Philadelphia to Bellone Valerio on the 2nd of April, 1937. The letter says: "With reference to a preceding correspondence, I invite you to inform me if 'Connazionale' is still residing in the same place and if and in what kind of political activity he engages."

The Committee also received in evidence a letter from Consul Decicco of New Haven, Connecticut, which reads, in part, as follows:

There are a big number of Italian-American societies in the State of Connecticut. It is necessary that this office be in possession of the names and addresses of all those who belong to such Italian-American societies.

Therefore I would appreciate it very much if you will send me the complete list of the names and the addresses of those who belong to your particular society.

The Committee obtained the form of application which is used by the Fascists when they apply for membership in the Black Shirts. On the front page of this application is the following notation:

> Fascist branches abroad.
> Branch of ....
> Name ....

The application requires the applicant to state whether or not he was in the World War and if he has been approved by the secretary of a particular branch. They also require the applicant to state how much he has paid to be admitted.

On the back of this application blank are lines where the consul of the particular town may approve the applicant before he is admitted, which means that every prospective member who applies to be admitted to the branches of the Black Shirts must be approved by the local Italian consul before he becomes a member.

The testimony before the Special Committee on Un-American Activities indicates that there are approximately 10,000 members of the Italian Black Shirts in the United States; and that approximately 100,000 people of Italian descent have participated in meetings of Fascist organizations. The Committee heard testimony that there is a branch of the Italian government secret police known as the O.V.R.A. operating in the United States. It was explained that this is a spy organization which has called at the homes of Italians and attempted to frighten them whenever they have participated in activities which do not conform to Fascist government policy. This spy organization is directly linked to the Italian consular service in the United States. The Committee was furnished the names of four agents of the O.V.R.A. who are operating in the United States.

The Fascist movement in the United States has followed the example of the Fascist Party in Italy with reference to Italian youth. Under the guise of education, children are indoctrinated with Fascist ideology.

The youth movement centers around the Dante Aligherie Society, with headquarters in the same building in which the Italian consul of New York has offices. The director of this society is Professor Mario Giani.

The Committee was told by an Italian witness that this society spends thousands of dollars in free distribution of pamphlets, books, and prizes to pupils.

This witness testified that many groups of children of Italian descent have been taken to Italy each year, ostensibly for their vacations, but, in reality, to be imbued with Fascist doctrines.

According to this same witness, the pamphlets distributed by this society contain such material as speeches by Mussolini, accounts of the achievements of the Fascist regime, and the military grandeur of the Italian army and navy, its colonial conquests and its promise in the building of a new Roman empire.

We were told by this witness and others who appeared before the Committee, that textbooks, some of which we received in evidence, which were used in teaching Italian pupils, contained a great deal of Fascist propaganda. These books are printed in Italy. One of them has a heading, "Books for the Italian Classes Abroad." In this book, there is portrayed a young Fascist saying that he salutes his flag, and he always thinks of his far-away fatherland. "God assist, now and forever, Italy. God help me to become a good Italian," the youth is pictured as saying.

Two of the books secured by the Committee had printed or stamped on the inside, the following statement: "Abraham Lincoln High School, Ocean Parkway and West Avenue, Brooklyn, N. Y." On the next page, there was stamped "Property Board of Education, City of New York, June 17, 1937." On page 7 is a portrait of Benito Mussolini, and on page 6 is the Fascist hymn, Liorinezpa.

Another textbook obtained by the Committee has the

same stamps, and its title is "Andiamo in Italio." This book was written by two American professors of Italian extraction. On page 38, there is an account of the rebirth of Italy. As translated to the Committee by the witness, it contains the following statement: "All the liberal and democratic governments which preceded the Fascist one were incapable of keeping order."

The witness further testified that the textbook branded labor unions and strikes as disruptive; and praised the Black Shirts for having seized the government of Italy by force. The book, according to the witness, glorifies the corporate state.

The witness testified that the book contained statements that the governments which preceded the Fascist were impotent to solve the Vatican problem, and that only the government of Mussolini, with its daring, could accomplish this great thing, and that now the Pope and the Italian government are at peace.

The Special Committee on Un-American Activities received in evidence a book written in the Italian language which is called *A Vow of Fealty to Mussolini*. The book contains thousands of pages. It was published, according to its own statement, in "New York, 1937, the Year 15 of the Fascist Era." The publisher is designated as the Economic Printing Service of New York City. There is a portrait of Mussolini, with his own autograph: "Mussolini, Rome, the 9th of May, the 14th Year."

This book contains the names of thousands of manufacturers in the clothing industry, contractors, designers, foremen, and workers. The book also contains letters from certain Italian-Americans, praising Mussolini. A letter on page 138 was translated by the witness, as follows: "As each immigrant feels in his heart the sentiment of the continuous progress of the empire, which is destined to become powerful, I give my salute and my devotion to you, Duce of Italy." A line from another letter, as translated to the Committee, reads: "We love our fatherland." Another letter, as translated, reads: "In the disorder in which Italy found itself when it was governed by unstable government, Italy has found now the power to redeem itself and become one of the first nations of the world, thanks to Mussolini." This letter is signed, "Nicholas Santoriello."

There are hundreds of letters of the same nature containing expressions of admiration for Mussolini. The witness testified that not only had the manufacturers written these testimonials of regard and devotion to Mussolini, but that they had also contributed money to Mussolini. The witness said:

> One of the sad notes in all this Fascist activity in the United States is the fact that many of the Italian-Americans who are engaging in subversive activities are actually on relief rolls or employed by W.P.A. and other Government agencies.
> Here we have the spectacle of men and women who are American citizens or aliens and earning their bread from the hands of the Federal Government, while at the same time working quietly to undermine and destroy the very democracy that is feeding, sheltering, and clothing them.
> Many signs point to the fact that the American Fascist movement is marching side by side with the American Nazi movement toward the common goal of a united front for a desired upheaval and destruction of our American form of democratic government.

The Committee was also told that the Fascist government of Italy ships in to the United States, for distribution through Fascist organizations in this country, hundreds of decorations, medals, and ribbons, all conveying the spirit of Fascism.

It was further testified that the American children of Italian extraction who were sent to Italy were given Fascist uniforms and taken to training camps where they received instruction in military formations, drills, and exercises; that these children participated in services, meetings, and parades on the streets of Rome, Genoa, and other cities; and that these children, in some cases, returned from Italy to the United States dressed in Fascist uniforms and always imbued with Fascist spirit and ideology.

The Committee received in evidence photographs which had been printed in official magazines published in Italy. A witness testified that one of these photographs showed a group of American school children, from Detroit, Michigan, photographed on their return from Italy, where they had spent their vacation time in the Fascist camps. The children are dressed in Fascist uniforms, as Gelillas (young Fascists). In their group, we were told, is the local consular agent, G. Ungarelli.

In another photograph, identified by this witness, there appears a group of American boys coming back from their trip to Italy. The boys are giving the Fascist salute to consul Siroana of the Italian government in Pittsburgh, Pennsylvania.

Still another photograph shows a group of American school boys who are guests of the Italian government doing exercises at the Fascist camp at Cortina d'Ampezzo.

The witness submitted for evidence another photograph which, he avowed, showed American boys in Fascist uniform marching to the tomb of the unknown soldier in Rome. The witness stated that the Italian government officers led the children, who were dressed in black shirts.

MUSSOLINI'S TROJAN HORSE IN AMERICA 341

The witness further testified as follows:

On July 17, 1937, on the Rex sailed a group of 95 children, parochial school, class A; they landed in Genoa the 25th day of July. They returned to the United States on the Saturnia the 26th of August. On July 17, on the Rex, sailed a group of 95 children, parochial school, class B. They landed in Genoa. Returned on the Saturnia the 26th of August.

On July 31, 1937, on the Conte di Savoia sailed a group of 72 school girls—public schools. They landed in Genoa on August 8, 1937. Returned to the United States on the Conte di Savoia on the 9th of September. On July 31, on the Conte di Savoia, sailed a group of 159 boys—public school. Landed in Genoa on August 8. Returned on the Rex on the 2d of September.

The next photograph shows Italian Black Shirts on the "Circolo Morgantini," in Harlem (New York City), participating in a Nazi celebration in Camp Siegfried in Yaphank, Long Island, on Sunday, August 29, 1937. The chief of the Black Shirt squad is John Finzio. This Black Shirt organization is identical in character with the German-American Bund.

The Committee received in evidence photographs showing Fascist Black Shirts and members of the German-American Bund meeting together.

There was a photograph of a celebration attended by thousands of Italians. According to testimony and photographs, the general consul of the Italian government in New York, Gaetano Vecchiotti, Count Facchetti Guiglia, and other Fascist officials participated; and all of them, including Consul Vecchiotti, wore black shirts.

During the Ethiopian conquest, according to evidence in the possession of the Special Committee on Un-American Activities, the Fascist representatives in the United States enlisted 1,000 Americans of Italian descent for military service in the Italian campaign; and many of these Americans returned to the United States in Fascist uniforms, which they wear at demonstrations. These veterans of the Ethiopian campaign have been actively organizing branches of the Fascist movement in this country.

The Special Committee on Un-American Activities has photographic evidence showing Fascists leaving the United States to join Mussolini's army. It shows the departure of a large group of Italians from the United States to join Mussolini's army fighting against Ethiopia. The Italians left on the steamship Rex from the port of New York on December 19, 1935.

An exhibit, which is now a part of the Committee's record, is a photostatic copy of *Progresso Italo-Americano* (a Fascist organ, according to testimony before the Committee). This newspaper carries a story relating to the return to the United States of Angelo Gloria, an artist, who left this country and enlisted in Mussolini's army in the Ethiopian adventure.

There are seven dailies published in the Italian language in the United States. All of them are Fascist publications under direct guidance from Rome. In the editorial department of each of these seven newspapers, there is an agent of the Fascist government who supervises editorial policy to make certain that these publications do not deviate from Fascist lines.

One witness before the Special Committee on Un-American Activities gave the following summary of Fascist propaganda in the United States:

> For instance, at the *Progresso Italiano Americano*, the largest daily newspaper published in the Italian language and owned by an American citizen, Generoso Pope, there is one Dr. Vincenzo Comiti. He is an agent of the Italian Fascist Govern-

ment. It is his job to see that the daily newspaper renders 100 per cent loyalty to the Italian Fascist Government.

By the way, this gentleman was preceded by a gentleman named Angelo Flavo Guidi, who is now in Rome. They seem to change them.

The *Progresso*, as well as the other six Fascist dailies, receive free wire service from Rome under the Fascist ministry of press and propaganda.

In addition to the *Progresso*, the publications are as follows: *Il Corriere D'America*, New York; *Il Popolo Italiano*, Philadelphia; *l'Italia*, Chicago; *l'Italia*, San Francisco; *Le Notzia*, Boston; and *La Voce del Popolo*, San Francisco.

Then there are more than 100 periodicals, weekly newspapers, magazines, bulletins, and so on, all of which are openly pro-Fascist.

The radio stations which mostly identify themselves with the organizations which disseminate Fascist propaganda are WBNX, WBIL, WOV, WHOM, all operating in and in the vicinity of New York City.

. . . They never play The Star Spangled Banner (on the phonograph records taken while Fascist propaganda is going on), but they always play the Fascist hymn Liorinezpa. They praise the Fascist government and speak against and attack the Government we have here.

The Fascist government in Italy is also shipping into the United States a steady stream of motion-picture films of a propaganda character. Most of these films are projected at the notoriously Fascist moving-picture house, the Cinema Roma, on Broadway in New York City.

A number of Fascist propaganda films are also shown in the meetings of Italian Fascist organizations and in Italian churches throughout the United States.

The Fascist government also sends to the United States Fascist speakers, frequently under the guise of commerce and education. Their real purposes, of course, being to spread foreign propaganda.

These speakers make appearances at American colleges, universities, and before American-Italian societies.

Their expenses are paid for by the Italian Government out of its fund for propaganda abroad.

The ends to which the Fascist movement in the United States will go to support the Italian Government is vividly portrayed in the fact that during the Fascist conquest of Ethiopia, the American-Fascist movement raised $1,000,000 supposedly for the Italian Red Cross, but actually for the military campaign of the aggressor.

In addition, the American Fascists, with Italian consuls participating, collected thousands of dollars worth of articles containing gold and silver, such as earrings, matrimonial rings, watch chains, and gold fillings from their teeth. This precious metal was shipped to Rome.

A branch of the American-Fascist movement also resorted to the clever method of collecting copper plates for the Italian Government to help offset the sanctions imposed upon it by the League of Nations. These plates were printed and sold in the form of post cards. On these copper cards were inscribed:

Before the altar of the fatherland we place this offer and our devotion.

Other similar copper cards bore the following inscription:

This sheet of copper which we offer to the fatherland symbolizes the faith of the Italians in America.

After the sale of these copper cards in the United States, they were mailed to Italy, and there they were melted for purposes of ammunition.

Whatever became of the money raised in the United States from the sale of the copper cards, American-Italians were never told.

Now, I can offer some evidence.

These (indicating) are the cards that were used in the Ethiopian War. They sold them to the Italians here at 15 or 25 cents apiece. We do not know what became of the money they exacted, but they told them they should mail them to

Italy so that the Mussolini government could use them for melting into ammunition.

The American clothing trade is a fertile field for Fascist agents to raise funds. In this trade field, both in the management and labor ends, are many American-Italians.

Periodically, Fascist agents descend on these American citizens and milk them of funds for purposes of Fascist propaganda in the United States. These Fascist agents have succeeded here in raising thousands of dollars from both employers and workers in exchange for printed greetings and messages of devotion to Mussolini.

Mr. E. Clements, an Italian citizen who has been residing in the United States since 1926 and whose occupation is that of a printer, told the Committee:

Well, the Fascist movement here in Chicago is not such as in New York and the east side of the United States, because we are so far from the Atlantic coast. The psychology of the people here in Chicago is not so near the Fascist movement as on the eastern coast of the United States, but the newspapers, the consul and the radio, they are making big propaganda for the Fascist movement. During the Ethiopian war, I was editor of the *La Parole*, an Italian newspaper, weekly, and I was against the Ethiopian war, as was my group in my movement. We got twice a letter, without signature, from Fascists, in which they told us if we don't stop our propaganda—and it was not propaganda but to be against the Ethiopian war—they would send some bombs to us.

Mr. Clements testified that there are four or five schools for Italian children in Chicago where Fascist games are played and where textbooks sent from Italy are taught the children. The witness said that these textbooks contain **Fascist propaganda glorifying Mussolini and the Fascist regime in Italy.** He described mass meetings of Italians in the

United States which he had attended where the Fascist salute was given. He said that the Fascist press service, with headquarters in Rome, sent press releases every day to the Italian newspapers in the United States; and that these Italian newspapers reprinted these releases. He also charged that Italian radios carried speeches in Italian praising Mussolini and Fascist Italy.

Mussolini's Trojan Horse in America differs from those of Stalin and Hitler chiefly in the fact that it has received much less general attention in the regular press of the country. For the most part, it is concealed behind the barrier of the Italian language. To the extent that one Trojan Horse is more secret than another, it is also the most dangerous.

For the present at least, Mussolini is one of the Axis Partners. He is also a passive partner in the contemporary rapprochement between Stalin and Hitler which bodes so much ill for democratic institutions the world over. His interference in the affairs of this country, through the now widely publicized Trojan Horse methods, is as intolerable as that of his more powerful allies.

CHAPTER XXVIII

AMERICA'S ANSWER TO THE TROJAN HORSE

DEMOCRACY and the principles for which it stands are gravely menaced throughout the world today. Over vast areas comprising at least two thirds of the world's population, both self-government and the hope of its early resurrection are dead. Of such incalculable magnitude is this tragic set-back to human progress that our finite minds must fail to grasp the full of import of its disaster. Where men had struggled and died for centuries to achieve a measure of freedom, the torch of liberty has been extinguished.

This havoc of the totalitarian destruction of free and civilized institutions has been wrought, in part, by a tactic which derives its name from the wars of ancient Troy, but surely the men of Greece who invented that tactic would blush with shame if they could know what modern dictators have done with their wooden creature of deception. As we measure the tragedy and horrors of totalitarian conquest today, even so must we measure the perfidy of the Trojan Horses which have been used in making these conquests.

The dictators have embarked upon a world war of ideologies. This war of ideologies is something new in the world. Already it has changed the map of Europe with a speed that would have startled Julius Caesar and Napoleon Bonaparte. What Stalin and Hitler have done on the continent of Europe, they are prepared to attempt throughout the world tomorrow. Only a few months ago, the three largest empires in the world were the British, the French, and the Dutch. Two of these have collapsed. The other is in graver peril than at any other time since Trafalgar. Four new empires are rising upon the ruins of the old—Stalin's, Hitler's, Mussolini's, and the Mikado's. Each of these new empires has behind it the driving, fanatical force of a totalitarian ideology. Each employs the strategy of the Trojan Horse followed by the blitzkrieg of total war.

The experience of this generation, more than that of any other, has demonstrated that the enemies *within* a country constitute a peril as great as any foreign foe. Treason from *within*, aided by invasion from *without*, has been responsible for the speed with which modern governments have collapsed in the face of totalitarian assaults. Stalin and Hitler have pushed their Trojan Horse tactics to the point of perfection.

The use of the Trojan Horse tactics by the Communists and Nazis has proven to be very effective. Indeed, the Trojan Horse, as we have seen, has been drawn into labor organizations, political parties, peace societies, educational institutions, civic clubs, and even into the government itself.

To date, the most notable tragedy wrought by the Trojan Horse tactics of Moscow is the destruction of France. Her once proud armies in rout, her great capital city in the hands of the Nazis, her government in complete capitulation, her vast industrial resources expropriated by Hitler—France today is the supreme warning to the rest of the world what ruin the Trojan Horse can accomplish through treason. When France finally recognized the nature and menace of the Trojan Horse and resorted to repressive measures against the Communists and the Nazis, it was too late! The People's Front of France, initiated by and controlled from Moscow, had destroyed the unity of the French people, had drained its resources, and had left the country relatively defenseless before the blitzkrieg of Hitler's invading hordes. This is not to say that the People's Front was alone responsible for the downfall of France, but there can hardly be any doubt now that it was in a large measure contributory to her undoing.

It is now apparent to every thinking person that the Trojan Horse minorities within a democracy constitute a major threat that cannot be ignored or minimized, and that cannot be measured in numerical terms. At the time the Communist Party seized Russia, it constituted less than one-half of one per cent of the total population of the country. The Nazi Party in Germany was always a minority party before Hitler seized the reigns of power.

Because of our great resources and strategic position in world affairs, the United States has been assigned to the cleverest Trojan Horse conspirators of Hitler, Stalin, and Mussolini.

It is difficult for the average American to appreciate the inroads which these Trojan Horses have made in the United States. Perhaps the best illustration of this was the opposition which the Special Committee on Un-American Activities encountered. What it was telling the people and what its witnesses were testifying to were branded as fantastic and unbelievable by many editorial writers, columnists, government officials, college professors, union leaders, and even some industrialists. Comic cartoons derided the Committee in many newspapers. Some of the important conservative people entertained grave doubts about the investigation. Even the President of the United States joked at one time about its revelations. Secretary Perkins and Secretary Ickes contributed their laughter; and in New

Deal circles the Dies Committee was considered by some a menace and by others a farce. Yet the witnesses were telling the truth, as has been verified by subsequent evidence and events. What they were telling the country in 1938 and 1939 is now generally recognized as true even by the Committee's severest critics.

The President no longer views the revelations of the Committee as ridiculous or unfounded or inconsequential. Only recently he admitted in his press conference that much of the information of the Committee was good and he referred people to the Committee's Hearings for pertinent information on the Fifth Column.

The Department of Justice, after years of indifference, has announced its intention of dealing with the Fifth Column. Two years ago, when the chairman of the Committee was pleading with the Department of Justice and the President for cooperation, it would have been relatively easy to secure the names of thousands of Fifth Columnists in America. They were then so confident, that they were operating more or less openly. Now they are working underground and the work of the Department of Justice will be extremely difficult.

For years the Department of Justice and the other agencies of the Federal Government failed to keep informed with reference to subversive organizations. In fact, these organizations were aided, as we have seen, by the agencies of the government in numerous ways. Now, however, when the truth has at last been hammered home to the heads of the Departments, they are trying to repair, through frantic measures, the damage due to their negligence.

Fortunately, however, for the country, the Special Committee on Un-American Activities has made a record of about twenty volumes which include the names, addresses, identities, methods, and plans of many of the Fifth Columnists in this country and the majority of their leaders. The information which was gathered during the past two years could not now be obtained, because the conspirators have destroyed their records and, in the parlance of the Communist Party, "gone underground."

Now that the whole country recognizes the menacing facts, what can be done about the Fifth Column and its Trojan Horse organizations? This is the question which has been asked by many people.

The very first answer to that question is for every American to cease justifying the Trojan Horses and their builders on the ground that they are the natural and inevitable result of adverse economic conditions.

Some so-called progressive and liberal leaders contended for a while at least that the answer to the Trojan Horses of the Nazis and the Communists lay entirely in the abolition of poverty and unemployment. They asserted that unemployment and poverty were the sole causes of subversive activities. They maintained that the government could and must solve these problems and that when this was done the Fifth Column would cease to exist. We were told that the rise of Stalinism in Russia, Fascism in Italy, and Hitlerism in Germany was due to the stress of economic conditions which existed in those countries. These so-called liberals have insisted, therefore, that remedial legislation should be confined to a correction of economic injustices.

It is undoubtedly true that poverty and unemployment facilitate the work of subversive groups. It was the stern Roman, Cato, who once observed that "the empty belly hath no ears." This was true in the days of the Roman Republic and it has been true in every generation.

But to place upon democratic government the responsibility for abolishing poverty and unemployment as a condition for its perpetuation is to seal its doom as a form of government and as the spirit of a free people. Economic distress is no justification for treason.

Many of our farmers carry on their work under adverse economic conditions that have been largely brought about by discriminatory legislation. Those who are familiar with the farmer's situation will acknowledge that it is extremely difficult to pay high taxes, cultivate depleted soil, and sell farm products upon a highly competitive market, and then buy industrial products on a tariff protected market.

In spite of the adverse conditions under which farmers have been compelled to work, subversive groups have made less progress among the farmers than among any other group in this country. In the course of the investigation into the un-American and subversive activities of those who give allegiance to foreign dictators, we have been impressed with the fact that one group more than any other in our population—the farmers—has withstood the appeals of the false philosophies of class hatred and racial and religious intolerance. These philosophies have enlisted the support of some men in labor unions, of some students in our schools and colleges, and of some sophisticated leaders in our crowded cities, but they have left the American farmers uncorrupted in their devotion to the principles which have made America great.

And yet many of our farmers labor under conditions far worse than the conditions which so-called liberals point to as the cause, even if not the justification, of subversive activities in the cities. If economic conditions were the cause of Communism and Nazism there would be more Communist farmers than there are Communist urban workers, students, and professional people.

In the second place, America's answer to the Trojan Horse conspiracies must be found in a speedy abandonment of that type of class legislation which does, indeed, produce economic distress.

With respect to poverty and unemployment caused or aggravated by monopolistic practices and governmental discrimination there is much that a democratic government can do, even though in a negative fashion, to correct or relieve the situation. No small part of economic injustices can be directly traced to class legislation and discriminatory policies on the part of government. It is a matter of common knowledge that much of our tariff legislation was written to please certain organized interests. In fact, the log-rolling and political trading which went on in connection with tariff legislation became a national scandal.

The manner in which the National Labor Relations Act was prepared and is administered is another typical example of class legislation. While the principle of collective bargaining is sound and just, everyone in Washington now knows that the C.I.O. not only helped to write this measure but dictated the appointments of the great majority of administrators who were chosen to enforce the act.

These instances could be multiplied a hundred-fold if it were necessary to do so. The ability of organized minorities to secure passage of discriminatory legislation has become one of the serious threats to the proper functioning of democratic government in America. It has not only brought about ridiculous inconsistencies, with one law contradicting another and thereby creating general confusion and inefficiency, but it has also brought about an expensive and undemocratic bureaucracy. We have one bureau devoted to the task of curtailing production and another bureau seeking to increase production. We have established agencies to prevent and dissolve monopolies and others to encourage and promote monopolies. Bureaus in Washington have usurped much of the legislative functions of the Congress. They not only administer laws, but many of them, through interpretation of laws, perform important legislative functions. The waste and extravagance practiced by these bureaus and their general attitude of meddling discourage private initiative and thrift.

A volume could be written to demonstrate that much of our poverty and unemployment have been brought about by class legislation, extravagance, and bureaucratic inefficiency and meddling. All that can be done here, however, is briefly to mention this fact in connection with subversive activities. It should, however, be stressed that the government itself has played an important role in the growth of Communism by providing Communists with jobs and opportunities for recruiting members and fellow travelers. There are few subversive organizations in America which cannot produce letters of endorsement and encouragement from prominent government officials. All this is a form of feeding the Trojan Horse. It can be ended promptly and effectively by those in government who have been responsible for it.

It is true that a democratic government can do much to abolish poverty and unemployment. It can repeal discriminatory laws. It can practice economy and thrift to avoid the crushing effect of high taxation which in all countries has produced poverty and unemployment. It can act as an umpire to administer the rules of the game fairly and impartially. It can refrain from grabbing the ball and running down the field on the side of some class or race or religion. In short, it can assume a wise and intelligent leadership by becoming the government of *all* the people.

In the third place, America's answer to the Trojan Horses must lie in a new appraisal of the function of government to guard the fundamental liberties of the people.

If democratic government assumes the responsibility for abolishing all poverty and unemployment, it is simply preparing the way for dictatorship. Such a theory of government is a powerful ally of the Trojan Horses. Democratic government must insist that its primary function is to protect life, liberty, and property, and to do everything within its power to give everyone a chance in the race of life. This does not mean that in times of great stress and calamities governments should permit people to starve. But it does mean that democratic government cannot and must not acknowledge a duty to furnish everyone with the kind of job he wants regardless of whether or not he is able to fill the job after he gets it. Government can, of course, abolish unemployment if it is willing to pursue dictatorial methods. Nothing is easier than to put everyone in this country to work if we are willing to pay the price of slavery. Stalin, Hitler and Mussolini have all boasted that they have done away with unemployment in their countries. This is true, but the price of their accomplishment must be considered. Liberty and the rights of man have been completely scrapped, and the people have been compelled to give up what is infinitely more precious than economic security. They have surrendered their liberty and in exchange have received "economic security." There are, however, many other forms of security which are vastly more important and desirable than economic security. To be secure in one's liberty, in one's home, in one's church, and in one's intellectual life means more than to be made secure by legislation in one's job. The people of Russia, Germany, and Italy have lost all their security because even the miserable wages which they receive under the regimented economy of the totalitarian governments fall far short of compensating them for the loss of their more basic liberties.

If there is anything that has contributed to the Fifth Column in America, it is the doctrine of those who imply that people have a right to conspire against the government unless their economic problems are solved for them by the government. As a matter of fact, everyone in this country, whether he be poor or rich, employed or unemployed, is infinitely better off than he would be in like circumstances under the dictatorships of Stalin, Hitler, and Mussolini. If, therefore, a citizen in this country is encouraged to believe that his loyalty to our democratic government is contingent upon the government's ability to give him the kind of job he wants, or thinks he should have, American democracy is doomed.

The only hope for any appreciable correction of social and economic injustices lies in the perpetuation of our free institutions, and those most interested, economically speaking, in the correction of such abuses should be the last to join or encourage subversive or un-American movements.

The argument that we have no right to combat the activities of Fifth Columnists and their Trojan Horse organizations until the economic conditions which they exploit are removed is absolutely false. Since the world began, mankind has been afflicted with the ravages of disease. Millions of people have died of diseases which were once considered incurable but which we can now prevent or cure. It required patience, intelligence, hard work, and self-sacrifice on the part of the medical profession to find the causes and the remedies. They have not yet found a way to protect mankind from the ravages of cancer and tuberculosis, although untold energy and effort have been expended in that direction. Nevertheless, it is universally agreed that government has the right to prevent quacks and charlatans from preying upon the miseries of tubercular and cancer patients. This does not mean that we should content ourselves with measures designed to curb these quacks. We must continue an energetic effort to discover the cause and cure of cancer and tuberculosis. But until this is done, it is the right and duty of government to keep medical quacks from preying upon these unfortunate victims. We have the same right to prevent Fifth Columnists and their Trojan Horse organizations from preying upon the economic misery of the poor and unemployed. This should be done not only in the interest of the great majority who are employed but also in the interest of the unemployed themselves. We must continue to search for the cause and cure of avoidable poverty and unemployment, but we must above all things also preserve our rights as free men. Such is the principal task of government.

In the fourth place, America's answer to the Trojan Horses lies in a re-assertion of the obligations of citizenship in our democracy. In the clamor for rights, obligations have been ignored.

For many years now we have been stressing the rights of the people. For ten years we have listened to members of the House and Senate orating about the rights of the people to jobs and security. Volumes have been written on this subject. Organizations have been formed to secure passage of a wide variety of crack-pot bills designed to guarantee jobs and economic security.

During all of this period little or nothing has been said about the duties and obligations of the people to the government. For every right there must be a corresponding duty. Those who enjoy the blessings of freedom have the responsibility for preserving freedom, not only for themselves but for their fellow citizens as well.

During the post-war period, the democracies generally were absorbed in attempting to satisfy the demands of their people for social and economic rights. While the democracies were talking about the rights of their citizens, the totalitarian governments were talking about the duties of their citizens. In Germany, Italy, and Russia, stress was laid upon the duty of the citizen to his government. No one will contend for a moment that this sole emphasis upon duty was desirable or right. In Germany, Italy, and Russia, it developed peoples who are the servants of the state. On the other hand, it has been fatal for the democracies to stress the rights of the people without, at the same time, emphasizing their duties and responsibilities.

Unfortunately, a generation has been brought up in the democracies which lacks any adequate appreciation of the great responsibilities of citizenship in a free country. Many seem to take liberty for granted and fail to appreciate its value. They have heard so much about economic rights that liberty has been relegated to a secondary place in their appraisal of values.

The leaders of the democracies should have had the courage to tell their people that a government which accepts the responsibility to support the people must have the corresponding right to discipline them. The same law which requires the father to support his children obligates the children to obey the father—if papa must support the child, papa must have the right to spank.

The men and women who fled from the oppressive tyranny of Europe to the wilderness of America were not seeking economic security. As a matter of fact, they left the comforts, the safety, and the conveniences of civilized society in the old world with the knowledge that they were headed for a wilderness peopled by savages and wild beasts. What was it that they sought above everything else in life? The answer may be found in every history of the United States. They wanted freedom of speech, and of conscience —the right to worship God according to the dictates of their conscience. They wanted to be free men.

The people in a democracy must decide that liberty is the most desirable of all human possessions and that its enjoyment compensates the beneficiary for any disadvantage of a democracy. This is fundamental in any answer to the problem of the Trojan Horse.

It is the duty of every citizen, whether employed or unemployed, poor or rich, to be loyal to this country and true to its traditions, principles, and ideals. There are no circumstances which excuse or justify treason. No one was more unfairly treated than Benedict Arnold; he was denied the recognition which he had earned by his courage and his ability as a leader. He was discriminated against and victimized by jealous and shortsighted politicians. Notwithstanding this fact, Benedict Arnold has gone down in American history, and deservedly so, as a horrible example of ingratitude and treachery.

In recognition of this loyalty of the citizen, but not in payment for it, the government owes him a duty; first, to protect his God-given rights to be free; and, second, to do everything that is consistent with the maintenance of his liberty to afford him an opportunity to make a living. Those who contend, or imply, that it is the duty of the government to support the people are preaching a fallacious doctrine which will eventually lead to dictatorship in this country.

The very basis of our approach to the problem of the

Trojan Horse must be sound thinking with respect to our economic and political institutions—a new and profound appreciation of our foundations of liberty.

In the fifth place, we must come to understand that there is an intimate relationship between liberty on the one hand and our economic arrangements on the other hand. Our economic system is not so perfect that it cannot be improved; nor so sacred that it is above criticism. But the cure for the ills of private enterprise is more private enterprise, a wider diffusion of private property in order that there may be a firmer foundation for personal liberty.

Private property rights are not in conflict with the most sacred human rights, as the radicals would have us believe. Everywhere throughout the world today, where men have been persuaded to sacrifice the rights of private property on the altar of bureaucratic and totalitarian state capitalism, there has followed a complete destruction of those fundamental human rights which were widely achieved in the century of liberalism.

If we retain our liberty and free institutions in America, we must reject the rule of monopoly of either the state or private variety, in either the economic or political realm. And since this is so, the real friends of liberty will be zealous to make our economic system function successfully. But the system cannot work with notable success, if public monopoly is advanced as the cure for private monopoly, and if those who administer the policies of government as they relate to legitimate business are the bitter enemies of legitimate business. You cannot superimpose upon a free and competitive economic system the crushing superstructure of totalitarianism. We decry, and properly so, the trend toward totalitarianism in Europe, but we do not seem to understand, or fully appreciate, the fact that the same trend exists in the United States. The same forces, the same philosophies, the same appeal to hatred exist in America and have made wide-spread progress.

It is evident, therefore, that we cannot successfully combat totalitarianism until we understand the meaning of democracy. We must be able to distinguish between democratic principles and totalitarian principles. There must be an intellectual awakening and a spiritual rearmament for the defense of democracy. This is not less essential than military rearmament. In fact, it is the prerequisite to any national defense. A democracy which is divided and confused on fundamental principles is incapable of marshaling its resources and manpower to resist the aggressions of a unified totalitarian state.

In the sixth place, the Trojan Horsemen must be ousted from their government positions. In July of this year, a Communist was indicted by a grand jury in Pittsburgh for obtaining, by fraud, signatures to a nominating petition of the Communist Party. At once, it was disclosed that this Communist was an employee of the Civil Aeronautics Authority in Washington. For two whole months thereafter, this indicted Communist continued uninterruptedly in her job in a federal agency which is vital to national defense. Only after the lapse of two months was she discharged "with prejudice" for her illegal Communist activities. There is, of course, no possible excuse for keeping Communists on the public payroll *until* they are indicted, to say nothing of keeping them there for weeks and months after they are indicted.

The Fifth Column and the Trojan Horse organizations can never be properly dealt with so long as we retain in the government service—even in its key positions—hundreds of left-wingers and radicals who do not believe in our system of private enterprise.

Even where these government job-holders are not directly linked with the agencies of foreign powers, or do not commit overt acts of illegality, they still believe in the principles of totalitarian rule. This is not less true where they pose as the antagonists of the totalitarian regimes. What they are trying to do in America is to substitute bureaucratic state Capitalism for our present political and economic system. They are trying to make New Dealism into a cross between Communism and Fascism. Some of them are foolish enough to suppose that they can retain liberty under a regimented and planned economy. They think they can do what Hitler, Stalin, and Mussolini have done in the "planning" business without impairing or sacrificing the Bill of Rights. They ignore the lessons of history, and seem never to learn that the principles of Socialism if applied to any country or under any conditions will inevitably lead to dictatorship.

These left-wingers are scattered throughout the government service and occupy key positions which enable them to oppose any efforts to combat the Fifth Column. They themselves are too deeply compromised to permit any vigorous action against the Trojan Horse organizations with which they have been affiliated. They do not understand that liberty and the Bill of Rights cannot survive the destruction of the American economic system. It is this group in the government that constitutes the spearhead of the Trojan Horse movement in this country. Until they are removed from their positions, we may expect at best only half-hearted and ineffectual action. They do not believe in the system of free, private enterprise, and if they had had their way, it would have been scrapped already.

They represent the same thought and movement in this country that Communism, Fascism, and Nazism represented in Europe. They have been doing everything in their power to make it impossible for our economic system to function. They have done more to promote class hatred in America than the Communist Party could ever hope to do. For eight years they have been attacking the political and economic system of this country under the guise of progressive thought.

Too long have these fellow travelers and purveyors of class hatred been at work. We cannot wisely expect any sincere change of conviction or attitude. And even if they tried, there are too many wounds which they can never heal. They represent the same type which led France to destruction and England to the brink of ruin. While their prototypes in France and England were condoning general strikes and otherwise sabotaging production, which left those countries unsupplied with necessary armaments, our own left-wingers were justifying the sit-down strikes in America.

In France and England, the merchants of class hate were finally driven from public life but it was too late to repair the damage they had done to French and English economy. Fortunately for us, it is not too late to profit by the experiences of the other democracies; there is still time, if we act promptly and courageously.

The issue is before the President. He must take the initiative in performing this necessary task in the interest of adequate preparedness.

The President cannot supply the leadership on which our national security rests until he inaugurates a thorough and genuine house-cleaning in government service. This is the plain truth, and to deny or avoid it may prove fatal in the end.

The President must surely realize by this time that his left-wing followers in the government are the fountain head of subversive activities. They may not think they are, and they may not consciously serve the ends of Stalin and Hitler, but the history of the totalitarian states shows that class hatred inevitably leads to racial hatred and that hatred, whether class, racial, or religious, when fully developed, means that three-fourths of the battle for dictatorship has been won. Hatred has paved the way for every dictatorship in Europe. It is a prerequisite to the suppression of liberty and free government.

Whether or not we can develop courageous leadership in this country remains to be seen. It depends upon an awakening of the people. The totalitarian psychology of Communism and Fascism has taken root in the minds of many of our people. It must be eradicated before the nation is prepared to defend itself against the assaults of totalitarianism.

In the seventh place, all organizations in this country which have been shown by the Special Committee on Un-American Activities to be linked to the totalitarian regimes must be outlawed. The President has been urged to take the initiative in this because anyone must realize the futility of any effort along this line without presidential sanction and cooperation. It is indefensible to permit the representatives of Hitler, Mussolini, and Stalin to operate in this country under the cloak of legality. We would not knowingly permit their paid spies to do it, and yet the Trojan Horse organizations are even more dangerous to this country than paid spies. To sit idly by and permit these organizations to spend millions of dollars in this country to destroy us *from within* is suicidal.

In the eighth place, the false interpretation of civil liberties which permits and justifies the existence of Trojan Horses has been brought about by the propaganda and activities of the very people who are seeking to destroy the Bill of Rights. For years they have been building up this utterly senseless idea of civil rights. How can we deal with the enemies of this country when we permit them to operate legally and get their names on the ballot? The whole thing is preposterous and a sad commentary upon the perversion of the meaning of the Bill of Rights.

We, in America, know that in the event of war we would be compelled to outlaw these organizations just as other countries have been forced to do. Why wait until the eleventh hour? If these organizations cannot be trusted in times of war then certainly they cannot be trusted in times of peace. Their subversive activities and propaganda in times of peace are just as dangerous to the country as their espionage and sabotage in times of war.

In the ninth place, another measure which must be adopted if we intend to tackle this problem with vigor and firmness is to stop the immigration of aliens who have been infected with the virus of Communism, Fascism, and Nazism. Thousands of them have been admitted to the United States in recent years under the guise of refugees. The country is filled with Sinons who are opening Trojan Horse doors. Many other so-called refugees are pro-Communist or pro-Nazi in ideology and background. Many of the leaders and guiding spirits in the Trojan Horse organizations have been admitted to the United States in the past twenty-five years, and yet we continue to let them come in. Why? The answer is to be found in political cowardice.

The political parties vie for the votes of the foreign element. Frankness is in order, but it should be distinctly understood that there are no aspersions cast upon the great majority of loyal and patriotic citizens of foreign stock. Everyone knows, however, that in the cities there is great demand for the admission of alien relatives and friends. The politicians from the big cities are afraid to antagonize these voters.

No one contends that there is any economic reason for the admission of aliens—we have more people now than we have jobs for them to hold. This is the only country in the world that will admit aliens to any considerable degree. All other democracies long ago stopped immigration and refused to permit aliens to hold jobs so long as there were citizens unemployed.

Finally, we must make up our minds to deport undesirable aliens. For eight years, many patriotic citizens have been urging Secretary of Labor Perkins to do her duty in this respect. But again politics intervened. Secretary Perkins apparently did not want to antagonize the organizations and groups which besieged her with appeals to withhold deportation orders. The President recently recognized this disgraceful situation when he transferred the Immigration Service to the Department of Justice. It remains to be seen whether or not the situation will be improved.

One may seriously doubt whether effectual measures will be adopted to deal with the enemies within this country until public sentiment forces it. Some steps will be taken by official Washington; but the political situation is such that we cannot expect any adequate or vigorous action until the public demand becomes so vocal and insistent that politicians are compelled to heed it.

Anti-Movements in America

An Arno Press Collection

Proceedings of the Asiatic Exclusion League, 1907-1913. 1907-1913

Beecher, Edward. **The Papal Conspiracy Exposed.** 1855

Beecher, Lyman. **A Plea For the West.** 1835

Budenz, Louis F. **The Techniques of Communism.** 1954

Burr, Clinton Stoddard. **America's Race Heritage.** 1922

Calhoun, William P[atrick]. **The Caucasian and the Negro in the United States.** 1902

Ministers of the Established Church in Glasgow. **A Course of Lectures On the Jews.** 1840

Dies, Martin. **The Trojan Horse in America.** 1940

Dilling, Elizabeth. **The Red Network.** 1935

East, Edward M. **Mankind At the Crossroads.** 1926

Evans, H[iram] W. **The Rising Storm:** An Analysis of the Growing Conflict Over the Political Dilemma of Roman Catholics in America. 1930

Fairchild, Henry Pratt. **The Melting-Pot Mistake.** 1926

Fulton, Justin D. **The Fight With Rome.** 1889

The Fund for the Republic, Inc. **Digest of the Public Record of Communism in the United States.** 1955

Ghent, W[illiam] J. **The Reds Bring Reaction.** 1923

Grant, Madison. **The Conquest of a Continent.** 1933

Hendrick, Burton J. **The Jews in America.** 1923

Huntington, Ellsworth. **The Character of Races.** 1925

James, Henry Ammon. **Communism in America.** 1879

King, James M. **Facing the Twentieth Century.** 1899

Kirwan (pseudonym of Nicholas Murray). **Letters to the Right Rev. John Hughes, Roman Catholic Bishop of New York.** 1855

Ku Klux Klan. **Papers Read at the Meeting of Grand Dragons Knights at Their First Annual Meeting.** [1923]

McCarthy, Joseph. **McCarthyism: The Fight for America.** 1952

McDougall, William. **Is America Safe for Democracy?** 1921

Monk, Maria. **Awful Disclosures.** 1836

[Morse, Samuel Finley Breese]. **Foreign Conspiracy Against the Liberties of the United States.** 1835

National Americanism Commission of the American Legion, Compiler. **ISMS:** A Review of Alien Isms, Revolutionary Communism and Their Active Sympathizers in the United States. 1937

Nevins, William. **Thoughts on Popery.** 1836

Pope, Or President? Startling Disclosures of Romanism as Revealed by Its Own Writers. 1859

[Priest, Josiah]. **Slavery.** 1843

Reed, Rebecca Theresa. **Six Months in a Convent** and **Supplement.** 1835

Roberts, Kenneth L. **Why Europe Leaves Home.** 1922

Ross, Edward Alsworth. **Standing Room Only?** 1927

Schaack, Michael J. **Anarchy and Anarchists.** 1889

Schultz, Alfred P. **Race or Mongrel.** 1908

Stripling, Robert E. **The Red Plot Against America.** 1949

Tenney, Jack B. **Red Fascism.** 1947

[Timayenis, Telemachus T.] **The Original Mr. Jacobs:** A Startling Exposé. 1888

Wiggam, Albert Edward. **The Fruit of the Family Tree.** 1924

Anti-Catholicism in America, 1841-1851: Three Sermons. 1977

Anti-Semitism in America, 1878-1939. 1977